HOMICIDE ON HYDRA
GEORGE JOHNSTON'S CRIME NOVELS

I0039947

Derham Groves

With a Preface by Des Cowley
and Susan Millard
And a Foreword by Ian Morrison

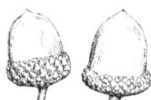

HOG PRESS

Hog Press
an Imprint of Culicidae Press
PO Box 620647
Middleton, WI 53562-0647
hogpress.com
editor@hogpress.com

HOG PRESS

ISBN: 978-1-941892-70-1

Library of Congress Control Number: 2023948221

Our books may be purchased in bulk for promotional, educational
or business use. Please contact your local bookseller or the
Culicidae Press Sales Department at +1-515-462-0278
or by email at sales@culicidaepress.com

twitter.com/culicidaepress – facebook.com/culicidaepress
threads.net/@culicidaepress

Designed by the author and polytekton © 2023

In Memory of Chester Eagle (1933-2021)

Contents

Preface

George Johnston's Shane Martin Novels

George Johnston's dual Miles Franklin Awards – Australia's most prestigious literary prize – for the first two volumes of his David Meredith trilogy has few parallels. Perhaps Hilary Mantel's Man Booker Prizes for the first two novels of her Cromwell trilogy best mirrors Johnston's late career feat. In Mantel's case, it sent readers scurrying to her backlist, which for too long had flown under the radar, especially her masterful **A Place of Greater Safety.** Sadly, in Johnston's case, **My Brother Jack** and **Clean Straw for Nothing** had the opposite effect, overshadowing his earlier work, which seemingly receded in readers' minds at the same pace that the Meredith books assumed their classic status.

Nowhere was this eclipse more apparent than with Johnston's series of novels published under the pseudonym Shane Martin. At the time he wrote them, money was in short supply, a simple truth providing ample fuel for those wanting to view them as little more than financial exercises on Johnston's part. Certainly, Johnston did not help matters with his passing reference to them as "potboilers." The five works, written between 1957 and 1962, mostly while Johnston lived with his family on the Greek island of Hydra – in the years directly leading up to his work on **My Brother Jack** – have never been reprinted, and to this day are little known, even amongst Johnston's most avid readers.

The 'Shane Martin' books were never published in Australia, and few copies appear to have entered the country or were circulated at their time of publication. The State Library Victoria, based in Melbourne – the city of Johnston's birth – holds all five titles, though, at present, they are catalogued under 'Shane Martin', with no link whatsoever to Johnston. The Baillieu Library, at the University of Melbourne, despite housing an extensive collection of Australian literature, to date holds none. Johnston's 'Shane Martin' books surface only occasionally on the antiquarian book trade, and those book dealers listing them are generally unaware of their link to a major Australian literary figure.

Derham Groves' new book goes some way toward restoring the Shane Martin novels back into Johnston's corpus, while at the same time mounting a case for their literary worth. It is, in many ways, an act of restitution, one that clearly required personal passion, along with a single-minded, dogged pursuit of its subject. His project evidences a detection prowess worthy of Johnston's eponymous hero Professor Challis.

Groves makes a strong case that these novels meant more to Johnston than has been previously recognised and are of a higher order than those few critics who have broached them have conceded. After all, few writers leave their literary pretentions – and Johnston most definitely aspired to be literary – at the door when switching genres. While it might well be the case that John Banville's Benjamin Black novels fail to live up to the literary high-water mark of his Man Booker Prize-winning **The Sea**, they remain relevant fodder for critics and readers wanting to grapple with his wider *oeuvre*.

Derham Groves' book is timely, building on a continuing wave of interest in the life of George Johnston and his wife, author Charmain Clift, a wave that sees few signs of waning. Tanya Dalzeill and Paul Genoni's award-winning **Half a Perfect World** (2018) documented the post-war artists' colony on the island of Hydra, of which the Johnstons were principal players. The Johnstons featured as characters in Polly Samson's 2020 novel **A Theatre for Dreamers**; and loomed large in Nick Broomfield's 2019 documentary **Marianne and Leonard: Words of Love**, about Leonard Cohen's love affair with Marianne Ilhen on Hydra. Biographical works on Charmain Clift, along with reprints of her writings, abound. More to the point, Johnston's **My Brother Jack** has never been out of print since first publication.

Groves brings to his book a background of interest and research into the field of detective fiction. He has pursued a lifelong interest in architecture and crime fiction, and has written extensively and curated exhibitions on Sherlock Holmes, as well as on Australian crime writers like June Wright, Arthur Upfield, and Sidney Hobson Courtier.

Given that George Johnston's 'Shane Martin' novels are largely unavailable to readers, Groves has performed an invaluable service in outlining – in detail – the intricate plotlines of each novel. More to the point, he has read the works closely, drawing correspondences with Johnston's own life, as well as with Johnston's alter-ego, David Meredith, from the trilogy. Groves has tracked down real-life models on which characters are based, and identified locales that Johnston drew upon. He details the publishing history of the books and analyses contemporary reviews and responses. In a first-rate feat of detection, he even managed to track down – and acquire – the original cover art to several of the books.

In **My Brother Jack**, the young David Meredith teaches himself to read and write hieroglyphics and spends his first journalistic earnings on a battered three-volume work **Wonders of the Past**. Does the origin of Johnston's archeologist sleuth, Professor Challis, lie in his fictional alter-ego's youth? The George Johnston that emerges from the pages of Derham Groves' study manifests a complexity that calls into question the long-held belief that the Shane Martin novels were written as cynical cash grabs. At the heart of this complexity is a series of masks that Johnston, to a greater or lesser degree, donned as part of his literary *modus operandi*. With Derham Groves' re-appraisal of the Shane Martin novels, this intricate play of masks is brought vividly and sharply into focus.

Des Cowley,
Former Principal Librarian,
State Library Victoria.

Susan Millard,
Curator, Rare Books,
Baillieu Library,
University of Melbourne.

Foreword

On Not Reading Shane Martin

George Johnston is all at once the most and the least autobiographical of Australian novelists. His reputation rests on the 'Meredith trilogy' — **My Brother Jack** (1964), **Clean Straw for Nothing** (1969), and **A Cartload of Clay** (1971). The first two books are narrated in the first person, and the third – unfinished and published posthumously – is in the third person. The protagonist, David Meredith, also appears in two earlier novels, **Closer to the Sun** (1960) and **The Far Road** (1962).

In **The Far Road** — a commercial failure but a work of which he was immensely proud[1] — Johnston used his experiences as a war correspondent to interrogate journalistic ethics. Since he referenced the events of this novel in **My Brother Jack**, perhaps it should be recognised as the first novel in the Meredith quartet.[2]

Johnston's prefatory note in **Closer to the Sun** insists, "The island of Silenos, the incidents of which I have written, the native inhabitants, the expatriate colony, the transient visitors, are all quite imaginary. This is completely a work of fiction."

Well, he would say that, wouldn't he. **Closer to the Sun** draws heavily on Johnston's life in Greece in the 1950s and reads like an early attempt at what became **Clean Straw for Nothing**. His wife and frequent collaborator, Charmian Clift, overdosed on barbiturates shortly before the latter novel's publication, without reading it, fearing it would portray her in a bad light.[3] The tragic irony is that the reality was quite opposite: in **Clean Straw for Nothing**, David Meredith's wife Cressida is a flawed but ultimately sympathetic character.

And let's say it again for emphasis. **A Cartload of Clay** was published in its unfinished form, shortly after Johnston's death. It is narrated in the third person.

You cannot — you really cannot — entwine fiction any more tightly with an author's life. And yet. To use real life incidents in a novel is not the same as writing an autobiography.

Garry Kinnane's biography makes it clear that the brooding, introverted David Meredith is anything but a simple self-portrait of George Johnston. Meredith is a carefully constructed character, a less than entirely reliable narrator, the central figure in a series of novels that cumulatively build into a complex, nuanced exploration of concepts of heroism and the construction of myths both personal and national. As Johnston himself put it, "the almost tragic irony of the final situation where Davy becomes his brother Jack's hero … the contrast with Jack's honesty, guts and, in a real sense, his uncomplicated nobility."[4]

Nor were George Johnston or David Meredith anything like Professor Ronald Challis.

When Derham Groves asked me to write a short piece for his book on Johnston's Professor Challis novels, written under the pseudonym Shane Martin, I answered, "One small problem. I've never read them." To which Derham replied, "Nobody else has either!" An exaggeration perhaps, but not far from the truth.

As Derham notes, Johnston himself referred to the Challis novels as "pot-boilers." Most people who have written about them have taken that self-deprecating, throwaway line much too seriously. Johnston, the talented child of a suburban working-class family, earned his living as a writer. In the sense that he was writing to put food on his family's table, *every book he wrote was a pot-boiler.* Some achieved critical acclaim, some did not. Some were bestsellers, and some failed dismally. The most widely acclaimed was also the most commercially successful — the autobiographical **My Brother Jack.**

Johnston's younger contemporary Jon Cleary (another working class boy who had followed the road through journalism into popular fiction) was similarly complicated about pot-boilers, but took a more confrontational approach, once telling an interviewer, "If I was a pot-boiler I would never take eight months to write a novel."[5] Cleary reconciled himself early in his career to the realisation that he was "more fitted to entertaining people than passing on messages about the state of the world" and was determined to "be as good a craftsman as I might be."[6]

A few years ago, I was on the selection panel for **Untapped: The Australian Literary Heritage Project**, a collaborative venture to identify significant Australian books that had fallen out of print and make them accessible again, initially as e-books and eventually in paper.[7]

Most of George Johnston's books were out of print, and despite our mixed feelings – Charmian's suicide casts a deep shadow – he seemed an essential inclusion. The panel agonised over the selection, eventually opting for his first collaboration with Charmian and winner of the **Sydney Morning Herald** novel prize, **High Valley** (1949). Somebody (it might have been me) mentioned the Shane Martin novels, but none of us had read them. We were looking for works that had *undeservedly* fallen out of print. We weren't interested in the thousands of genre pulps pumped out by the likes of Horwitz and Cleveland,[8] so given Johnston's pot-boilers remark, we bracketed the adventures of Professor Challis in that category.

The distinction we failed to make is that — even when he was desperate enough for money to consider a return to journalism — Johnston never wrote actual pulps. However, several of his books were published and promoted in pulp-adjacent forms.

Penguin issued **Death Takes Small Bites** (1948) as a paperback in 1959; the French translation (**A Petit Feu**, 1951, published in a series that included translations of such leading American crime writers as David Goodis, Cornell Woolrich, and Erle Stanley Gardner) sold a hundred thousand copies and was re-issued in 1975.

Horwitz, whose stable included the prolific thriller writer Carter Brown (aka Alan Yates), published a paperback edition of **High Valley** in 1965, but in their up-market, decidedly non-pulp "Horwitz Australian Library" series.

Collins highlighted the erotic elements of **The Sponge Divers** (1956) on the covers of Fontana paperback editions in 1964 and 1971, while obscuring Charmian's co-authorship of the novel.

The Darkness Outside (1959) is a psychological drama generally recognised as Johnston's most accomplished literary novel before the Meredith sequence, and arguably his most complex and sophisticated work, full stop, earning comparisons with Joseph Conrad. The 1964 Fontana paperback includes advertisements for Alistair MacLean (**Night Without End, The Last Frontier**), Hammond Innes (**The Strange Land, Killer Mine, The Angry Mountain**), and Ian Fleming's old drinking pal, Geoffrey Jenkins (**A Grue of Ice, A Twist of Sand**). Also, the front cover has a quote in large block type from a review proclaiming it "macabre, hypnotic, frightening" below the image of a man and a woman leaning over a bloodied corpse.

Genuine pulp writers, though, pumped out formulaic work to order at the rate of tens of thousands of words every week. Like Cleary, Johnston did not — could not — do that. A conscientious craftsman, constantly writing and re-writing, he finished some books in months, but took many years over others.

Even the thoroughly noir **Death Takes Small Bites** cannot resist absurdist notes and metafictional touches: the protagonist Cavendish C. Cavendish (the middle C is not an initial but his entire middle name) claims to be thinking of writing a crime thriller, with the title **Death Takes Small Bites.** The French translation, **A Petit Feu**, takes this ironic playfulness further. To cook "a petit feu" is to cook on low heat. Metaphorically, it can also mean to die a slow death. An explanation of the grim joke would require too many spoilers.

Death Takes Small Bites has been dismissed as "spurious and poorly plotted." Johnston himself, never a gentle critic of his own work, called it "pretty lousy."[9] It is wildly implausible, and could have done with some editing. But here's the thing. It is a Romance, in the early modern sense. You don't go to Edmund Spenser for coherence and plausibility. Like the Redcrosse Knight in Spenser's **Faerie Queene (1590)**, Cavendish sets out brimming with confidence but quickly finds himself way out of his depth. And like Spenser, Johnston had a moral purpose. If you stop reading more than ten pages before the end, you too will think **Death Takes Small Bites** a "pretty lousy" genre piece, a low-grade Fu Manchu knock-off, riddled with racism, sexism, and more than a hint of sadism. The denouement upends all that. As often in Chandler and Hammett, and Johnston's contemporary Ross Macdonald, the bigger picture reveals a sickening betrayal.

There is also a nod to Camus. **The Plague** (1947) was published the year before **Death Takes Small Bites**. Cavendish's quest takes him to a plague-stricken city, where he encounters a selfless doctor who knows he is ultimately powerless but nevertheless persists in the face of overwhelming horror. As a device for advancing the plot, this episode is indeed "spurious," but it opens up themes of heroism and integrity that are core concerns of the Meredith novels.

Death Takes Small Bites is ultimately a dark comedy of errors — a violent adult **Wizard of Oz**: Cavendish is the cowardly lion, and there is also an enigmatic figure behind a curtain and a poppy field! Cavendish and his love interest, the gorgeous Charmian, are set upon by gangsters. It's a case of mistaken identity. But the gangsters are dim-witted and befuddled by the assumptions they make, while Cavendish and Charmian — like the isolated archaeologists in the **The Darkness Outside —** fail to interrogate their own mental frameworks. Alfred Hitchcock would have made a great movie of it.

Professor Ronald Challis, by contrast, is highly observant and never allows himself to assume anything – except his entitlement to pry into pretty much anything, anywhere, whenever the mood takes him. **Twelve Girls in the Garden** opens with Challis peering into a stranger's loungeroom window. In **The Myth is Murder**, his curiosity is piqued by a young woman wearing unusual earrings.

The Shane Martin novels feel very different from the rest of Johnston's fiction due to this quality in the protagonist, and it also helps to explain why he adopted a pseudonym, openly acknowledged it, and continued to write under his own name. Starting with the Penguin edition of **Death Takes Small Bites**, the author biographies in Johnston's novels consistently note his authorship of "suspense" or "detective" novels "under the pseudonym of Shane Martin."

Regardless, the identity of Shane Martin would have been easy for anyone close to Johnston to solve: the Challis novels use Greek settings, including islands where the Johnstons lived, and Shane and Martin were the names of two of his children.

To spell it out, Shane Martin was not a mask but a brand. By publishing the Challis novels pseudonymously, Johnston was not attempting to conceal his association with them from the world at large but creating a distinct authorial persona to enable himself to write in a different style. In a sense, Shane Martin is as much a fictional narrator as David Meredith.

Here's another thing. Johnston trained as a lithographer before becoming a journalist. He was a very visual writer, fond of lavishing detailed physical descriptions even on relatively minor characters.

So, what do you think Shane Martin looked like, given that Shane is a unisex name, and that Shane Johnston was a girl?

Thanks to Derham Groves, I have now read two of the adventures of Professor Challis, **Twelve Girls in the Garden** and **The Myth is Murder**. Whether I have read Shane Martin is another question. I agree they deserve more recognition and wish I had pushed to include them in **Untapped**.

Ian Morrison,
Heritage Librarian,
Libraries Tasmania.

Endnotes

[1] Garry Kinnane, **George Johnston: A Biography** (Melbourne: Nelson, 1986), p.194. Kinnane reports that 82 copies of the first edition were sold in Australia. This does not necessarily mean that it failed to find an audience: lending slips in the State Library of Tasmania's surviving copy show that it was constantly on loan from July 1962 until at least March 1964.

[2] Greer Johnson and Chris Tiffin, 'The Evolution of George Johnston's David Meredith,' **Australian Literary Studies**, vol. 11, no. 2, 1983, pp. 162-170.

[3] Kinnane, p. 280.

[4] Quoted in Johnson and Tiffin, p. 169.

[5] Christopher Day, 'The Golden Years of Jon Cleary'. **Sydney Morning Herald**, 28 August 1966, p.84.

[6] Quoted in Roger Osborne, 'Jon Cleary and Sundowner Productions Limited: The Making of a Textual Craftsman', **Script & Print**, vol. 45, no. 4, 2021, pp. 141-155 [146, 147].

[7] **Untapped: The Australian Literary Heritage Project**, https://untapped.org.au/, accessed September 2023.

[8] For a detailed account of mid-twentieth century Australian pulp publishing, see Andrew Nette, **Horwitz Publications, Pulp Fiction and the Rise of the Australian Paperback** (London: Anthem, 2022).

[9] Quoted by Kinnane, p. 91.

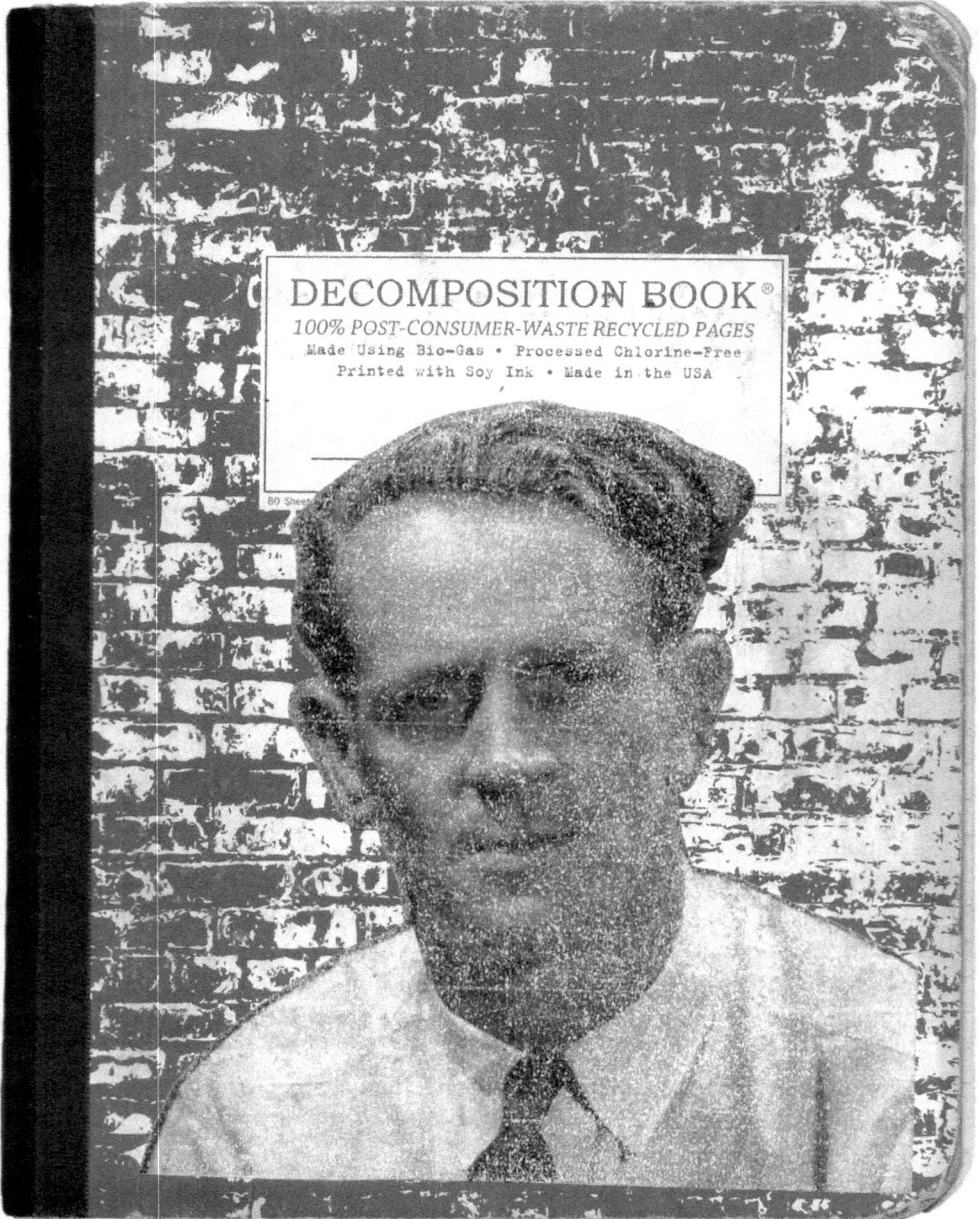

Plate 1 Front cover of Derham Groves' notebook.

Introduction

George Johnston & Professor Ronald Challis

Reading and Writing

In 2008, I curated an exhibition called **Murderous Melbourne** at the Baillieu Library, the University of Melbourne, which focused on three 'golden age' crime writers from Melbourne, Victoria, Australia — Arthur Upfield (1890-1964), Sidney H. Courtier (1904-1974), and June Wright (1919-2012). But in preparation for this exhibition, I read many crime novels of the period by other Melbourne writers, including, to my surprise, George Johnston (1912-1970), the winner of two Miles Franklin Awards for his autobiographical novels **My Brother Jack** (1964) and **Clean Straw For Nothing** (1969).

While most famous for writing **My Brother Jack** — arguably the great twentieth-century Australian novel — Johnston wrote many books, including six crime novels. The first was **Death Takes Small Bites** (1948), featuring the American journalist and accidental detective Cavendish C. Cavendish. Johnston's other five crime novels were **Twelve Girls in the Garden** (1957), **The Saracen Shadow** (1957), **The Man Made of Tin** (1958), **The Myth is Murder** (1959), titled **The Third Statue** (1959) in the

USA, and **A Wake for Mourning** (1962), titled **The Mourners' Journey** (1963) in the USA, which all feature the American archaeologist and amateur sleuth Professor Ronald Challis. (Some have suggested that Johnston's **The Cyprian Woman** (1955) and **The Far Road** (1962) are crime novels, but I do not consider them as such.) Johnston wrote the Challis novels using the pseudonym Shane Martin, based on the names of his daughter Shane (1949-1974) and son Martin (1947-1990). Their mother was Johnston's second wife, the Australian author Charmian Clift (1923-1969), whom he married in 1947.

Johnston wrote **Death Takes Small Bites** shortly after he and Clift moved from Melbourne, his hometown, to Sydney late in 1946. He wrote the first four Challis novels on the island of Hydra in Greece, where the Johnstons lived between 1955 and 1964. And he wrote the fifth Challis novel in Stanton, England, where the Johnstons lived for six months over 1960-61.

Generally speaking, in the five Challis novels, the Professor searches for somebody who is, in turn, looking for someone or something. Money was always very tight for the Johnstons on Hydra. According to Clift, the Challis novels "were bread and butter [...] which [George] wrote at white-heat at the rate of a couple of months for each one as insurance policies for me and the kids."[1] (**Fig. 1**)

Like everything that Johnston wrote before **My Brother Jack**, the Challis novels are out of print and pretty much forgotten. Fortunately, I bought second-hand copies of them in the lead-up to the **Murderous Melbourne** exhibition. Now, they are very hard to find and often expensive.

Homicide On Hydra: George Johnston's Crime Novels is my attempt to recover and restore Johnston's Challis books from obscurity. They deserve much more attention than they have received because, besides being excellent thrillers, they reveal much about Johnston, one of Australia's best-loved and most successful writers.

Fig. 1 The Johnstons: (L-R) George, Shane, Charmian, Jason, and Martin.

What's In A Name?

Because George Johnston wrote the Challis novels under a pseudonym and once called them "pot-boilers,"[2] many people have assumed Johnston was ashamed of them and they are not worth reading. However, it is nowhere near as simple as that.

People have made far too much of Johnston telling Kay Keavney of **The Australian Women's Weekly** the Challis novels were pot-boilers because, even when the author was the one who said it, that does not necessarily mean they are no good. Sir Arthur Conan Doyle (1859-1930) was very contemptuous of his Sherlock Holmes stories, but that does not mean they are no good either. As someone who has read a lot of detective fiction over the years, the Challis novels are very well written and very entertaining to read. Whether Johnston was ashamed of writing them is a tricky question, once again without a simple answer. The thoughts of two characters Johnston based on himself and created after he wrote the Challis novels might provide some clues.

David Meredith was the alter ego of Johnston in his three acclaimed autobiographical novels, **My Brother Jack**, **Clean Straw for Nothing**, and **A Cartload of Clay** (1971) — with the latter being unfinished and published posthumously. In the first novel, while learning to become a lithographer, the teenaged Meredith began writing articles about sailing ships on the side for the **Morning Post**, calling himself 'Stunsail' (i.e., an extra fair-weather sail used on square-rigged ships) "because of a shy *shame* that overcame me."[3] [My italics.] But after writing only two articles, Meredith "wrote to the magazine editor suggesting that the pseudonym [...] be discarded in favour of my own name."[4]

Much of what Meredith did in those three novels, Johnston had done in real life, including precisely that. While learning to become a lithographer, the sixteen-year-old Johnston started writing articles about sailing ships on the side for the **Argus** (1848-1957), calling himself 'Stunsail.' They published his first article, 'The Glory That Was — Coal Hulks with Proud Histories' (1929), under his pseudonym,[5] but all of his subsequent articles under his own name.[6]

Secondly, another Johnston surrogate was the (unnamed) narrator in his short story, 'Vale Pollini' (1965), who lived on Hydra exactly for the same reasons that Johnston did: "A house could be bought for almost nothing and rented for even less," the narrator said. "Living was quite possibly cheaper than anywhere else in Europe. So were wine and cigarettes."[7] And also like Johnston, he wrote thrillers using a pen name, explaining, "I wrote suspense stories under a *shamed* pseudonym."[8] [My italics.]

Since Johnston's two stand-ins used pseudonyms because, in the case of Meredith, he was ashamed of being a writer — albeit briefly, and in the case of the unnamed narrator, he was ashamed of what he wrote, perhaps Johnston had similar feelings about the Challis novels. But if that was true, then it is hard to judge to what extent he was ashamed of them, given that his pseudonym comprised the names of two of his children, and he dedicated the books to his family and friends. So, if Johnston was hiding behind 'Shane Martin,' it was in plain sight because you did not have to be much of a detective to figure out that Johnston was Martin, especially if you were Australian and interested in writers and artists. Furthermore, Johnston never disowned the Challis novels and was also happy to include them among his books. For example, the author's bio on the back of the 1959 Penguin edition of **Death Takes Small Bites** states, "George Johnston, under his own name in collaboration with his wife, or, more recently, under the pseudonym of 'Shane Martin,' is the author of many war books, travel books, novels, and thrillers."[9]

Johnston used a pseudonym, in my view, to separate the Challis novels from his other work. Of course, he was not the first writer to do this for that reason and not because they were ashamed of their work. For example, Dame Agatha Christie (1890-1976) used the pseudonym 'Mary Westmacott' to separate her detective novels from her psychological thrillers. A couple of book reviewers also suspected something like this with Johnston. Reviewing **Twelve Girls in the Garden** for the **Spokane Chronicle** in Washington, Bob Hill said, "Perhaps Shane Martin is a pseudonym for an author whose previous works have dealt with weightier themes."[10] While Pamela Ruskin of the **Australian Jewish News** in Melbourne, Australia, said, "This is a first-class mystery written so well that I feel Shane Martin must be a pseudonym that cloaks either a writer or another professor."[11]

In 'The Case of a Very Loose Canon: The Shane Martin "Potboilers" of George Johnston' (2017), authors Paul Genoni and Tanya Dalziell rather timidly suggested that the name "Professor Challis might prompt readers to recall Arthur Conan Doyle's popular detective Professor Challenger, although the two characters are very unlike."[12] Professor George Edward Challenger, to give him his full name, appeared in three science fiction novels by Doyle — **The Lost World** (1912), **The Poison Belt** (1913), and **The Land of Mist** (1926). He was an adventurer, an anthropologist, and a zoologist but not a detective. Nevertheless, Genoni and Dalziell might be right about him since Johnston was familiar with **The Lost World**, mentioning it in two articles he wrote about Sikang in East Tibet.

In 'Strange Tales Come Out of Tibet … Asia's Enigma' (1945), Johnston said, "I am not prepared to believe that hidden somewhere in silent Sikang is Hilton's Shangri-La or Conan Doyle's Lost World — but I am not prepared to disbelieve that behind its mountain barriers are strange secrets about which the world of today knows nothing."[13] And in 'Modern Politics Have Come to Sikang's "Lost World"' (1950), Johnston wrote, "I had the feeling then that I was about to enter **The Lost World** of the late Sir Arthur Conan Doyle."[14] Later, I argue that Johnston based Edmund Grosteller in **The Myth is Murder** on Doyle's Professor Challenger and was a fan of Doyle's Sherlock Holmes detective stories.

Regarding the origin of the name of Johnston's Professor Challis, there are other equally — if not more likely — sources than Doyle's Professor Challenger, in my opinion. For example, Johnston moved from Melbourne to Sydney in 1946 to work for the *Sun* (1910-1988). Its offices were at 60-66 Elizabeth Street, Sydney, not far from Challis House (1906-present) at 4-10 Martin Place, opposite the cenotaph, and the Sydney Post Office. Johnston would have regularly walked past Challis House — its name etched in stone above the door. (**Fig. 2**)

Fig. 2 Challis House, Martin Place, Sydney.

The University of Sydney built Challis House as a commercial rental property with money bequeathed by the English-born Australian merchant and philanthropist John Henry Challis (1806-1880). (**Fig. 3**) The University used the rest of his generous bequest to fund various professorships. As the Challis Professor of this, or the Challis Professor of that, was regularly mentioned in the press, perhaps Johnston reversed this familiar title to get the name, Professor Challis. He also might have liked that it was a homonym for 'chalice,' a suitable aptronym for an archaeologist.

Fig. 3 John Henry Challis (1806-1880).

I wondered whether the Ned Kelly Award-winning Australian crime writer Garry Disher (b. 1949) named his detective, Inspector Hal Challis, who has appeared in seven novels (1999-2016), as a tip of the hat to George Johnston. But, alas, no. "I must admit I collect names from film credits, newspapers, anywhere at all, and would have collected the name Challis from somewhere," Disher told me. "I wish it were a homage to Johnston, but it is not. I remember listening to CDs by The Tallis Scholars [a British early music vocal group] at the time but dismissed Tallis as not quite right for my character. For some reason, I agonise over names. They have to fit somehow."[15]

Likewise, I wondered whether my late friend Chester Eagle (1933-2021), winner of the **Age** Book of the Year in 1985, had named his heroine Victoria Challis in his eponymous 1991 novel after the Professor since he was a Johnston aficionado. In 1980, Chester interviewed George Johnston's brother Jack and sister-in-law Pat at their home in the Melbourne suburb of Doveton. "I had two of the best nights of my life with Jack and Pat — two of nature's gents,"[16] he said. Chester also reviewed **George Johnston: A Biography** by Garry Kinnane for the **Age**. "The closer you get to Johnston and Clift, the harder they are to see,"[17] remarked Chester. And he tidied up the manuscript of **Charmian and George: The Marriage of George Johnston and Charmian Clift** by his late friend, Max Brown (1916-2003), for its posthumous publication in 2004.

I took three months of Long Service Leave in 2018 to visit Greece. Hot on the trail of Johnston and Challis, I emailed Chester from Hydra to ask him about Victoria Challis. "I wasn't even aware George Johnston had invented a Professor Challis," replied Chester, to my surprise. But I think his take on the plight of the Johnstons on Hydra was very insightful:

> I feel connected to George, even though he's not a man I would have liked. In many ways, I feel sorry for him because, although he had talent to spare, he had to struggle desperately to become the writer he wanted to be. I believe George suffered terribly when he wrote the books for which he is now famous. And even more so when he wasn't writing them, because he didn't know what he needed to write. I think George and Charmian were very bad for each other, even though there's no question

they were bonded more deeply than either could manage. The dream they set off in search of turned into a nightmare, and neither could find a way to avoid what was happening. It's all too sad to think about. Thanks for writing from Greece, Derham! When you return to Melbourne, let's share a bottle of red. Supplies are holding well at my end.[18]

Roots

The ancestors of Professor Challis "crossed the Atlantic to Massachusetts in the brig *Jupiter* in 1754."[19] (**Fig. 4**) Challis's father was "a stern and opinionated judge of the Supreme Court."[20] Little is known about the Professor's mother apart from that she always insisted they set their clock twenty minutes fast."[21] Challis

Fig. 4 The HMS Brig Jupiter.

was six years old on 1 January 1897,[22] which means he was born in 1891. He grew up in Boston, Massachusetts. "On good days when I was a kid back in Boston, I was allowed to help [arrange] my uncle's collection of botanical specimens,"[23] Challis recalled. And he spent his "childhood holidays" on the coast of Maine.[24] That was all George Johnston told us about his archaeologist-detective's early years.

Why did Johnston make Challis American instead of Australian or British? In **Clean Straw For Nothing**, David Meredith said, "Australians were good cricketers and confidence men, swashbuckling soldiers, inveterate sportsmen and gamblers, but not to be taken seriously in other fields."[25] If Johnston agreed with his alter ego, archaeology was one of those "other fields," so Challis could not be Australian. And in 'From Narragonia to Elysium: Some Preliminary Reflections on the Fictional Image of the Academic' (1990), Richard Sheppard explained there had been a trend away from British academics to American ones in fiction following the publication of **Lucky Jim** (1954) by the English author Kingsley Amis (1922-1995), which had created "the sense [...] that something [was] going wrong with British higher education and its relationship with society."[26] Therefore, "the same systematic considerations suggest why Shane Martin's post-**Lucky Jim** academic sleuth Professor Ronald Challis [...] had to be non-British,"[27] said Sheppard. I believe he is correct, but it seems Johnston had a soft spot for Americans regardless, especially New Englanders. Besides Challis, who came from Boston, Cavendish C. Cavendish in **Death Takes Small Bites** came from Canaan, Connecticut,[28] and Eliot Purcell, the protagonist in Johnston's dystopian novel **The Darkness Outside** (1959), studied archaeology at the University of Pennsylvania in Philadelphia.[29]

A Face Difficult to Forget

Throughout the five Challis novels, the Professor was in his sixties. He had a "shock of white thistledown hair,"[30] also often described as a "mane of white hair."[31] Challis had "China-blue eyes,"[32] which were "bird-bright."[33] To add to his avian appearance, he moved with "quick, bird-like hops"[34] or "bird-like skips"[35] and thus "looked like some queer, crested bird."[36] Challis had "a thin face pink and pointed that looked rather like the face of an elderly pixie."[37] Indeed, people often described him as "pixie-like,"[38] "gnome-like,"[39] or "elfin,"[40] especially since he was "uncommonly short"[41] and never weighed "more than one hundred and twenty-six pounds."[42]

Sefton Halliday, the sixty-year-old artist in Johnston's short story, 'Requiem Mass' (1952 or 1953), written four or five years before **Twelve Girls in the Garden**, was the predecessor of Challis. He was also "imp-like"[43] and "not human at all," with a "great mane of silky white hair tossed above his narrow face like thistledown as if at any moment he might burst with a puff and scatter tiny white seed-darts into the air all about him."[44] (More about him later.)

Did Johnston have someone in mind when he envisaged Halliday and Challis? Perhaps it was the English philosopher Lord Bertrand Russell (1872-1970). In an article on the influence of America on global economics that Johnston wrote in his weekly column in 1952, he suggestively described him as "that incorrigible and mischievous intellectual pixie."[45] Russell also had an unruly mane of white hair, a bird-like appearance, and a slight build like Challis. (**Fig. 5**)

The Professor's distinctive features became something of a go-to for Johnston. In **My Brother Jack**, he modelled David Meredith's friend Sam Burlington on his own friend, the Australian artist Sam Atyeo (1910-1990). (**Fig. 6**) However, Johnston's description of Atyeo sounded more like Challis because he had "a kind of skittery, bird-like quality," and the way "his nondescript feather-coloured hair would fly into spiky little crests, enhanced the avian look

Fig. 5 Lord Bertrand Russell *(left)* and Professor Challis by William Randell.

Fig. 6 *Sam Atyeo* (1930) by Sybil Craig (1901-1989).

he had."[46] Another example was Conrad Fegel, the Czech artist in **Closer to the Sun** (1960), the first of Johnston's novels that featured David Meredith, who, once again, sounded like Challis since he looked like a "little pixie"[47] with "brilliant blue eyes"[48] and "a mane of thin, dusty hair around his temples."[49]

It is worth noting that George Johnston wrote only two series of books. The first was the five Professor Challis novels (1957-1962) — **Twelve Girls in the Garden, The Saracen Shadow, The Man Made of Tin, The Myth is Murder**, and **A Wake for Mourning**. The second was the five David Meredith novels (1960-1971) — **Closer to the Sun, The Far Road, My Brother Jack, Clean Straw for Nothing**, and **A Cart Load of Clay**. Regarding the latter series, the first two novels are generally not given as much weight as the last three. Perhaps the reason is that in **Closer to the Sun**, Meredith's brother was called Mark, not Jack, and his wife was called Kate, not Cressida, and **The Far Road** was set in China during World War II when Meredith was single and a war correspondent. Although, in the scheme of things, this hardly seems relevant.

Lawyer First, Archaeologist Second

Young Ronald Challis had "every intention of ultimately embracing a career in the law,"[50] and following in the footsteps of his father, who gave him a thick gold pocket watch inscribed with the cautionary advice, "Never take no for an answer,"[51] when he graduated from Harvard Law School. However, one rainy day in New York in April 1915, a female student from Vassar, having "suddenly become more interested in the new phenomenon

Fig. 7 Foyer, Algonquin Hotel *(left)* and the Metropolitan Museum of Art (c. 1915).

of Dadaism than in Challis's rather immature observations on constitutional law," stood him up in the foyer of the Algonquin Hotel. Unexpectedly at a loose end, he wandered into the Metropolitan Museum of Art and "found himself attending a lecture on the Mycenean excavations and was promptly lost both to matrimony and the legal profession."[52] (**Fig. 7**)

The fact that Challis studied law helps to explain his interest in crime. Moreover, he believed that crime detection and archaeology were similar. "I like piecing things together," Challis told Bimbo Grasset in **Twelve Girls in the Garden**. "Unlike you, I very much enjoy mysteries. It is my profession, in a sense."[53] And the reason why they were similar was that their methodologies were the same:

> "In my profession," said the Professor, "there is a system we often have to work on which involves the establishment of an initial hypothesis. We may have discovered a section of crumpled wall, some fragments of pottery, a heap of charred ash, a bronze arrowhead, a coin or two. The fragments are scattered and seem to be unrelated. The levels are confusing. The gaps to be filled in seem impossibly blank. What we try to do is establish a working

33

hypothesis and try to build the pieces around it. If the picture begins to fit together, we press on with it. [...] If it doesn't, we discard it altogether and look around for something different. [...] Chance comes into it. It is an elastic combination of expert knowledge, pure chance, luck, deduction, and the ability to master jigsaw puzzles. [...] Now, on the basis of this rather hit-or-miss system, would you like to hear my theory on your brother's disappearance?"[54]

According to the Professor's close friend and eminent colleague, Sir Granville Peart, Challis was "the most brilliant of living archaeologists [...] whose imaginative discoveries in Crete and Syria and Anatolia had entirely reshaped man's knowledge of two thousand years of ancient history."[55] After working in Greece for over thirty years, his achievements included "the discovery of the

Fig. 8 The British archaeologist, Sir Arthur Evans (1851-1941).

Gournian Treasury, a distinguished professorship and an impressive number of honorary doctorates, enough excavated material to fill a good-size museum, and a series of monographs which the Royal Society had designated as the greatest single contribution to knowledge of the preclassical past since Evans."[56] (**Fig. 8**)

The Gournian Treasury

Professor Challis was best known for discovering the Gournian Treasury. Thus, when Peter Judd first met him in **The Saracen Shadow**, he asked, "You aren't the Challis, by chance, who dug Gournia? [...] How awfully nice to meet you. I was fascinated by your book." Then Judd turned to his friend and patron, Doctor Talbot Fillingham-Ausling, and said, "It was Professor Challis, you will recall [...] who excavated the great Minoan Treasury at Gournia, in Crete,"[57] Ironically, he found the Gournian Treasury by chance, "having been let down by an irresponsible Cretan muleteer who had failed to bring three promised donkeys for a hard journey across the mountains to Krista, he set out to walk the first six miles or so, and in doing this had inadvertently stumbled onto both the remains of an ancient wall and everlasting archaeological fame."[58]

In real life, a team of American archaeologists led by Harriet Boyd Hawes (1871-1945) first excavated Gournia between 1901 and 1904. (**Fig. 9**) They found a palace, a town square, sixty-four houses, two cemeteries, and a network of streets. But they did not find a treasury.[59] Johnston knew enough about it to reserve this absent but plausible building for Challis to discover. In **A Wake for Mourning**, the Professor told Tony Saben that he had found the Gournian Treasury "in a very confusing labyrinth below a most confusing palace."

> The place was overthrown, sacked, burnt, rolled around by earthquakes, trodden down and ploughed under. It was lost and quite forgotten for

Fig. 9 The American archaeologist, Harriet Boyd Hawes.

four thousand years, covered over for centuries by two hundred feet of rock and earth. It became only a barren hill without a name in a wasteland on the coast of Crete miles and miles from anywhere. And would you believe this, Saben? — I guessed where it was and I went and dug it all up![60]

George Johnston was always interested in archaeology. "Whenever he had money to spend on books, right through his life, he very often spent it on works of history of one kind or another, or [...] archaeology or ancient civilisations,"[61] said Garry Kinnane

(b. 1938) in **George Johnston: A Biography** (1986). Indeed, in **My Brother Jack**, David Meredith, aged fifteen, spent his first pay cheque for writing "on second-hand library books in Cole's Book Arcade," which included "a rather battered three-volume set called **Wonders of the Past**" (1923) by Sir John Alexander Hammerton (1871-1949). "This was concerned with ancient history and archaeology, and I didn't quite know why I had bought it, except that it had wonderful colour-plates of the finds in King Tutankhamen's tomb, and I was surprised that none of the eager, grasping bargain-hunters at this book sale seemed to want it,"[62] said Meredith. He also taught himself "to read and write the hieroglyphics of Ancient Egypt."[63] Thus, Challis was an extension of Johnston and, as far as that went, a forerunner of Meredith. "You look the real bloody old absent-minded professor, don't you?"[64] Meredith's brother Jack told him. But despite the highly autobiographical nature of the Challis novels, Kinnane dismissed them, saying they were neither deeply researched nor very serious,[65] which was untrue.

In the Footsteps of Sherlock Holmes

Professor Challis was often a law unto himself, prying through the windows of strange houses, reading a newspaper or even a private letter over the shoulder of the person seated next to him on a train or a bus, peeping through keyholes, listening in to telephone calls, and eavesdropping on private conversations.[66] "I am an interfering old busy-body who keeps asking far too many questions,"[67] he said. In this respect, Challis was more like Miss Jane Marple by Dame Agatha Christie (1890-1976) than Sherlock Holmes by Sir Arthur Conan Doyle (1859-1930). Even so, Challis had some noteworthy similarities — as well as differences — to the Great Detective. For example, he was also a bachelor. When the Professor was not on an archaeological dig somewhere in the Mediterranean, he lived in a "small bachelor flat [...] in a tall and rather unprepossessing building at 93 St. George's Square" in London.[68] The landlord of

Challis, Mr. Valentine, was just as fussy as the landlady of Holmes, Mrs. Hudson, but had it over her for colour. (More about him later.) However, Challis did not have a permanent sidekick like Holmes. The person who came the closest to Doctor Watson was Sir Granville Peart in **The Man Made of Tin**.

Challis was also eccentric like Holmes. "He took his hot bath and shaved himself while he was in the tub, did four minutes of yogi breathing by the open window, and brewed himself two cups of thick Turkish coffee over the small, spluttering gas ring in the corner of the room." Indeed, the Professor liked Turkish coffee so much that he always travelled with a long-handled Greek copper coffee pot or *briki,* given to him by the owner of a *kafenéion* in Piraeus, with which he could brew coffee to his liking, black, gritty, and thick, over just a few charcoal embers almost anywhere.[69] (**Fig. 10**) He was also a great gourmet — like another classic detective,

Fig. 10 The Professor's *briki* or Greek coffee pot.

Nero Wolfe, created by Rex Stout (1886-1975) — dining at fine restaurants like *Chapon Fin* in Bordeaux and *Restaurant Bourgogne* in London, and typically having *Coquilles à la Flamberge,* a broccoli vinaigrette, soft Camembert, and a half-bottle of Moselle from Trarbach for lunch.[70]

Challis claimed to have only two hobbies — painting and murder.[71] He exuded a convincing air of Christian integrity in public, but, in private, his beliefs were almost entirely pagan.[72] The Professor could ride a bicycle and drive a speedboat but not a car. He regretted that one never sees an opera singer nowadays with a cheetah, nor a prima ballerina with a leopard.[73] Challis could get a bee in his bonnet about the most surprising and trivial things. "You could never possibly trust, for example, a marriage manual written by a man with a hyphenated name," he once declared. "I don't know why this should be. There is no reason or logic […] it just waives validity."[74] Challis was gregarious[75] even when alone, talking[76] and sometimes singing Gilbert and Sullivan

Fig. 11 The American journalist, Art Buchwald.

to himself.[77] He liked to read crime thrillers by the French writer Maurice Dekobra (1885-1973)[78] and what the American satirist Art Buchwald (1925-2007) had to say in the Paris edition of the **Herald Tribune**.[79] (**Fig. 11**) But the Professor was sick to death of the erudite posturing of some of his academic colleagues.[80]

Admittedly, the Professor's eccentricities were insignificant compared to the Great Detective's. For example, Doctor Watson was astonished to discover that Holmes was ignorant of the Copernican Theory and the composition of the Solar System on the one hand[81] but could identify the ash from one hundred and forty different varieties of pipe, cigar and cigarette ash on the other.[82] "What the deuce is it to me [...] that we go round the sun," protested Holmes. "If we went round the moon, it would not make a pennyworth of difference to me or [...] my work."[83] However, Watson revealed the true extent of Holmes's peculiarities when he grumbled that he "keeps his cigars in the coal-scuttle, his tobacco in the toe-end of a Persian slipper, and his unanswered correspondence transfixed by a jack-knife into the very centre of his wooden mantelpiece." Watson also believed "that pistol practice should distinctly be an open-air pastime" and objected to "when Holmes in one of his queer humours would sit in an armchair, with his hair-trigger and a hundred Boxer cartridges, and proceed to adorn the opposite wall with a patriotic V.R. done in bullet-pocks."[84]

Lastly, whenever Challis spoke ponderously or thought deeply, he would make steeples with his fingers like Holmes. In **Twelve Girls in the Garden**, he "placed his fingertips together and examined them thoughtfully."[85] Likewise, in the third Challis novel, **The Man Made of Tin**: "He nodded, placed his fingertips neatly together and stared into the fire."[86] In the fourth Challis novel, **The Myth is Murder**: "The Professor made churches and steeples with his fingertips."[87] And in the fifth Challis novel, **A Wake for Mourning** (1960): "He placed his fingers together carefully."[88] Holmes was very fond of doing this, too. For example, in **The Sign of the Four** (1890), he put his fingertips together, leaned his elbows on the arms of the chair, and made a steeple with his fingers, "like one who has a relish for conversation."[89] It was one of Holmes's quirky mannerisms that many actors who played him over the years jumped on, including the one who perhaps interpreted him the best, Jeremy Brett (1933-1995).

Since most boys of George Johnston's generation were fans of Sherlock Holmes, it is not surprising that he enthusiastically reported the Great Detective's one-hundredth birthday celebrations in London in 1954 in his newspaper column:

> The BBC gave half an hour to a special programme of tribute. Because of the inclement weather they were obliged to apologise for the absence of Holmes himself from the programme — he is, of course, a very old man now living a secluded life bee-keeping in Sussex — but there were plenty of others in the studio to pay homage. There was ex-Detective-Superintendent Fabian of Scotland Yard to thank Holmes for his invaluable help on many a sticky case; Holmes's old music teacher, Herr Professor Willi Notenschlager, to testify to the detective's brilliance with the violin; a clergyman whose father had taught Holmes at school, who had tales to tell of the great detective's audacity, even as a boy. Even Lord Peter Wimsey was in the studio to pay tribute to "The Master." He recalled how, when he was a boy of eight, Holmes had solved the mystery of his missing kitten. This was a case in memory of which he still treasured the receipt for two shillings and ninepence signed by Holmes, himself, and endorsed "for professional services."[90]

Worth a Second Look

In Professor Ronald Challis, George Johnston created a charming, eccentric, well-rounded protagonist who inhabited the unique and fascinating world of archaeology and crime. As such, Johnston sits very favourably alongside other Australian 'golden age' crime writers, such as Arthur Upfield; sisters Anne (1887-1966) and Margot (1896-1975) Goyder, writing as Margot Neville; Sidney H. Courtier; Pat Flower (1914-1977); Geraldine Halls (1919-1996), writing as Charlotte Jay; June Wright; Patricia Carlon (1927-2002), etc. Johnston also holds his own internationally and, in my opinion, at his best, comes close to the likes of Sir Arthur Conan Doyle, Dame Agatha Christie, Rex Stout, Georges Simenon (1903-1989), Eric Ambler (1909-1998), and Ross Macdonald (aka Kenneth Millar, 1915-1983), which is high praise, indeed, I know.

I suspect that, deep down, Johnston liked to think of himself as Australia's Ernest Hemingway (1899-1961). Imagine if Hemingway scholars chose to ignore five of the books he wrote, even though they were vehicles for trying out different things — some later used in his other books — and revealed his personal and professional contacts and views on all sorts of things from food and wine to homosexuality, all because he wrote them using a pseudonym and once suggested they were lurid tales written to make some desperately needed money. That would not be very scholarly, would it? Well, that is what most Johnston scholars seem to have done. They have chosen to ignore **Twelve Girls in the Garden**, **The Saracen Shadow**, **The Man Made of Tin**, **The Myth is Murder**, and **A Wake for Mourning** because he once described them as "pot-boilers" and wrote them under the name Shane Martin. And then Garry Kinnane inanely dismissed them in his otherwise first-rate biography. But, hopefully, not anymore. At the very least, Johnston's five Professor Challis novels are worth a second look.

Endnotes

[1] Charmian Clift (1969), 'On **Clean Straw for Nothing**' in Nadia Wheatley (ed.), **Sneaky Little Revolutions**, Sydney: NewSouth Publishing, 2022, p. 402.

[2] Kay Keavney, 'From George, With Sadness,' **Australian Women's Weekly** (Sydney, Australia), 27 August 1969, p. 13.

[3] George Johnston, **My Brother Jack**, London: Collins, 1964, p. 81.

[4] Ibid., p. 116.

[5] Stunsail (George Johnston), 'The Glory That Was — Coal Hulks with Proud Histories,' **Argus** (Melbourne, Australia), 2 February 1929, p. 2.

[6] For example, see George H. Johnston, 'Ill-Fated Voyages: Tragic Wrecks on Australian Coast,' **Argus**, 20 April 1929, p. 10.

[7] George Johnston, 'Vale Pollini' (1965), in Garry Kinnane (ed.), **George Johnston and Charmian Clift: Strong-man from Piraeus and Other Stories**, Melbourne: Nelson, 1983, p. 174.

[8] Ibid.

[9] George H. Johnston (1948), **Death Takes Small Bites**, Harmondsworth, UK: Penguin Books Ltd., 1959, unpaged back cover.

[10] Bob Hill, 'Looking at Books,' **Spokane Chronicle** (Spokane, Washington), 6 June 1957, p. 34.

[11] Pamela Ruskin, 'Thumbnail Book Reviews,' **Australian Jewish News**, (Melbourne) 5 July 1957, p. 8.

[12] Paul Genoni and Tanya Dalziell, 'The Case of a Very Loose Canon: The Shane Martin "Pot-boilers" of George Johnston,' **Southerly: A Review of Australian Literature**, vol. 77, issue 1, p. 62.

[13] George H. Johnston, 'Strange Tales Come Out of Tibet … Asia's Enigma,' **Argus**, 6 January 1945, p. 12.

[14] George H. Johnston, 'Modern Politics Have Come to Sikang's "Lost World,"' **Sun**, (Sydney) 31 October 1950, p. 17.

[15] Garry Disher (Australian author), Email to Derham Groves, 25 May 2018.

[16] Chester Eagle (Australian author), Email to Derham Groves, 17 April 2018.

[17] Chester Eagle, 'Links with Greatness,' **Age**, 11 October 1986, p. 178.

[18] Chester Eagle, 17 April 2018.

[19] Shane Martin (George Johnston), **Twelve Girls in the Garden**, New York: William Morrow and Company, 1957, p. 5.

[20] Shane Martin, **The Saracen Shadow**, London: Collins, 1957, p. 39.

[21] Ibid., p. 186.

[22] Ibid., p.

[23] Ibid., p. 83.

[24] Shane Martin, **The Man Made of Tin**, London: Collins, 1958, p. 132.

[25] George Johnston, **Clean Straw For Nothing**, London: Collins, 1969, p. 131.

[26] Ibid., p. 41.

[27] Richard Sheppard, 'From Narragonia to Elysium: Some Preliminary Reflections on the Fictional Image of the Academic,' in David Bevan (ed.), **University Fiction**, Amsterdam: Rodopi, 1990,

[28] George H. Johnston, **Death Takes Small Bites: A Novel**, London: Victor Gollancz Ltd., 1948, p. 9.

[29] George Johnston, **The Darkness Outside**, London: Collins, 1959, p. 17.

[30] Shane Martin, **The Saracen Shadow**, 1957, p. 10

[31] Shane Martin, 1958, p. 137

[32] Shane Martin, **The Myth is Murder**, London: Collins, 1959, p. 19.

[33] Shane Martin, **Twelve Girls in the Garden**, New York: William Morrow and Company, 1957, p. 23.

[34] Shane Martin **The Saracen Shadow**, p. 9

[35] Ibid., p. 60.

[36] Shane Martin, **Twelve Girls in the Garden**, p. 32.

[37] Ibid., p. 23

[38] Shane Martin 1959, p. 70.

[39] Shane Martin, 1958, p. 171

[40] Shane Martin, **The Saracen Shadow**, p. 133
[41] Shane Martin, **Twelve Girls in the Garden**, p. 5.
[42] Ibid.
[43] George Johnston (1952 or 1953), 'Requiem Mass,' in Garry Kinnane (ed.), **George Johnston, Charmian Clift, Strong-man from Piraeus**, Melbourne: Thomas Nelson Australia, 1983, p. 74.
[44] Ibid., p. 65.
[45] George H. Johnston, 'London Diary: British Labor Broods on American Dollars,' **The Sun** (Sydney, Australia), 1 October 1952, p. 20.
[46] George Johnston, 1964 p. 102.
[47] George Johnston, **Closer to the Sun**, London: Collins, 1960, p. 93.
[48] Ibid., p. 80.
[49] Ibid., p. 95.
[50] Shane Martin, **Twelve Girls in the Garden**, p. 171.
[51] Shane Martin, **The Saracen Shadow**, p. 39.
[52] Shane Martin, **Twelve Girls in the Garden**, p. 171-172.
[53] Ibid., p. 37.
[54] Ibid., p. 72.
[55] Shane Martin, **The Man Made of Tin**, p. 18.
[56] Shane Martin, **Twelve Girls in the Garden**, p. 14.
[57] Shane Martin, **The Saracen Shadow**, p. 22.
[58] Shane Martin, **Twelve Girls in the Garden**, p. 171.
[59] Livingston Watrous, Email to Derham Groves, 28 September 2022.
[60] Shane Martin (1962), **Mourners' Voyage**, New York: Doubleday & Company, Inc., 1963, p. 160.
[61] Garry Kinnane, **George Johnston: A Biography**, Melbourne: Nelson Publishers, 1986, p. 12.
[62] George Johnston, 1964, pp. 81-82.
[63] Ibid., p. 74.
[64] Ibid., p. 159.
[65] Garry Kinnane, pp. 154-155.
[66] Shane Martin, **The Saracen Shadow**, p. 69.
[67] Ibid., p. 125.
[68] Shane Martin, **Twelve Girls in the Garden**, pp. 3-4.
[69] Ibid., p. 19.
[70] Ibid., p. 43.
[71] Shane Martin, **The Saracen Shadow**, p. 12.

[72] Shane Martin, 1963, p. 157.

[73] Ibid., p. 34.

[74] Shane Martin, **Twelve Girls in the Garden**, p. 21.

[75] Shane Martin, 1963, p.3.

[76] Shane Martin 1958, p. 36.

[77] Ibid., p. 12.

[78] Shane Martin, **Twelve Girls in the Garden**, p. 56.

[79] Ibid., pp. 107-108.

[80] Ibid., pp. 10-11.

[81] Sir Arthur Conan Doyle (1887), **A Study in Scarlet**, in William S. Baring-Gould (ed.) (1968), **The Annotated Sherlock Holmes**, London: John Murray, 1973, vol. 1, p. 154.

[82] Ibid., vol. 2, p. 148.

[83] Ibid., vol. 1, p. 154.

[84] Ibid., p. 123.

[85] Shane Martin, **Twelve Girls in the Garden**, p. 106.

[86] Shane Martin 1958, p. 87.

[87] Shane Martin, 1959, p. 221.

[88] Shane Martin, 1963, p. 2.

[89] Sir Arthur Conan Doyle (1890), **The Sign of the Four**, vol. 1, p. 611.

[90] George Johnston, 'Sherlock Holmes "Can Never Die,"' **Newcastle Sun** (Newcastle, New South Wales), 14 January 1954, p. 12.

The Books

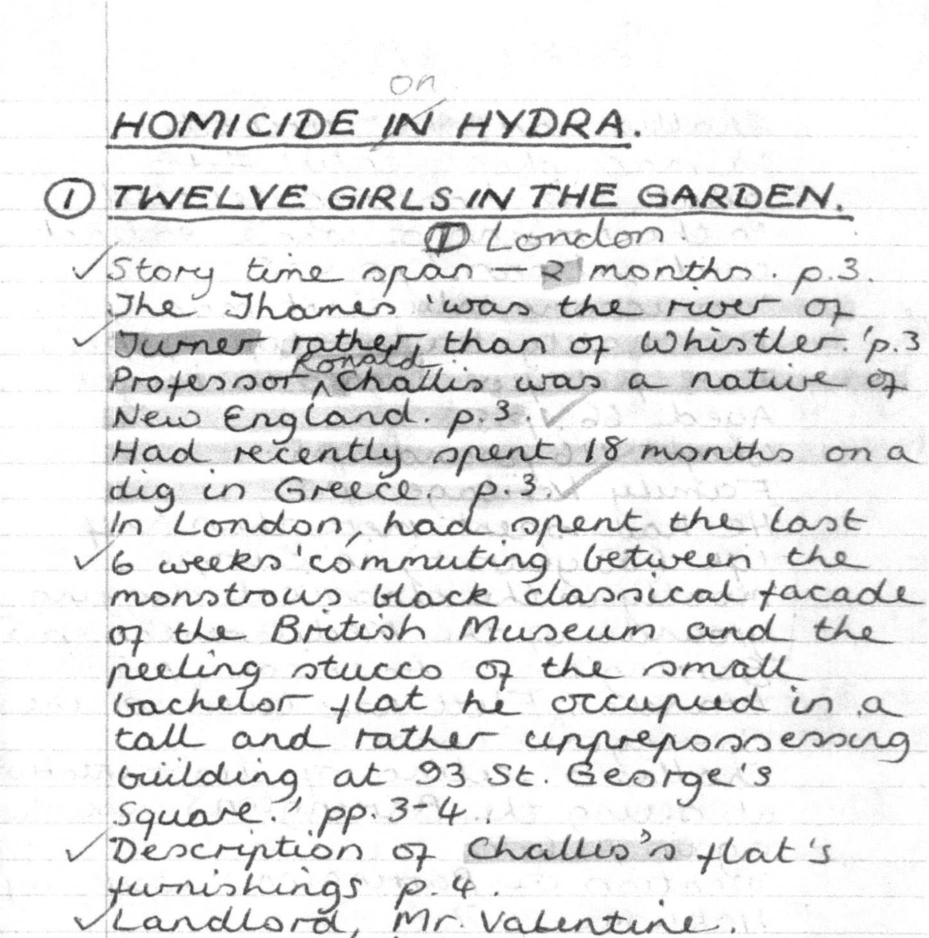

HOMICIDE *on* IN HYDRA.

(1) TWELVE GIRLS IN THE GARDEN.

(1) London

✓ Story time span — 2 months. p.3.

The Thames 'was the river of
✓ Turner *rather* than of Whistler.' p.3

Professor *Ronald* Challis was a native of
New England. p.3.

Had recently spent 18 months on a
dig in Greece. p.3.

In London, had spent the last
✓ 6 weeks 'commuting between the
monstrous black classical facade
of the British Museum and the
peeling stucco of the small
bachelor flat he occupied in a
tall and rather unprepossessing
building at 93 St. George's
Square.' pp. 3-4.

✓ Description of Challis's flat's
furnishings p. 4.

✓ Landlord, Mr. Valentine.

Had a desire to walk along the
Chelsea Embankment to see the
house of his friends, Erica and
✓ John Barrington, again.

Georgian house in Tite Street.
Description of house p. 4.

Plate 2: Page from Derham Groves' notebook.

48

1. Twelve Girls in the Garden

Like everything George Johnston wrote before his award-winning autobiographical novel **My Brother Jack** *(1964),* **Twelve Girls in the Garden** *(1957), his first crime novel featuring Professor Ronald Challis, written using the pseudonym Shane Martin, is long out of print. It takes place in London and Greece over two months in late 1957. Collins published the book in Great Britain and William Morrow in the USA, but no Australian edition was published. It is still possible to pick up a reasonably priced second-hand copy of the American edition, but finding a copy of the English one is almost impossible. A summary of* **Twelve Girls in the Garden** *follows, with comments, opinions, and reviews afterward.*

Dramatis Personae

Professor Ronald Challis	An archaeologist and amateur detective.
Mr. Valentine	The Professor's landlord.
John and Erica Barrington	The Professor's friends.
Paul Grasset	An artist who bought the Barringtons' house.
Bimbo Grasset	An artist and Paul's younger brother.
Claude Fanlec	Paul's agent.
Curtis J. Grantheim Jr.	An art collector and client of Fanlec.

Frida Lindstrom	Paul's favourite model.
Joákimos	Paul's art dealer.
Stephen Roach	The junior partner of Joákimos.
Brandon Flett	A student of architecture who rents Paul's house.
Charlie	A taxi driver and Flett's odd job man.
Joe Kelly	A private eye hired by Flett.
Gigi	Flett's girlfriend and Paul's model.
Helen Sorelle	Paul's girlfriend and model.
Polly Sorelle	Helen's younger sister and Paul's model.
Vassilis Klonaris	A sea captain employed by the Sorelles' father.
Theódoros Milos	The owner of a *Kafenio* on Astypalaia.
Cyril Bloom	A British diplomat.
Bunty Williams	Bloom's scatty friend.

London

After spending eighteen months on an archaeological dig in Greece, Professor Ronald Challis comes to London to do research at the British Museum. He has a small bachelor flat in an eighteenth-century Georgian building at 93 St. George's Square, Pimlico, London. (**Fig. 12**) It contains too much antique French furniture and too many mid-Victorian objects for either comfort or the Professor's liking. There are also mezzotints decorating the walls and ornate chandeliers hanging from the ceilings.

After six weeks in London, Challis is bored with just travelling between his flat and the museum. So, for a change of scenery, he decides to visit the house in Tite Street, Chelsea, where his American friend John Barrington and his Greek wife Erica used to live. Having arrived unannounced, the current occupant of the house, a handsome, thick-set American in his mid-thirties named

Brandon Flett, obligingly shows the Professor around. "Did you know Whistler lived here once?" asks Flett. "Just before he went broke over that business with Ruskin. That's what they say, anyway." (**Fig. 13**)

Fig. 12 St. George's Square, Pimlico (recent photograph).

Fig. 13 James McNeill Whistler (left) and his house at 31 Tite Street, Chelsea.

Flett is studying architecture in London and renting the house from Paul Grasset, a French artist whom he met in New York three or four years ago. Grasset is a fine sculptor only some of the time, according to Flett, because when he is distracted by a woman, he neglects his work. "When Grasset came to London, you wouldn't know whether it was to see Butler's sculpture or Epstein's or to meet some woman at the Savoy," says Flett.

To end the tour, Flett shows Challis twelve statues of young women in the garden sculpted by Grasset. The Professor admires his brilliant virtuosity as the statues are imbued with warmth, life, and vitality, even though they are cast in rough concrete and treated with paint and acids to simulate old bronze. Challis appreciates Grasset's ability to imitate the great sculptors of history, too — a Donatello hand, here, a Rodin foot, there, etc.

But Challis also sees a carelessness in Grasset's work as some of the heads and bodies do not match. But then he recalls that the Roman Emperor Hadrian (76-138) did something similar, having four hundred and seventy-two heads of himself made to be attached to generic torsos throughout his empire. (**Fig. 14**) So maybe he is not careless, just quirky.

Professor Challis recognises one of the twelve statues as Jenny, the name Flett gave a young woman in tight black trousers and a striped shirt in the portrait above the fireplace. Since Grasset is a philanderer, Challis wonders if the statues are his 'hunting trophies.'

Flett's twenty-three-year-old Greek friend, Polyxéna 'Polly'

Fig. 14 Bronze head of Hadrian.

Sorelle, joins them in the garden. She is a slim and singularly attractive girl, wearing a red handkerchief knotted at the neck of a black fisherman's-knit jersey and blue jeans rolled up a turn or two above soft moccasins. Her casualness, assurance, vitality, and intelligence remind Challis of the young people attending art classes and drama schools and staying in youth hostels on the Continent. He recognises Polly as another of Grasset's statues, which she says he made three or four years ago in Paris when she was on an excursion with a Swiss finishing school. Polly was seventeen, and Grasset was twenty-eight. She loved him, but he did not care for her.

Flett and Polly tell Challis that Grasset mysteriously disappeared about six months ago, even though he had a big art show coming up, and no one knows where he is or what happened to him. "All the top-notchers would have been there," says Flett. "Did you know Picasso had promised to come? It was the biggest thing that ever happened to Grasset, the crux of his career."

When Challis returns to 93 St. George's Square, Mr. Valentine tells him Polly called and wishes to meet him at five-forty-five p.m. tomorrow at the Woburn Arms in Oxford Street, Bloomsbury, near the British Museum.

The next day at the pub, Challis and Polly discuss Paul Grasset over a beer. She says he liked success but did not care how he got it. Even his agent, Claude Fanlec, used to say he was incapable of moral distinctions. As Polly wants to discover what happened to him, she invites the Professor to a party later that evening at the Chelsea studio of one of Paul's former models, Frida Lindstrom, who she thinks might know something. Before they leave, Challis notices a small, swarthy, neatly dressed man sitting in the corner watching them.

Frida Lindstrom has nothing good to say about Paul Grasset. "When he disappeared, I shed no tears," she says. "Nor anyone else, I imagine. He was the most despicable man I have ever known — and I have known some unpleasant men." Challis also hoped to meet Giji, another of Paul's former models, who Brandon Flett told him about, but no one knows where she is. But the party is not a waste of time because Challis meets Paul's brother, Charles 'Bimbo' Grasset, who is also an artist but not as successful as his older sibling. He says a second-hand dealer named Joákimos has the sculptures Paul made for the show they had to cancel when he disappeared.

After hearing nothing from Brandon Flett or Polly Sorelle for a fortnight, Professor Challis writes to his colleague Jacques Monfreid at the Académie Française to discover more about Paul Grasset and his circle. While Monfreid had nothing new to say about him, he sent the Professor a newspaper article about Grasset's agent, Claude Fanlec. It says he was a thirty-seven-year-old art dealer from Nantes who went bankrupt and committed suicide on Dieppe Pier.

In 1948, Fanlec was responsible for discovering the so-called Rocamadour Reliefs, an early medieval church group of eighteen small figures in sandstone, part of a Romanesque frieze depicting pilgrims adoring the Virgin of Rocamadour. Despite protests by French antiquarians and churchmen, these priceless fragments were disposed of by Fanlec to the New York collector Curtis J. Grantheim, Jr. for a sum reputed to have been in the vicinity of forty million francs. At present, they are in the Grantheim Collection on Long Island.

On 17 November, Professor Challis prepares to leave London for Athens by the evening boat train. However, he has been thinking about Paul Grasset's disappearance. So, after lunch, the Professor strolls to the second-hand shop in Paddington that belongs to Paul's art dealer, Joákimos. He has a bald, pear-shaped head. No eyebrows. But Oriental-looking hen's eyes. Massive dewlaps. A benevolent smile. A fat, pear-shaped body. Sallow skin like celluloid. And a gentle and cultured voice flavoured with a faint Near Eastern accent.

To the Professor's surprise, Joákimos informs Challis that Brandon Flett left the Tite Street house because he is leaving the country. Initially, he wanted to sell Joákimos the twelve statues by Paul, but at the last minute, he changed his mind and destroyed them. "Destroyed?" asks Challis, shocked. What was the setup when the moment a man disappeared, everyone was apparently at liberty to dispose of his property and effects?

Just as Challis is about to leave, Joákimos introduces him to his junior partner, Stephen Roach — the same man who, nearly three weeks before, had sat at the corner table in the saloon bar of the Woburn Arms, watching Polly and the Professor. In Paris the next day, Challis writes to his landlord, Mr. Valentine, asking him to visit the Tite Street house and see whether Paul Grasset's twelve statues are still in the garden.

Simplon-Orient Express

Professor Challis finds travelling on the Simplon-Orient-Express rather disappointing because, in his view, it never lives up to how it is depicted in the popular thrillers by the French crime writer Maurice Dekobra (1885-1973). (**Fig. 15**) Yet each time he travelled, the hope would spring anew, and beneath the great, glass

Fig. 15 The French thriller writer Maurice Dekobra.

canopy of the Gare de Lyon, he would feel that this time something must happen. So, as the train leaves Milan station, Challis is delighted to see Bimbo Grasset sprinting to catch it.

Later, during a train stop, they finally catch up in a bar at Venice station. Bimbo shows Challis a cable he received from Polly Sorelle, who is in Athens: "PAUL SEEN HERE SOME MONTHS AGO STOP FLETT ARRIVED YESTERDAY GRANDE BRETAGNE STOP SUSPECT THEY KNOW STOP LOVE — POLLY."

"Who are *they*?" asks Challis. "Brandon Flett or Joákimos?" Bimbo is unsure. The Professor also asks whether Paul made the Rocamadour Reliefs. Bimbo believes he did, which would mean they are fake.

Returning to the train, they see Stephen Roach walking along the platform. He must have flown to Venice and caught the train from there. Bimbo recalls meeting him a decade ago in Paris, but his name was Rakmet then. "He was studying art, and I got to know him vaguely because he was interested in sculpture," says Bimbo, noting that he had an extraordinary knowledge of art and wrote articles and books.

Bimbo also tells Challis about his brother Paul. Growing up in Cherbourg, France, he protected Bimbo from their eldest brother, Victor, who was a bully. Paul became a sculptor because his uncle was a monumental mason. And Bimbo became a sculptor because he idolised Paul. At the same time, he also hates him and is jealous of him. Paul is ambitious, clever, and vain, says Bimbo. He is technically brilliant but lacks originality and has stolen other people's ideas, including his and Rakmet's.

Paul is a womaniser who uses people to get ahead, including Brandon Flett, Grantheim's protégé. He used Flett to get into Grantheim's good books. But then Paul ran off with his girlfriend. "It isn't the portrait of the artist as a young man or the portrait of the young man as an artist," says Bimbo. "It's the portrait of the artist as a bastard."

Bimbo also tells Challis about Paul's agent, Claude Fanlec. He traced stolen art for the allied military governments in France, Germany, and Italy during World War II. Fanlec then worked for UNESCO before becoming an art dealer in Paris. But six months ago, he got into financial trouble and shot himself on Dieppe Pier. "A man whose body is found floating in the water with a bullet in the head may have taken his own life," says Challis. "Equally, he may have been the victim of a murderer."

The Professor suspects Paul might have murdered Fanlec over the faking of the Rocamadour Reliefs. He was a young sculptor with incredible technical skills, extensive knowledge of stonecutting, and an uncanny capacity for reproduction. But Paul was also unscrupulous and prepared to use his talents dishonestly to achieve success.

If Paul had made the Romanesque-style figures that Fanlec 'discovered' and sold to Grantheim for one hundred and fifty thousand dollars in 1948, he would have received a sizeable cut, which might explain how he could afford the house on Tite Street. "It is significant, I think, that the disappearance of your brother and the death of Fanlec happened at the same time," says Challis. Although he admits he is only guessing, and just as likely, Paul could be hiding somewhere and turning out counterfeit antiques, chasing a girl and fleeing a jealous husband, or lying low because he is about to be exposed. Or he could be dead.

On the train later that night, Challis hears Stephen Roach trying his door. But by the time he puts on his overcoat and slippers, Roach is standing by an open door at the end of the corridor. While sounding each other out, Roach manoeuvres Challis so his back is to the door. But before he can push him off the moving train, Bimbo rushes Roach from behind and knocks him out. Bimbo explains that he was Grantheim's art adviser until he sacked him, probably over the Rocamadour Reliefs. Therefore, Claude Fanlec, Paul Grasset, and Roach probably all knew they were fake. "That's a lively little setup for all sorts of possibilities, like blackmail," says Bimbo.

"Or murder," says Challis.

Athens

Professor Challis stays at the Grande Bretagne (1842-present) in Athens because Brandon Flett is also there. (**Fig. 16**) He wishes to meet him, but Flett is always out. So Challis contacts Polly Sorelle and meets her at nearby Syntagma Square, and from there,

Fig 16 Hotel Grande Bretagne in Athens where Challis and Flett stayed (2018).

59

they catch a bus to the Acropolis for a quiet chat. She says that after her crush on Paul Grasset fizzled out, she left school and returned to Greece. But as Polly's mother was dead and her father, a shipping magnate, had business in New York, she went to live with her older sister Helen in Paris.

As it happened, independent of Polly, Helen met Paul by chance in Marseilles, and they have been together ever since. But when Paul disappeared, so did Helen. Polly befriended Flett soon after because he lived in Paul's house, and she thought he might lead her to Helen. "You see, I had already met his brother Bimbo, and he was naturally rather worried about it, and it seemed perfectly logical that this man who had known Paul in New York and who had taken his house would have some information that might be helpful."

However, as Polly did not trust Flett, she did not tell him that the woman in the portrait above the fireplace, whom he called Jenny, was Helen. She fears that to protect Paul, Helen might have murdered Fanlec. "Yes, it's all a deal more complicated than I think we had realised," says Challis.

Polly arranges to have dinner later that evening with Bimbo and Challis. She will meet Bimbo at the Hotel Majestic, where he is staying, and they will pick up the Professor at the Grande Bretagne at eight p.m. Also, Flett contacts Challis, and they arrange to meet tomorrow evening.

At eight-thirty p.m., Bimbo calls Challis to ask whether Polly has arrived, as there is no sign of her. He also asks if he has read today's **Athens News**. As the Professor has seen neither, Bimbo comes to the hotel alone. He shows Challis a newspaper report about a man's body found in a well near the Acropolis. Some letters he had on him suggested it was Stephen Roach. "I might call into the embassy and offer my services on the matter of identification," says Challis.

Since Polly has still not arrived at the Grande Bretagne, Bimbo calls her house. "She left her home at ten past seven," says Bimbo.

"That's more than two hours ago. She got a taxi from her door. It shouldn't have taken her more than fifteen minutes."

Then the telephone rings. "This is the Hotel Majestic. The message Mr. Grasset was expecting has come through, sir," a receptionist tells the Professor. "Miss Sorelle asks that you and Mr. Grasset go on to dinner without her as she had to leave the city suddenly on urgent business." Suspiciously, an unnamed man phoned the Majestic on Polly's behalf. Challis suspects she has met Flett, but Bimbo is doubtful. In the end, they decide to skip dinner.

The next day, Challis visits police headquarters to identify the body of Stephen Roach. A toffee-nosed diplomat from the British embassy named Cyril Bloom accompanies him. The body is not Roach, however. "This man was big, fair-complexioned, inclined to stoutness; my man was short, rather compactly built, very swarthy — and, I would guess, a year or two younger," says the Professor. As luck would have it, Bloom sometimes went dancing with Helen Sorelle. But he has not seen her for about two months and promises to enquire into her whereabouts. When Challis returns to the Grande Bretagne, he receives a hurried note from Flett, cancelling their meeting as he must go out of town on unavoidable business. The Professor had half expected it.

The Venetian House

A taxi is waiting to pick up Polly Sorelle outside her house. "Hotel Majestic," she tells the driver. Instead, he takes her to a secluded and rather shabby area of decayed old houses with crumbling walls and tangled gardens and stops in front of an old, dilapidated stone house of Venetian design, standing in an unkept garden behind a high stone wall. To her surprise, Brandon Flett greets her. Outraged, Polly refuses to go inside.

"If you don't, I have an idea things might go pretty badly for your sister Helen," says Flett. He had conflicting loyalties because his father and Curtis J. Grantheim Jr. ran a small bakery before Grantheim became rich. After Flett's father died, Grantheim put him through college. However, Flett knows Grantheim will seek revenge for being tricked by the fake Rocamadour Reliefs. So he hired a private eye named Joe Kelly to find Paul Grasset and Helen Sorelle before Grantheim and his cronies did. But Kelly was murdered before he could tell Flett where they were hiding. So Flett 'abducted' Polly to warn her who she was up against. "They have killed two pretty smart operators already," Flett tells Polly. "Now, what chance do you think there is for you? Or for your funny old Professor friend? I don't want to see anybody else get hurt. In particular, I don't want to see *you* get hurt."

Flett suspects that Stephen Roach shot Claude Fanlec on Dieppe Pier and threw Joe Kelly down the well near the Acropolis, but the police believe Fanlec killed himself, and Kelly fell accidentally. However, Flett knows Roach is a homicidal maniac, and if he gets to Paul and Helen first, he will kill them because he is the sort of tidy little man who likes a clean blotter on his desk. Flett asks Polly for three days without interference from her, Bimbo, or Professor Challis so he can find Paul and Helen. However, they are interrupted when Charlie, Polly's taxi driver-cum-abductor, who does odd jobs for Flett, rings the doorbell.

Just then, Bimbo Grasset arrives and knocks Charlie out. He did not trust Flett, so he dug around himself and discovered he sometimes used this house. When Flett opens the door, Charlie is on the ground, and Bimbo is itching for a fight. But Flett is no pushover and knees him in the groin. Charlie, still the worse for wear, watches Bimbo and Polly while Flett sees if he can learn anything at Joe Kelly's hotel.

Cyril Bloom calls Professor Challis to say the dead man was an American named Joseph Parnell Kelly. Also, a flibbertigibbet named Bunty Williams told him Helen Sorelle was pregnant and living on the island of Kos. Afterward, the Professor investigates where they found Kelly's body and bumps into Brandon Flett doing the same thing. "I'm damned sure it wasn't an accident," says Flett. "You've got to explain first how or why anyone would get himself into a godforsaken place like this at night."

Flett tells Challis that he knew Helen Sorelle was Paul Grasset's girlfriend and the girl in the painting, whom he named Jenny after his girlfriend who ran off with Grasset and became a goodtime girl called Giji (French for Jenny). "She's at the end of the road — except it's more like a sewer than a road — and do you know, she won't be thirty until the year after next," says Flett bitterly. "That's Giji. Just one of the girls from Paul Grasset's garden."

Charlie locks Bimbo Grasset and Polly Sorelle in the living room of the Venetian house. Polly tells Bimbo she knows where her sister Helen and his brother Paul are hiding. Vassilis Klonaris, a sea captain who worked for her father, told her he had seen them on the small Greek island of Astypalaia four days ago. But they must first break free of Flett and Charlie. So Bimbo starts a fire, and Polly screams on cue. When Charlie goes to investigate, Bimbo knocks him out as soon as he unlocks the door. Then they race outside and escape in Charlie's taxi. If all that drama is not enough, Bimbo and Polly suddenly realise they are in love.

Brandon Flett and Professor Challis share a taxi from Limnae, where Joe Kelly's body was found, to the Grande Bretagne. Waiting there for Flett is Charlie with the news of Bimbo and Polly's escape. Charlie suspects the address of Vassilis Klonaris that he found on an envelope in her handbag might be significant. Flett enquires at the hotel desk and discovers he is a sea captain, and his boat, the *Barbara*, sailed from Piraeus that afternoon. So Flett and Charlie immediately dash off there. "Why Piraeus?" asks Charlie.

"I have a hunch that's where we might find your cab," says Flett. At Piraeus, he quickly establishes that Captain Klonaris' boat sailed for Astypalaia and heads there himself.

Coincidentally, Cyril Bloom and Bunty Williams are having a drink at the Grande Bretagne. Bloom sees Challis and casually tells him that Stephen Roach visited the embassy to find out about boats to Astypalaia. "There's a folk industry they have there for making rather charming knives and forks," explains Bloom. Talk of the island prompts Williams to let drop that she was mistaken the other day — Helen Sorelle was living on Astypalaia, not Kos. The chase is now on, and all roads lead to Astypalaia.

The Island

Professor Challis sees Astypalaia for the first time — a sprinkling of square white houses against a rumpled green blanket of rolling hills and, to the left, a ridge of red earth and stone rises steeply above the sea to a line of bare-armed windmills and an imposing monastery. (**Fig. 17**)

Fig. 17 The seaport of Pera-yalo on Astypalaia (recent photograph).

The Professor knows the *kafenio* or coffeehouse nearest the landing steps will be the best place to ask about Paul Grasset and Helen Sorelle. The owner, Theódoros Milos, tells him they are staying at a farmhouse about seven kilometres away but advises him to wait until tomorrow as it will soon be dark, and the road is muddy and dangerous. So they go inside to arrange a room for Challis, but when he sees two bags belonging to Stephen Roach in the corridor, he tells Milos he wants to leave now because they might be in danger, so they head off riding mules. When they finally reach the farmhouse, the Professor tells the man who greets them, "My name is Challis. I am a friend of your brother's." He also says that Stephen Roach is somewhere nearby, and his brother Bimbo, his sister-in-law Polly, and Brandon Flett will probably arrive tomorrow morning.

"They are coming to find Paul Grasset?" asks the man. "How sad, then, that they will be disappointed, having journeyed so far." They go inside. Challis waits in the living room while the man goes upstairs to fetch Helen. "My husband tells me you know my sister," she says, wearing a brown maternity dress. "I do not wish to see her." As they seem unaware of the danger, Challis tells Helen that Roach has come to murder her husband. "Why should he want to do that?" asks Helen.

"I think the Rocamadour Reliefs have something to do with it," says Challis. A dog starts barking outside. The man grabs a shotgun and goes to investigate. Challis follows him. Helen stays inside and locks the door. "There's something over there, near the hedge," whispers the Professor. So the man dashes off in that direction while Challis heads back to the farmhouse and runs into Bimbo and Polly. "My God! How did you get here?" asks Challis, helping Polly off her mule. "Ah, here comes Grasset now."

"Hello, Polyxéna. Hello, Grasset," the man with the shotgun says.

"Where is Paul?" asks Bimbo. "Where is my brother?"

"I regret to say your brother is dead," the man says.

"Then, in God's name, who are you?" asks Challis.

"My name is Fanlec. Claude Fanlec."

Helen loved Paul, but he made her feel smirched and tainted. One time, when he was in New York, she had dinner with Fanlec in Paris. They had too much to drink, and Fanlec asked her to marry him. Then, when Paul returned from New York on another occasion, she went to Dieppe to meet him, but he never showed up. Fanlec knew she was going there and went to find her. They met in the street by chance and decided to elope on the spot. Fanlec did not even bother to check out of his hotel. They had been in Rouen on their honeymoon for two days when they were surprised to read a newspaper report about Fanlec's death! The police thought they had found his body floating near the pier at Dieppe. (**Fig. 18**) "What papers were in the man's pocket were illegible," explains Helen.

66

The revolver which had killed him was found on the sea bed, not far from where the body was floating. I think perhaps the police investigations were a little careless, but, anyway, in the course of these inquiries, they learned that a certain Claude Fanlec had disappeared from his hotel several days before, leaving all his clothing behind and an unpaid hotel bill.

Of course, it was Paul Grasset's body. But since he and Fanlec looked like brothers, the hotelier thought Paul was his missing guest. At the inquest, the finding was suicide. But Paul did not kill himself, according to Fanlec. Roach did. "He simply followed Paul to Dieppe, enticed him to the end of the pier at night, shot him, and tossed his body and the gun into the sea," says Fanlec.

Now, Roach wants to tidy up any loose ends by killing Fanlec, which is why he and Helen have been hiding on the island. But he has no regrets about cheating a despicable profiteer like Curtis J. Grantheim, Jr. The trouble was that a wretched little swine like Paul needed lots of money, so he was blackmailing him, Joákimos, and Roach, Fanlec told Challis.

Fig. 18 The pier at Dieppe, France (recent photograph).

After mulling things over, Challis concludes that Fanlec murdered Paul. He was alone in Dieppe for a couple of days before meeting Helen, so he had the opportunity to kill him. And since Fanlec was in love with Helen and thus had a motive to kill Paul as well. So Challis tells Bimbo to go to Pera-yalo with Milos to find Flett and bring him to the farmhouse. "Why the devil do we want him?" asks Bimbo, puzzled.

"It will be more complicated, still, if we do not clear up this question of identity," explains Challis. But it is only a ploy to get Bimbo away because "it might be safer not to have Bimbo and his brother's murderer together in the same house," thinks the Professor.

Later that night, Roach mistakes Fanlec for Paul and shoots him dead. He then takes off down the hill, only to meet Brandon Flett coming up, and they wrestle in the mud. Roach loses his footing and tumbles over a cliff to his death.

Professor Challis, Brandon Flett, Bimbo Grasset, and the Sorelle sisters, Polly and Helen, return to Athens with Captain Klonaris. Bimbo and Polly are already a couple, and given Flett's concern for Helen, they may well become a couple. While. Challis finally reads the letter he received from his landlord, Mr. Valentine.

> The statues are there all right. I counted twelve of them. Very nice, I thought they were. One, in particular, took my fancy — the second one down from the pensioner's garden on the wall nearest the Embankment. Do you remember the second-floor landing, just down from your room, where I used to

keep the chest? Well, I fancy that would be a lovely place for that statue if they are willing to dispose of it. The price would have to be reasonable, of course.

While Professor Challis and Mr. Valentine often clash over the décor of 93 St. George's Square, they agree that the statue of Polly would look lovely on the second-floor landing.

THE END.

Comments, Opinions, Reviews

You Can't Tell A Book By Its Cover

Twelve Girls in the Garden was the first of the five Professor Challis novels by George Johnston, written using the pseudonym, Shane Martin. Collins published the book in the UK and hired the English illustrator William Randell to design the dust jacket. He depicted the fight between Brandon Flett and Bimbo Grasset, with Polly Sorelle in the foreground, her back to them, looking anxious but very smart in her pearl earrings, yellow pullover, yellow gloves, and tan suit with a sprig of narcissus in her lapel, which prompted Challis to remark, "Narcissus in November! It was no wonder that the Greeks had once worshipped the earth."[1] (**Fig. 19**)

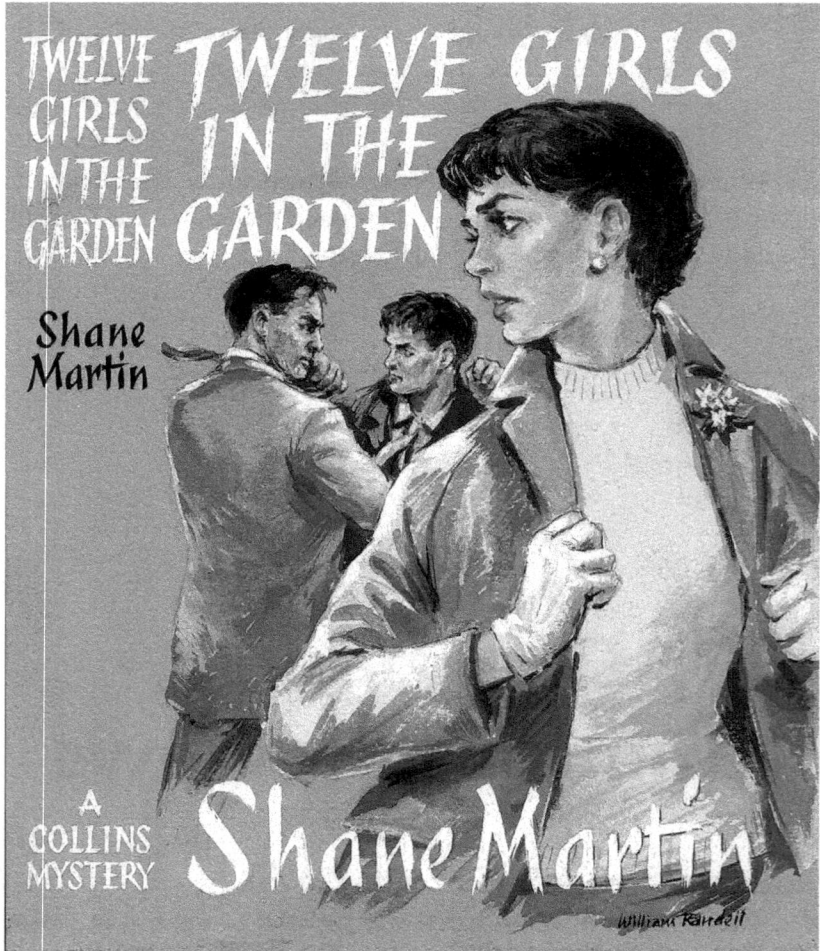

Fig. 19 Dust jacket by William Randell.

Randell specialised in crime fiction and also designed the dust jackets for three other Challis novels — **The Saracen Shadow** (1957), **The Man Made of Tin** (1958), and **The Myth is Murder** (1959). Despite being very prolific and one of the best in the business during the 1950s and 1960s, we do not know much about him.[2] In 2020, I purchased Randell's original artwork for **Twelve Girls in the Garden**, dated 26 September 1956, and **The Myth is Murder**, dated 29 September 1958. He painted everything by hand, including the book titles and the author's name — they did not use stick-on letters or anything like that in those days. Believe it or not, Collins threw these out along with the original artwork for about four hundred other dustjackets, which were rescued from a rubbish tip by a lucky book collector.[3]

William Morrow published the American edition of **Twelve Girls in the Garden** and hired Carol Doen, a freelance commercial artist from Wilmington, Vermont, to design the dust jacket. (**Fig. 20**) Her delicate pen-and-ink drawing of the twelve statues of the girls in the garden reflected Johnston's description in the novel quite accurately:

> An ornate stone pergola had been built against the wall facing the house, with a curved fan of steps running up to it from the lily pond. On either side of the pergola were two arched stone niches, and there were four identical niches spaced along each of the other two walls. In each of the twelve niches stood the statue of a girl, a little more than half-life-size. Some were nude, some half-draped; all seemed vaguely classical in pose until you looked more closely when you saw that they were not classical at all. And no two were alike.[4]

The American-run Dollar Book Club chose **Twelve Girls in the Garden** as one of its offerings in 1957, which guaranteed Johnston five thousand dollars. It came just in time because he had only three pounds and ten shillings in the bank.[5]

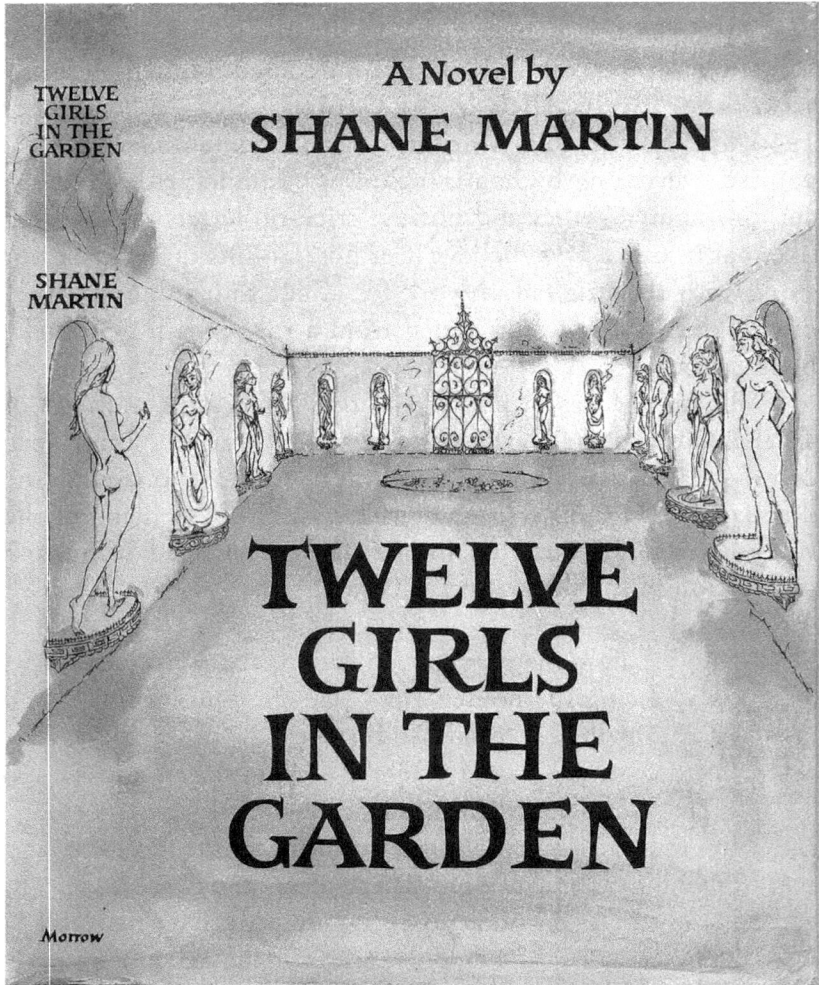

Fig 20 Dustjacket by Carol Doen.

Name Dropping

Twelve Girls in the Garden was the first time George Johnston had written something using a pseudonym since he was sixteen years. It combined the names of his youngest daughter, Shane (1949-

1974), and eldest son, Martin (1947-1990), to produce the name Shane Martin. Interestingly, and perhaps fittingly, Johnston also gave several characters in **Twelve Girls in the Garden** alternative names: Paul was sometimes called 'Pip' or 'Greg.' Charles was 'Bimbo.' Polyxéna was 'Polly.' Helen was 'Jenny.' Jenny was 'Giji.' Brandon was 'Ben.' Constantinos was 'Charlie.' And Roach was 'Rakmet.' I do not want to theorise about Johnston's use of a pseudonym too much. But by giving himself and his characters alternative names, maybe he was saying something about hidden identities and the nature of crime fiction.

In 'The Case of a Very Loose Canon: The Shane Martin "Pot-boilers" of George Johnston' (2017), Paul Genoni and Tanya Dalziell stated, "Issues of identity and identification are of course a standard trope in crime fiction, but in the Shane Martin novels they usually have little to do with concealing crime — they are simply a by-product of a modernity in which identity is (re) shaped by travel, migration, and the cosmopolitan impulse to craft one's identity."[6] While that is perhaps true of Polly Sorelle and Bimbo Grasset, events in **Twelve Girls in the Garden** do turn on identities, such as when, at different times, Professor Challis, the Dieppe police, and Stephen Roach all mistake Claude Fanlec for Paul Grasset or vice versa.

Twelve Girls in the Garden allowed George Johnston to air his considerable knowledge of art and artists acquired from when he studied drawing at the National Gallery School in Melbourne during the late 1920s and early 1930s while training to become a lithographer. It appears that he named Paul Grasset after the Swiss artist Eugene Samuel Grasset (1845-1917), a pioneer of

Fig. 21 Eugene Grasset by Grasset (left) and James Flett by Flett.

Art Nouveau, and Brandon Flett after the Australian artist James Edward Flett (1906-1986), best known for his pictures of pirates. (**Fig. 21**)

Johnston also casually dropped the names of many artists throughout **Twelve Girls in the Garden**, including Bernini (1598-1680), Braque (1882-1963), Butler (1913-1981), Cezanne (1839-1906), Constable (1776-1837), Corot (1796-1875), Cotman (1782-1842), Dürer (1471-1528), Epstein (1880-1959), Hokusais (1760-1849), Houdon (1741-1828), Maillol (1861-1944), Picasso (1881-1973), Renoir (1841-1919), Rubens (1577-1640), Verrocchio (1435-1488), Watteau (1684-1721), etc. Johnston also scattered colourful analogies concerning art throughout the book, such as "the river of Turner rather than Whistler,"[7] "like being pitchforked into an illustration by Doré,"[8] and "a world of old steel engravings."[9]

Art fakery was at the heart of **Twelve Girls in the Garden** and the second Challis novel, **The Saracen Shadow**, as I shall explain in the next chapter. Therefore, it is interesting to note that in **My Brother Jack**, Johnston's alter ego, David Meredith, faked a painting of his great-grandfather's ship, the *Grafton*, "in the exact mode of the marine painting of the time," aging and fading it with chemicals and smoke and putting it in a frame of the appropriate period. He gave the picture to his grandmother, telling her he had picked it up from an antique shop in Melbourne. While it was nothing like what Paul Grasset did by faking the Rocamadour Reliefs, I think the pleasure that Meredith got from his deception also applied to Grasset. "The unqualified success of this deception delighted me for years, less for the pleasure I had given my grandmother than for the testimony it provided of my own cleverness,"[10] Meredith said.

While Johnston chose writing over art as a teenager, he always felt most at home with artists. Some of his closest friends were the Australian artists Colin Colahan (1897-1987), Cedric Flower (1920-2000), Russell Drysdale (1912-1981), and Sydney Nolan (1917-1992). Johnston dedicated **Twelve Girls in the Garden** to Colahan and his wife Ursula (1915-1989).[11] He dedicated his third Professor Challis novel, **The Man Made of Tin,** to Flower and his wife Pat (1914-1977).[12] Johnston dedicated his dystopian novel, **The Darkness Outside** (1959), to Nolan and got him to design the dust jacket for **My Brother Jack**.[13] And he dedicated **Clean Straw for Nothing** (1969) to Drysdale and his wife Maisie (1915-2001).[14]

Death Takes Small Bites

George Johnston finished **Twelve Girls in the Garden** in March 1956,[15] while the growing Johnston family — George (44), his wife, the writer Charmian Clift (33), heavily pregnant with their son Jason (b. April 1956), and their two other children, Martin (9) and Shane (5) — were living on the Greek island of Hydra, "which doesn't even have a wheeled vehicle, and where nothing moves faster than donkey pace,"[16] said Clift.

Fig. 22 The Johnstons' house on Hydra (2018).

Despite the island's low cost of living, money was very tight for the Johnstons, especially since, in January 1956, they bought a sea captain's house built in 1788. It had three-storeys, ten rooms, metre-thick stone walls, great carved wooden doors, paved courtyards, mature fruit trees and vines, and a terrace facing the sapphire-blue Saronic Gulf.[17] (**Fig. 22**) Even though it was a bargain at only five hundred pounds, it took all the money they had saved. Johnston hoped that **Twelve Girls in the Garden** would put some cash in their pockets, just like his first crime novel, **Death Takes Small Bites** (1948), had done nine years earlier.

  Death Takes Small Bites is a suspenseful, fast-paced story "set on the now decaying Burma Road, with mysterious Chinese, landslides, murder, and oil franchise plottings," said the book reviewer for the **Telegraph** in Brisbane, Australia, adding that it "would make a first-class adventure film."[18] Johnston drew on his

76

memories of China as a journalist during World War II for the setting of **Death Takes Small Bites** and modelled its male lead, Cavendish C. Cavendish, aka 'Jed,' an American newspaperman from Canaan, Connecticut, on himself. After recounting his adventures to American oil man Harrison Fisher, like a true postmodernist, Cavendish channels Johnston and the book reviewer from the **Telegraph**. "Imagine the book I'll be able to write. I'll make it a thriller. I've always wanted to write a whodunit. I'll call it **Death Takes Small Bites**. Hollywood will make a film of it, and you can play the lead."[19]

Johnston named and modelled the female lead in **Death Takes Small Bites**, Charmian Anthony, an American nurse, after Charmain Clift. "The brightness of her beauty was almost as arresting as a sharp blow,"[20] says Cavendish of Anthony, who fall in love and marry each other, even though she and Russell Coates, an Australian doctor, are engaged. The love story of Cavendish and Anthony was similar to that of Johnston and Clift, who also had good looks and sex appeal in spades and fell in love and married each other even though she and Leo Kenney, an Australian airman, were engaged.

In Great Britain, Victor Gollancz published **Death Takes Small Bites** in hardback in 1948, and Penguin Books published it in paperback in 1959. While in America, Dodd, Mead & Company published it as a Red Badge Mystery, an imprint they supposedly reserved for only the best detective stories, in 1950. An abridged version of **Small Bites**, illustrated by Ben Turner, was published in the **Standard** in Montreal, Canada, on 20 October 1951. Several non-English editions of **Death Takes Small Bites** were also published. Librairie Gallimard published it in hardback in France in 1951. Johnston found its new French title, **A Petit Feu** (**Little by Little**), "quite inexplicable,"[21] perhaps because he mistook it for **Le Petit Feu** (**The Little Fire**). And Bladkompaniet published **Death Takes Small Bites** in paperback in Norway in 1961. Its new Norwegian title, **Mote I Tali-fu** (**Fashion in Tali-**

fu), referenced the small Chinese village of Tali-fu in the novel. It is worth noting that foreign languages, including Greek, were a mystery to Johnston. He once went into a shop on Hydra and, instead of asking for a hairbrush in Greek, asked for a hairy cunt![22]

Death Takes Small Bites sold very well, especially in France. Librairie Gallimard paid Johnston an advance of seventy-five thousand francs (equivalent to ten thousand pounds) for an initial print run of thirty-thousand copies.[23] Although, according to him, they ended up selling one hundred and ten thousand copies.[24] Nevertheless, Johnston thought it was "a pretty lousy book."[25] (See Ian Morrison's insightful discussion about **Death Takes Small Bites** in the Foreword.)

In **Clean Straw for Nothing**, George Johnston's surrogate David Meredith said he wrote his first thriller while living on his own in rough digs in Sydney, which is also what Johnston did while writing **Death Takes Small Bites**. In 1947-48, Meredith, his wife Cressida, and their newborn son Julian, along with Johnston, his wife Charmian, and their nearly-born son Martin, could not find suitable accommodation in Sydney. So, Cressida and Julian moved to Lebanon Bay to live with her parents, and Charmian and Martin moved to Kiama to live with hers. While Meredith "moved to a verandah room over a cheap restaurant run by 'Pop' Charlton,"[26] and Johnston had a tiny flat in Manly, described as "a dismal place to live,"[27] where they pushed ahead with writing their thrillers, trying to earn some extra money for their growing families. Their books ended up selling well but not making enough for them to leave their newspaper jobs and write fiction full-time, as Meredith explained:

There was a chance of escape — admittedly risky — when the novel which he had written after work on Pop Charlton's verandah was published, for while it had no particular *succès d'estime*, it was favourably enough reviewed, and by Australian standards, it made a respectable amount of money. In the end, he stuck to the safety of his position with the **Globe**, on the ground that he was not justified in jeopardizing to such a hazardous and precarious prospect the future of the children, a daughter, Miranda, having by this time been added to his responsibilities.[28]

Meredith and Johnston eventually found suitable accommodation in the Sydney seaside suburb of Bondi, which enabled them to reunite with their wives and children. However, Meredith was unimpressed with his new flat, so probably Johnston was too. According to Meredith:

> It was an unattractive flat on the ground floor of a hideous big block in liverish brick, enclosing the garbage area and communal incinerator, and set in a wasteland of tiled red roofs pressing down on dwellings all the same, all jostling for a treeless foothold, part of an enormous monotonous sprawl that crowded all the way to the very edge of the awesome coastal cliffs, and no doubt would have crowded half the way to New Zealand except that the Pacific Ocean got in the way. A huge brick sewerage stink-pole dominated this repellent vista like a monument to bad taste, and the sea beyond it was evilly curdled by the city's effluent.[29] (**Fig. 23**)

Fig 23 The Johnsons lived at Flat 7, 26
Simpson Street, Bondi (2022).

Unfortunately, Johnston turned into a working-class snob
concerning the Australian suburbs. He contributed a negative
critique of them titled 'The Citizen's Eye' (1968)[30] to **Look Here!**
Considering the Australian Environment (1968), edited by
John Button (1933-2008), later a Labor Party senator, which also
contained a negative critique by the Australian architect Robin
Boyd (1919-1971),[31] the author of **The Australian Ugliness**
(1960),[32] who made trashing suburbia popular in the 1960s.[33]
According to my late friend, the Melbourne writer Chester Eagle,
Johnston described the Australian suburbs, which produced men
like his brother Jack, "with a contempt that rivals [the Australian
satirist Barry] Humphries [(1934-2023), the Australian architect]
Robin Boyd at his most acerbic, and the [Australian writer] Patrick
White [(1912-1990)] who imagined Sarsaparilla [the suburb in
his play, **The Season at Sarsaparilla** (1965)]."[34] And judging by

her **Sydney Morning Herald** article, 'On Painting Bricks White' (1965),[35] Charmian Clift was just as bad as her husband on the subject.

In Australia in 1950 — six years before the introduction of television — Fidelity Radio of Sydney serialised **Death Takes Small Bites** for radio, producing twenty-six weekly episodes, which debuted on 3DB in Melbourne, Victoria, on 2 May 1950. John Appleton (1905-1990) adapted the book and produced the serial, which starred the Australian actors Howard Craven (1917-2000) as Cavendish C. Cavendish and Margaret Christensen (1921-2009) as Charmian Anthony.[36] (**Fig. 24**) Nigel Lovell (1916-2001), Walter Pym (1905-1980), and John Saul (1913-1979) played supporting roles.[37] "One radio paper recently voted **Death Takes Small Bites** the best production of last year,"[38] reported the **Sun**.

George Johnston submitted another crime novel, **Murder By Horoscope**, to Victor Gollancz in 1951, but they rejected it. "I am extremely sorry, but most regretfully, we shall have to let **Murder By Horoscope** go," wrote Sheila Hodges of Gollancz. While she thought it was "immensely interesting," they were nervous about publishing it "at the present difficult time."[39] Johnston's British literary agent, David Higham (1895-1978), suggested he shorten it before they tried another publisher, but he never did, and it was never published. However, once again, Fidelity Radio serialised the story for radio, but with the modified title, **Death by Horoscope**, which debuted on 2HR in the Hunter River region of New South Wales on 24 August 1951. John Appleton also adapted the story — but this time only "as fast as George writes it"[40] — and produced the serial. The Australian actor Don Crosby (1924-1985)

Fig. 24 Howard Craven and Margaret Christensen in **Death Takes Small Bites**.

played Pendennis, an English pilot, and John Saul was the series' announcer. On 1 August 1951, Johnston told Higham, "I have no intention of writing any more thrillers."[41] But he was not through with them yet because he had the five Challis novels still to write.

Money for Old Rope

George Johnston introduced the idea of an artist casting concrete statues of twelve of his models in a short story called 'Requiem Mass,' which he wrote about four years before **Twelve Girls in the Garden**. It was about sixty-year-old Sefton Halliday and his thirty-year-old wife Erica Kiranos. Observing Halliday's studio and garden, the narrator of the story, Brian Burton, said, "The tracery of the bare twigs seemed something almost contrived behind the solidity of the nudes, cast in concrete, half-life-size; the models he had had, twelve of them ranged around the walls."[42] Halliday was an older version of Paul Grasset, who also made a dozen concrete statues of his models and had a tragic influence on women, killing his wife and himself in the end. Burton was a younger version of Professor Challis, also an archaeologist working in Greece before visiting London to complete his research at the British Museum.[43] This short story was published posthumously in 1983, which is surprising given it was one of Johnston's "best pieces of writing, and probably his most serious-minded achievement to that time,"[44] according to Garry Kinnane. Perhaps he sat on it because he planned to turn it into a book. If that was the case, how ironic since the book was **Twelve Girls in the Garden**, which Kinnane suggested Johnston wrote because "domestic preoccupations prevented him undertaking anything very serious or requiring deep research."[45] Talk about praising something one minute and damning it the next.

'Astypalaian Knife' (1955) was another short story by Johnston that influenced **Twelve Girls in the Garden**. It was about a young Greek-American named Michael Tosaris, whose grandmother came from the Greek island of Astypalaia. While studying in London, he bought an antique knife from Astypalaia at Portobello Road Market for two shillings and ninepence, which inspired him to visit the island, where he met his wife, settled down, and lived happily ever after.[46] In **Twelve Girls in the Garden**, Stephen Roach told Cyril Bloom he wanted to import knives from Astypalaia, which prompted Professor Challis to dash there for the novel's dramatic denouement. It was all grist for the mill to Johnston.

I wonder if the idea of statues with mismatched heads and bodies in **Twelve Girls in the Garden** initially came from Johnston's colleague, the Hungarian-Australian newspaper cartoonist George Molnar (1910-1998), and not the Roman Emperor Hadrian? The timing of Molnar's book **Statues** (1954) and the helpful role Johnston played in its publication suggests he might. In February 1954, Johnston asked his British literary agent David Higham to help Molnar find a publisher for his book of cartoons about statues.[47] "We think it is one of the cleverest and most amusing things we have seen for a long while,"[48] said Higham positively. Later that year, Phoenix House published Molnar's book in the UK, and E.P. Dutton published it in the USA. One of his cartoons showed a perplexed-looking man standing next to the headless torso of a woman, trying to work out which of the heads on the ground was a match. (**Fig. 25**) It was just the sort of thing that would have amused Johnston and got him thinking.

Fig. 25 Cartoon from **Statues** (1954) by George Molnar.

I suspect George Johnston was a big fan of Sherlock Holmes and Sir Arthur Conan Doyle because their collective fingerprints are evident throughout the five Challis novels. For example, how Bimbo Grasset tricked Charlie into opening the door so he and Polly Sorelle could escape by starting a fire and getting her to shout "fire" on cue in **Twelve Girls in the Garden** was the same as how Holmes tricked Irene Adler into revealing where she had hidden a compromising photograph of her ex-lover, the King of Bohemia, by starting a fire and getting Dr. Watson to shout "fire" on cue in 'A Scandal in Bohemia' (1891).[49] Of course, Johnston was not the first crime writer to owe a debt to the dynamic duo of Holmes and Doyle.

A Sense of Place

Twelve Girls in the Garden involved Professor Challis and other characters travelling from place to place in pursuit of Paul Grasset and Helen Sorelle, which gave George Johnston plenty of opportunities to do what he did best — vividly describe everyday places. For example, the Professor went on a nostalgic visit to the former house of his friends John and Erica Barrington in Chelsea, London, where the American painter James McNeill Whistler (1834-1903) also once lived. After John shot himself — no reason given — in the drawing room of the historic house, Erica sold it and remarried the Professor's old friend, the English archaeologist Sir Granville Peart. The Barringtons' house now belonged to artist Paul Grasset, who leased it to architecture student Branden Flett. Challis was unreasonably disappointed not to see those things he recalled from the Barringtons' day, such as their Venetian chest, carved wooden Flemish Madonna, and woodblock print by the Japanese artist Katsushika Hokusai. (**Fig. 26**) Now there were "expressionist paintings on the walls, some queer pieces of semiabstract sculpture, and, in the far corner, a Scandinavian-looking drawing desk, a weird contraption of laminated wood and thin rods of tubular steel, above which hung the dull metal cowls of two modern work lamps. In the open fireplace, like some inexplicable intrusion from Upper Tooting, was one of those electric heaters with a spinning gadget inside, which is unreasonably supposed to suggest that a log fire is smouldering."[50] Challis experienced a "curious feeling of

Fig. 26 'The Great Wave off Kanagawa' (1831) by Hokusai.

disorientation that comes from returning to a house that one has known in the past with a reasonable familiarity but that in the interim has passed into other hands and become imbued with a different personality."[51]

The visit to the house was not only nostalgic for Professor Challis but also for George Johnston because his friends, the Australian artist Colin Colahan and his English wife Ursula Marx, also used to live in Whistler's house at 31 Tite Street. Since it was only a short drive from the Johnstons' flat at 4 Palace Court, Bayswater Road, they often saw each other before the Johnstons moved to Greece, and George dedicated **Twelve Girls in the Garden** to "Colin and Ursula — for fun."[52] But given that the Police suspected Colahan of brutally murdering his girlfriend and model, Mary 'Molly' Dean (1905-1930), for some time before confirming his alibi, crime may not have been his favourite genre. The still unsolved case captivated Johnson, who wrote about it obliquely in **My Brother Jack**.[53]

Johnston could very skilfully convey the lived-in quality of a room through the objects it contained. An excellent example was the Venetian House in Athens, where Brandon Flett and Charlie kept Polly Sorelle and Bimbo Grasset prisoners. It belonged to an old Korean War buddy of Flett's named Brown, who let him use it while he was away in Patras with "something to do with that Cyprus rioting."[54] Since Brown had not lived there very much, the living room still bore traces of former residents:

> A few photographs of stiff, poker-faced Greek family groups remained on the walls, and behind

the ill-fitting glass door of a high cabinet, half a dozen icons were gathering dust. In back of the couch was a picture of donkeys and cactus worked in cotton embroidery. To these fragments from an earlier life the sideboard was unrelated, with its bottles of Seagram's V.O. and White Rock and gin and Rose's lime juice, and a box of pretzels and a big can of coffee from the American commissariat; and there were stacks of American magazines littered around the room: **The New Yorker** and **Holiday** and the **Saturday Evening Post**, magazines that had a smell of nostalgia about them, and one or two old copies of the **National Geographic Magazine**. Next to the whiskey bottle was a chessboard with the pieces spilt across it, and a deck of playing cards laid out for a game of solitaire that had never been completed. To Polly it had the appearance of a bachelor establishment that had grown very tired of itself.[55]

Another good example was the dining room in the house where he and David Meredith grew up in Melbourne — 11 Buxton Street, Elsternwick.[56] "It had bay windows sealed off by heavy cretonne curtains and a long sofa across which no play of sunlight ever moved and a big sideboard cluttered with the cut glass and E.P.N.S. of innumerable gifts, and all the walls were crowded with Mother's paintings of flowers in vases and landscapes she had never seen — snow scenes and Swiss lakes and thatched cottages,"[57] said Meredith in **My Brother Jack. (Fig. 27)** In my view, Johnston's descriptions of Brown's house and his and Meredith's house are up there with Sir Arthur Conan Doyle's description of the sitting room at 221 Baker Street.

Fig. 27 The Meredith/Johnston family home (2023).

One of my favourite examples of George Johnston's vivid word pictures in **Twelve Girls in the Garden** is his description of the second-hand shop run by Joákimos in Paddington, London, which "had the dubious air of muddle and secrecy, with a flavour of ignorant stockpiling, that might lead one quite mistakenly to believe in the possibility of discovering a rare Memlinc or van Eyck or, at worst, a quite good Byzantine icon underneath its coating of discoloured varnish and grime."

> It followed the usual custom of displaying in its windows and on the pavement outside only the tawdriest of trash — cumbersome pieces of

furniture which were either blatantly spavined or suspiciously wormy; chamber pots of impressive size and florid *décor* but quite lacking in handles; chipped saucers filled with wedding rings, synthetic gems, old coins, and unmatched earrings; cases of medals concerned with forgotten gallantries in campaigns against Kaffir, Boer, and Afridi; mid-Victorian specimen cabinets choked either with geological fragments or brittle moths and insects; a tray of surgical instruments that looked as if they must have been used by Crippen; miscellaneous articles of *chinoiserie* brought from Foochow in that free-enterprising period when taste had declined in inverse ratio to the prosperity of the English tea trade; a varied but rather damaged selection of Spode, Staffordshire, and Rockingham; the usual china dog and Negro boy; a stuffed owl, solemnly dusty; and a group of hideously coloured plaster statuettes of girls in the cloche hats, shingles, and alluring postures of the Twenties.[58]

As this description seems too authentic to have been made up, I was not surprised to discover that in **My Brother Jack**, David Meredith, used to pass a second-hand shop like this on his way to school, which also had a saucer of wedding rings and a stuffed owl in the window.[59] In the lead-up to writing his masterpiece, undoubtedly, the Challis novels encouraged him to rake through his past for material and hone his powers of description. The mention of the French thriller writer Maurice Dekobra in **Twelve Girls in the Garden** is significant because he pioneered a documentary or journalistic style of writing fiction, sometimes called 'dekobrisme' after him, which Johnston also employed. In 'The Case of a Very Loose Canon: The Shane Martin "Pot-boilers" of George Johnston,' Paul Genoni and Tanya Dalziell said the reference to Dekobra was to distance **Twelve Girls in the Garden** from the sort of Jazz-age thrillers he wrote, such as **The Madonna of the Sleeping Cars** (1925).[60] But, quite the contrary, I believe that Johnston was doffing his hat to Dekobra.

Mr. Valentine

Professor Challis dreaded the smell of French polish because it meant his landlord Mr. Valentine, "a friendly and attentive man who subscribed to **The Connoisseur**,"[61] was restoring yet another antique that very well might end up in his already cluttered flat at 93 St. George's Square, which already looked like "a jungle of ormolu."[62] When George Johnston wrote **Twelve Girls in the Garden** — a decade before homosexuality was legalised in Great Britain — showing a passion for interior decorating and fussy furniture in books and films often signalled that a character was gay. Johnston may have intended to give Mr. Valentine a recurring role in the Challis novels like that of the Great Detective's landlady, Mrs. Hudson, in the Sherlock Holmes stories. But even though Challis was still living at 93 St. George's Square in the third Challis novel, **The Man Made of Tin**, Mr. Valentine sadly disappeared after **Twelve Girls in the Garden**.

Johnston named the Professor's landlord after his friend, the Australian journalist Victor Valentine (1918-1976). (**Fig. 28**) They met while covering the war in China during the early 1940s, and both worked for the **Sun** in London during the early 1950s. When Johnston was away, Valentine filled in for him, and when Johnston left the newspaper and went to Greece in 1954, Valentine inherited his column. Johnston dedicated his novel, **The Cyprian Woman** (1955), to him, enigmatically stating, "For Victor Valentine, But For Whom."[63] And Valentine lent Johnston the airfare to return to Australia in 1964.

Like Mr. Valentine, Victor was also gay. At midnight on 18 September 1947, the New South Wales Police arrested him for

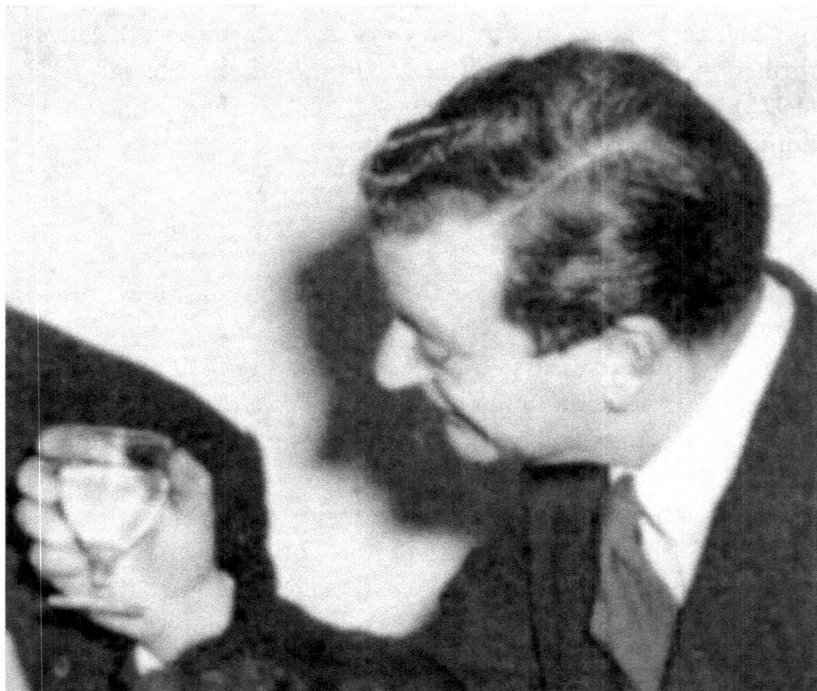

Fig. 28 The Australian journalist Victor Valentine.

indecently assaulting a man in Hyde Park, Sydney. When Constable Hurley questioned them, the man said Valentine had invited him to sit next to him on a bench in the dark. While going to the police station, Valentine punched Hurley, shouted, "I'm getting out of this — you are not putting this on me,"[64] and broke free. In the course of recapturing him, the other man escaped. In court, Valentine said he had never met the man before and denied doing anything illegal, explaining that after attending a boozy gathering in Oxford Street, Sydney, he decided to sleep it off in the park before going to his aunt's house in Pyrmont, where he lived.[65] In those less tolerant days, a conviction could be life-shattering, so fortunately for Valentine, he was acquitted.[66] He left for England in 1949.

While living in London during the early 1950s, Johnston wrote an article for the **Sydney Morning Herald** about the pros and cons of decriminalising homosexuality, but they rejected it. Johnston was furious and retaliated by sending them an article about London sewerage works, telling a colleague, "If they don't like what I write for them, I'll give them shit."[67]

Polly Sorelle and Charmian Clift

Professor Challis was smitten with Polly Sorelle because "he had a distinct feeling about [her] which, in a younger man, might well have been construed as a romantic excitement."[68] However, she

Fig. 29 Charmian Clift aged 33 in 1957.

did not have similar feelings for him, which was hardly surprising since he was sixty-six years old and looked like "a cross between a cassowary and a small Adélie penguin halfway through its moult!"[69]

I suspect George Johnston modelled Polly on Charmian Clift. When he wrote **Twelve Girls in the Garden**, she was ten years older than Polly but still only thirty-three and, by all accounts, very sexy and stylish. Greeba Jamison (1920-2012), the Women's Editor of the **Age** from 1953 to 1969, described her as "always extremely smart, chic, but with enough of the bizarre, to make her dressing interesting above average."[70] (**Fig. 29**)

The British blogger Moira Redmond thought Challis patronised young people but liked his descriptions of their clothes.[71] He was bemused by the partygoers' odd attire at Frida Lindstrom's. "It was ironic to reflect on the thought that English anthropologists spent so much time travelling to the islands of Melanesia when this fertile field of tribal research lay at their very doorsteps,"[72] Challis said to himself. And when he met Polly at the Woburn Arms, he noted her "French fisherman's shirt of thin horizontal stripes, red and white, worn beneath a severe charcoal-grey suit, was her only concession now to the world where colours were bright, Bechet was as big a word as Bach, and everyone read Strindberg."[73] (**Fig. 30**)

Fig. 30 (L-R) American saxophonist Sidney Bechet (1897-1959), German composer Johann Sebastian Bach (1685-1750), and Swedish playwright August Strindberg (1849-1912).

The Professor's description of Polly suggests she would have fitted in perfectly with the young bohemians living on Hydra during Johnston's day. They generally came from affluent countries such as West Germany, Sweden, France, and America, and aspired to be poets, painters, philosophers, or all three. They tended to be a bit younger than Johnston, who was like a big brother or father figure. However, occasionally he got annoyed with their naïve views, especially when they would criticise his writing for being too commercial one day and borrow money from him the next.[74] This group included the Canadian singer-songwriter Leonard Cohen (1934-2016). The English poet David Goschen (1931-1980) and his wife, Angela. The Swedish writer Axel Jensen (1932-2003) and his wife Marianne (1935-2016). She became Cohen's muse and lent her name to the title of his song, 'So Long, Marianne' (1967). The English painter Anthony Kingsmill (1926-1993), who had an affair with Clift. The flaky, flirtatious French artist Jean-Claude Maurice. And the American writer Gill Schwartz and his French wife, Loetitia.[75]

Like Johnston's circle on Hydra, a cosmopolitan group also inhabited **Twelve Girls in the Garden**. Professor Challis, Brandon Flett, Joe Kelly, John Barrington, Curtis J. Grantheim Jr., and Jenny were American. Paul Grasset, his brother Bimbo, and Claude Fanlec were French. Polly Sorelle, her sister Helen, Erica Barrington, Charlie, Captain Klonaris, and Theódoros Milos were Greek. Mr. Valentine, Cyril Bloom, and Bunny Williams were English. Stephen Roach was Syrian. Frida Lindstrom was Swedish. While the nationality of Joákimos was unspecified, the Armenian-American actor Akim Tamiroff (1899-1972) — best known for the movies, **For Whom the Bell Tolls** (1943), **Touch of Evil** (1958), and **The Trial** (1962) — easily could have played him. (**Fig. 31**)

Reviews

Twelve Girls in the Garden was reviewed widely in the USA, less in the UK, and hardly in Australia, mainly because it was not

Fig. 31 Akim Tamiroff could have played Joákimos.

published there — relatively few books were in those days — and Collins did not export many copies to Australia. No doubt there would have been greater local interest in **Twelve Girls in the Garden** if more people had known that George Johnston had written it or even if they had realised that Shane Martin was an Australian. Still, it is quite puzzling why Collins did not try harder to sell more books in the author's home country.

It was usual at the time for book reviews to consist of one or two-line summaries. For example, the review of **Twelve Girls in the Garden** in the **Marion Star** in Ohio noted, "An elderly archaeologist sets out to find a missing sculptor accused of forgery and amorous misdeeds."[76] Likewise, the **Nashua Telegraph** in New Hampshire stated, "An elderly archaeologist goes to Greece in an attempt to straighten out the affairs of some interesting people."[77] But even brief mentions like these helped to spread the word about the novel. But regardless of their length, most reviews praised **Twelve Girls in the Garden**. For example, the **Knoxville Journal** in Tennessee said, "Shrewd Prof. Challis of USA grows suspicious on London jaunt; finds fears confirmed on an Athens visit as corpses develop. Pleasant and intelligent performance."[78] The **Salt Lake Tribune** in Utah said, "During this period of scarce fiction that is well-written as well as light, it is satisfying to find a novel of suspense and sophistication that is good."[79] The **Pottsville Republican** in Pennsylvania said, "From a walk beside the Thames to a rocky island in the Aegean, this is polished storytelling with a heady, steadily mounting suspense and great dramatic appeal. All roads, in this novel, lead to Athens."[80] While on the other side of the Atlantic, Maurice Richardson of the **Observer** in London, UK, said, "Pleasantly literate, peripatetic thriller with elderly archaeologist hero searching for a missing sculptor in Chelsea and Greek islands. Some murder and art-faking. Cosy."[81]

Many reviewers liked Professor Challis. For example, Phyllis Stock of the **Bridgeport Post** in Connecticut said, "Lacking the Professor, **Twelve Girls in the Garden** would be an ordinary mystery story. With him, it becomes something more. Whether he is commenting on the vagaries of the human mind or pointing up the splendours of an Attic landscape, Professor Challis is a man worth knowing."[82] The **Longview News-Journal** in Texas said, "Introducing Professor Ronald Challis, archaeologist nonpareil, in a sophisticated and absorbing novel of Modern Greece."[83] The **Los Angeles Times** said, "Written with wit and sophistication, this is a lively, pleasing story and the white-haired, impish professor is worth a whole series of books."[84] And the **Times Literary Supplement** described the Professor as a Quixotic sort of character.[85]

They also liked the descriptions of Greece in **Twelve Girls in the Garden**. Louise E. Larrabee of the **Tulsa World** in Oklahoma wrote, "Interwoven with the delightfully inscrutable plot are the author's erudite siftings from the archives of art and bright word pictures of ancient and modern Greece that painlessly leave the reader more fully informed."[86] While exploring a sense of place was a focus for George Johnston, he always included enough red herrings and twists and turns in the five Challis novels to satisfy the most devoted reader of crime fiction. As Kathleen Freeman of the

Western Mail in Cardiff, UK, said in her review of **Twelve Girls in the Garden**, though the whole is a travelogue, it never loses the plot or forgets the action, even when describing Greece.[87]

Pleased with his archaeologist-detective Professor Challis, satisfied with how **Twelve Girls in the Garden** turned out, encouraged by good book reviews, and hopeful of healthy book sales, George Johnston began writing the second Challis novel, **The Saracen Shadow**, as soon as he had finished the first.

Endnotes

[1] Shane Martin (George Johnston), **Twelve Girls in the Garden**, New York, USA: William Morrow and Company, 1957, p. 94.

[2] Zoe Stansell (British Library), Email to Derham Groves, 30 August 2023. William Randell is not in either **The Dictionary of British Book Illustrators** (1994) by Alan Horne or the **Dictionary of British Book Illustrators** (1983) by Brigid Peppin and Lucy Micklethwait.

[3] Mark Skipper (Cheltenham Rare Books), Email to Derham Groves, 13 August 2020.

[4] Shane Martin, 1957, pp. 10-11.

[5] Garry Kinnane, **George Johnston: A Biography**, Melbourne, Australia: Nelson Publishers, 1986, pp. 162-163.

[6] Paul Genoni and Tanya Dalziell, 'The Case of a Very Loose Canon: The Shane Martin "Potboilers" of George Johnston,' **Southerly** (Sydney, Australia), vol. 77, issue 1, p. 66.

[7] Shane Martin, 1957, p. 3.

[8] Ibid., p. 67.

[9] Ibid., p. 80.

[10] George Johnston, **My Brother Jack**, London: Collins, 1964, pp. 26-27.

[11] Shane Martin, 1957, dedication, unpaged.

[12] Shane Martin, **The Man Made of Tin**, London, UK: Collins, 1958, dedication, unpaged.

[13] Shane Martin, **The Darkness Outside**, London: Collins, 1959, dedication, unpaged.

[14] Shane Martin, **Clean Straw for Nothing**, London: Collins, 1969, dedication, unpaged.

[15] Garry Kinnane, p. 155.

[16] Charmian Clift, 'Home from the Aegean,' **Australian Women's Weekly** (Sydney), 26 February 1964, p.7.

[17] Ibid.

[18] 'Book Reviews, The Truth About Oscar Wilde,' **Brisbane Telegraph** (Brisbane, Australia), 28 August 1948, p.4.

[19] George H. Johnston, **Death Takes Small Bites**, London: Victor Gollancz Ltd., 1948, p. 131.

[20] Ibid., p. 53.

[21] George Johnston, Letter to David Higham, 8 July 1954, at the Harry Ransom Center, University of Texas.

[22] Garry Kinnane, pp. 161-162.

[23] Arthur Polkinghorne, 'Sydney Diary,' **Sun** (Sydney), 19 May 1949, p. 21.

[24] George Johnston, Letter to David Higham, 8 July 1954.

[25] Ibid.

[26] Ibid., p. 72.

[27] Garry Kinnane, p. 91.

[28] Ibid., pp. 86-87.

[29] George Johnston, **Clean Straw for Nothing**, p. 75.

[30] George Johnston, 'The Citizen's Eye' (I) in John Button (ed.), **Look Here! Considering the Australian Environment**, Melbourne: F.W. Cheshire, 1968, pp. 11-17.

[31] Robin Boyd, 'The Nineteen-Sixties in Focus," in John Button (ed.), **Look Here! Considering the Australian Environment**, Melbourne: F.W. Cheshire, 1968, pp. 33-45.

[32] Robin Boyd, **The Australian Ugliness**, Melbourne: F.W. Cheshire, 1960.

[33] Derham Groves, 'Reframing "The Australian Ugliness,"' **Pursuit** (University of Melbourne), https://pursuit.unimelb.edu.au/articles/reframing-the-australian-ugliness, 2019, accessed 30 April 2023.

[34] Chester Eagle, 'Links with Greatness,' **Age** (Melbourne), 11 October 1986, p. 178.

[35] Charmian Clift (1965), 'On Painting Bricks White,' in Nadia Wheatley (ed.), **Sneaky Little Revolutions: Selected Essays of Charmian Clift**, Sydney: NewSouth Publishing, 2022, p. 50.

[36] 'Burma Road to Serial Background,' **Age**, 28 April 1950, p. 25.

[37] 'Studio News and Views,' **ABC Weekly** (Sydney), 25 February 1950, p. 32.

[38] Arthur Polkinghorne, 'Sydney Diary,' **Sun**, 15 August 1950, p. 21.

[39] David Higham, Letter to George Johnston, 27 December 1951, at the Harry Ransom Center, University of Texas.

[40] 'Studio News and Views,' **The ABC Weekly**, 4 March 1950, p. 32.

[41] George Johnston, Letter to David Higham, 1 August 1951, at the Harry Ransom Center, University of Texas.

[42] George Johnston (1953 or 1954), 'Requiem Mass,' in Garry Kinnane (ed.), **George Johnston, Charmian Clift, Strong-man from Piraeus**, Melbourne: Thomas Nelson Australia, 1983, p. 62.

[43] George Johnston, 'Requiem Mass,' pp. 69 and 71.

[44] Garry Kinnane, pp. 117-118.

[45] Ibid., pp. 154-155.

[46] George Johnston, 'Astypalaia Knife,' in Garry Kinnane (ed.), **George Johnston Charmian Clift: Strong-man from Piraeus and Other Stories**, pp.122-141.

[47] George Johnston, Letter to David Higham, 17 February 1954, Harry Ransom Center, University of Texas.

[48] David Higham, Letter to George Johnston, 12 February 1954, Harry Ransom Center, University of Texas.

[49] Sir Arthur Conan Doyle (1891), 'A Scandal in Bohemia,' in William S. Baring-Gould (ed.) (1968), **The Annotated Sherlock Holmes**, London: John Murray, 1973, vol. I, p. 363.

[50] Ibid., p. 8.

[51] Ibid., pp. 6-7.

[52] Shane Martin, 1957, dedication, unpaged.

[53] George Johnston, 1964, pp. 132-138.

[54] Ibid., p. 126.

[55] Ibid., p. 125.

[56] George Johnston, **Closer to the Sun**, London: Collins, 1960, p. 43.

[57] George Johnston, 1964, p. 46.

[58] Ibid., p.44.

59 George Johnston, 1964, p. 20.
60 Paul Genoni and Tanya Dalziell, pp. 56-57.
61 Ibid.
62 Shane Martin, 1957, p. 4.
63 George Johnston, **The Cyprian Woman**, London: Collins, 1955, dedication page.
64 'For Trial on Indecent Assault Charge,' **Truth** (Sydney), 28 September 1947, p. 21.
65 Ibid.
66 'Not Guilty of Indecency Charge,' **Daily Telegraph** (Sydney), 25 November 1947, p. 10.
67 Garry Kinnane, p. 135.
68 Shane Martin, 1957, p. 92.
69 Ibid., p. 22.
70 Garry Kinnane, p. 109.
71 Moira Redmond, 'Twelve Girls in the Garden by Shane Martin, **Clothes in Books**, http://clothesinbooks.blogspot.com/2018/09/twelve-girls-in-garden-by-shane-martin.html, 27 September 2018, accessed 27 August 2021.
72 Shane Martin, **Twelve Girls in the Garden**, p. 28.
73 Ibid., p. 22.
74 Garry Kinnane, pp. 164-165.
75 See Paul Genoni and Tanya Dalziell, **Half the Perfect World: Writers, Dreamers and Drifters on Hydra, 1955-1964**, Clayton, Australia: Monash University Publishing, 2018.
76 'New Books Fiction,' **Marion Star** (Marion, Ohio), 29 July 1957, p. 9.
77 'New Books in Review: Library Offers Education for Eleven Cents Monthly,' **Nashua Telegraph** (Nashua, New Hampshire), 13 July 1957, p. 10.
78 'Crime Corner,' **Knoxville Journal** (Knoxville. Tennessee), 9 June 1957, p. 44.
79 'Twelve Girls, Garden Are Good Mystery,' **Salt Lake Tribune** (Salt Lake City, Utah), 30 June 1957, p. 59.
80 'Books and News at the Pottsville Public Library,' **Pottsville Republican** (Pottsville, Pennsylvania), 2 July 1957, p. 2.
81 Maurice Richardson, 'Crime Ration,' **Observer** (London), 14 April 1957, p. 16.

[82] Phyllis Stock, 'Exciting World Through Eyes of a Gentleman,' **Bridgeport Post** (Bridgeport, Connecticut), 9 June 1957, p. 38.

[83] 'Library News and Reviews,' **Longview News-Journal** (Longview, Texas), 6 April 1958, p. 36.

[84] 'Suspense Story Called Superior,' **Los Angeles Times** (Los Angeles, California), 30 June 1957, p. 104.

[85] 'Trappings of Violence,' **Times Literary Supplement**, 17 May 1957, p. 301.

[86] Louise E. Larrabee, 'Mystery Features Ladies in Stone,' **Tulsa World** (Tulsa, Oklahoma), 7 July 1957, p. 81.

[87] Kathleen Freeman, 'Right and Wrong,' **Western Mail** (Cardiff, UK), 20 April 1957, p. 4.

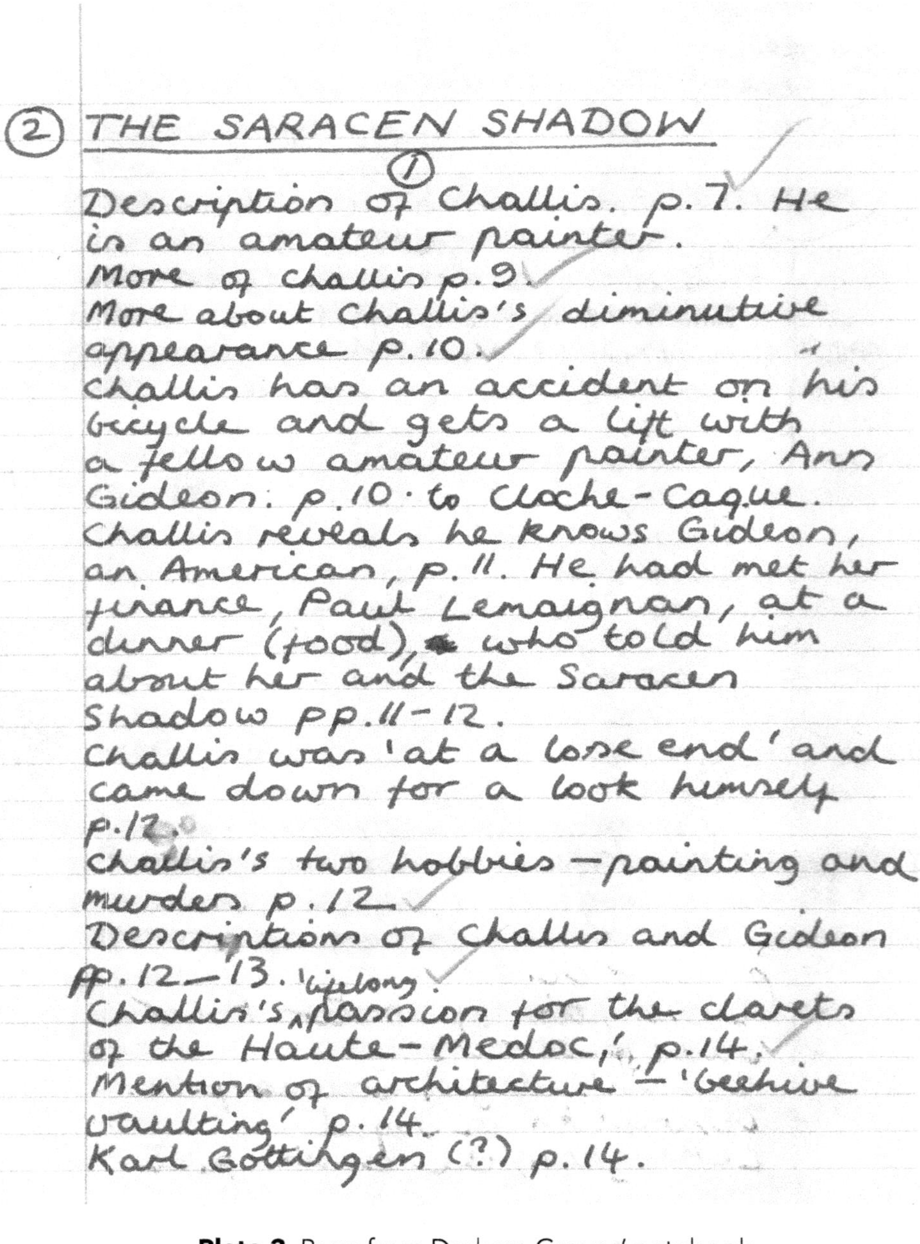

② THE SARACEN SHADOW

Description of Challis. p.7. He
is an amateur painter.
More of challis p.9
More about challis's diminutive
appearance p.10.
Challis has an accident on his
bicycle and gets a lift with
a fellow amateur painter, Ann
Gideon. p.10. to Cloche-Cague.
Challis reveals he knows Gideon,
an American, p.11. He had met her
fiancé, Paul Lemaignan, at a
dinner (food), who told him
about her and the Saracen
Shadow pp.11-12.
Challis was 'at a lose end' and
came down for a look himself
p.12.
Challis's two hobbies — painting and
murder p.12
Description of Challis and Gideon
pp.12-13. 'lifelong'
Challis's passion for the clarets
of the Haute-Medoc, p.14.
Mention of architecture — 'beehive
vaulting' p.14.
Karl Gottingen (?) p.14.

Plate 3 Page from Derham Groves' notebook.

2. The Saracen Shadow

The Saracen Shadow *(1957) is the second Professor Ronald Challis novel by Shane Martin/George Johnston. It takes place in France over seven days, sometime during the northern summer (June, July, and August) in 1957. Collins published it in Great Britain, but no American or Australian editions were published.* The Saracen Shadow *is now out of print, and copies are as scarce as hens' teeth. Following is a summary of the novel, with comments, opinions, and reviews later.*

Dramatis Personae

Professor Ronald Challis	An archaeologist and amateur detective.
Doctor Achille Brion	An archaeologist and the Professor's friend.
Madame Lemaignan	The matriarch of Château Cloche-Caque.
André Lemaignan	The eldest son of Madame Lemaignan.
Paul Lemaignan	The youngest son of Madame Lemaignan.
Jaquiline Lemaignan	The cousin of André and Paul.
Ann Gideon	Paul's fiancé.
Henri Casteret	The cellar master at Cloche-Caque.
Doctor Talbot Fillingham-Ausling	The owner of Château Erasmus.
Peter Judd	A writer and guest at Château Erasmus.
Josh Stowe	An artist and guest at Château Erasmus.
Michelet	The owner of Michelet's Bar.

Chapter I

After spending the last two summers digging in the stony aridity of southern Greece, Professor Ronald Challis wants to pass this one "in a more benevolent and tractable section of Europe." And since he has a lifelong passion for the clarets of the Haute-Medoc, he decides to holiday in the Dordogne River region of southwest France.

Challis attends a banquet of local vignerons at the Chapon Fin (1825-present) in Bordeaux, one of the first restaurants to achieve three Michelin stars. (**Fig. 32**) "I doubt I shall ever forget the *quenelles de brochet* [pike dumplings] or that *poularde à la vapeur* [steamed chicken]," he says. Challis meets Paul Lemaignan

Fig. 32 The Chapon Fin, Bordeaux, France (*recent photograph*).

of Châteaux Cloche-Caque, the "birthplace and temple of that particular claret which had given the Professor more moments of sheer bliss than any other wine he had drunk." Lemaignan tells him about his family curse — the Saracen Shadow. About six years ago, they found a twelve-hundred-year-old portrait of a "bearded man in a fur cap" in a sealed-off cellar in the foundations of Cloche-Caque. According to the curse found with the painting, this man was held captive on the site of the château, and every subsequent century, five males belonging to the family occupying the place will meet with violent deaths. The curse has delivered three victims so far this century — with Paul and his older brother André the only two remaining male members of the Lemaignan family.

Paul tells Challis he is welcome to visit Cloche-Caque anytime and see the painting of the Saracen. So, finding himself at a loose end a couple of days later, he decides to visit the château, look at the portrait, and investigate the family curse recorded and lately discovered in an ancient document.

Professor Challis heard so much about Paul Lemaignan's American fiancé from him at the dinner that he wants to meet Ann Gideon before he visits Cloche-Caque. Since he knows she is a keen landscape painter, he enquires in St. Estèphe where she might be before renting a bicycle far too big for him and heading off with "a paint box and a portable easel slung haphazardly across his shoulder" to try and find her, which he eventually does by the River Gironde. However, the Professor puts her off by criticising her for painting the water blue instead of grey and cuts his losses, packing up his paints, easel, and canvas and pedalling off furiously. But a short time later, he falls off his bicycle, buckling the front wheel and twisting the handlebars. Half an hour passes before Gideon charitably offers Challis a lift by the side of the road. "I am driving to the Château Cloche-Caque," she says. "Through Pauillac. If that is your direction."

"Thank you very much," says Challis. Now he can tell her about meeting her fiancé two nights ago at the Chapon Fin and being invited to visit the château and see the painting.

"At the river, why didn't you make yourself known to me?" asks Gideon.

"I'm afraid I'm rather like that," says Challis. "I have an insatiable curiosity and a penchant for doing things indirectly." He also asks her about the Saracen Shadow.

"I think the story is all rather far-fetched and absurd," says Gideon, adding that Cloche-Caque sometimes gives her the "heebie-jeebies." They finally arrive at the chateau and park in front. Challis follows her inside "like a small and well-trained pet." After passing through a labyrinth of vast gloomy rooms, they emerge onto "the most stupendous terrace Challis had seen outside Versailles." He panics when he sees that Paul Lemaignan is not amongst those gathered, but Gideon has the situation well in hand. "This is my dear friend, Professor Challis, from Boston," she says. "I have suggested he might stay with us a few days."

André Lemaignan, Paul's brother, greets Challis and introduces him to the others. Henri Casteret, a nervous and reluctant Frenchman, is Cloche-Caque's cellar master. Doctor Talbot Fillingham-Ausling, a red-faced Englishman with great wiry eyebrows, is the Lemaignan's neighbour. Peter Judd, a very tall and pale young Englishman who is a writer, asks the Professor whether he is the Challis who dug up Gournia. Jaquiline Lemaignan, André and Paul's pale and slender cousin who is at the beck and call of their mother and her aunt, the formidable but infirmed Madame Lemaignan. And, finally, Josh Stowe, a painter in his early thirties from Alabama or Tennessee, whom Challis saw paddling a boat on the river earlier in the day when he was with Ann Gideon. Judd and

Stowe are guests at Fillingham-Ausling's house, Château Erasmus. "Even if the story of the Saracen Shadow was no more than a diverting fable to amuse the gullible, there were enough queer little strains and tensions quivering on this bland, sunlit terrace to make his visit to Cloche-Caque worthwhile," thinks the Professor.

Chapter II

After the gathering on the terrace breaks up, André Lemaignan and Josh Stowe drive to St. Julien, Doctor Talbot Fillingham-Ausling and Peter Judd return to Château Erasmus, and Casteret, Jaquiline Lemaignan, Ann Gideon, and Professor Challis remain at Cloche-Caque. He would like to see the painting of the Saracen, but Ann doubts whether André will show it to him. "He's mulish and ungracious by nature," she says. "If he knows you're interested, he'll deliberately try to obstruct your interest." Henri Casteret found the portrait and a stack of ancient documents during alterations to the château's bottling room. André kept the picture even though he had no interest in art or culture and gave the documents to Fillingham-Ausling, who discovered the curse amongst them. "Nobody had ever heard of the Saracen Shadow before that," says Ann.

While it is not his area of expertise, Challis thinks the man in the portrait might be a Saracen Prince — the fifth son of Hisham (691-743), the tenth caliph of Umayyad. (**Fig. 33**) "Anyway, at some stage when the tide is turning against the Muslim invaders, the Prince suffers some form of treachery and betrayal in this area, is imprisoned in a dungeon on this very site, languishes for

Fig. 33 Hisham ibn Abd al-Malik, father of the Saracen Prince.

some years in miserable captivity, and ultimately perishes here — leaving behind the strange legend of the Berber Captive," says the Professor. He asks Gideon about Doctor Talbot Fillingham-Ausling and Peter Judd.

"Oh, it is a funny set-up," explains Gideon. They have been living together for years in the Château Erasmus. The doctor is extremely wealthy and is his patron. I heard Judd came down here to write a book, but now he seems to spend most of his time foraging out material for Fillingham-Ausling because he is writing the book, although I suppose Judd is doing the writing for him. The book, incidentally, is a sort of history of this château: it's not about his place at all, except indirectly."

Challis also wants to know how Josh Stowe fits in. "Oh, Josh is a comparatively recent acquisition," says Ann. "He's only been there since last winter. The doctor brought him back from Paris around Christmas. Oh, Judd's all right — at least he's much nicer than anyone else to poor Jaquiline — and Josh is a drunk, and he's not much good to himself or anyone else for that matter, but there's something about him that I like, and I feel terribly sorry for him, too." Paul Lemaignan is expected home from Bordeaux but is running late. Around ten thirty p.m., the telephone rings. "It just might be Paul," says Ann. "Would you excuse me?" But it is Fillingham-Ausling calling to say there has been a car accident and André Lemaignan is dead.

Chapter III

Shortly after Ann Gideon hears of André Lemaignan's death, Paul Lemaignan returns by car to Château Cloche-Caque. "He must have been very drunk by the time it happened," says Paul of his alcoholic older brother. "And if Josh Stowe were there, he would have been drunk, too." Professor Challis and Paul drive to Château Erasmus, where they brought André's body after the accident. He asks Paul why they did not take it to Cloche-Caque instead. "I don't know," says Paul. "Presumably, the villagers would have brought it up, and they know my mother. She is old and not well. Her heart is not strong. They would not want to upset her, I suppose. They would think it natural enough to take it, to take him to our neighbour." However, Fillingham-Ausling is upset with having "corpses delivered to my door," throwing his hands up in protest and wildly beating the air around his head as if he was afraid of bats getting tangled in his hair. In the meantime, Josh Stowe is unaware of André's death because he is still sleeping off his hangover.

Peter Judd tells Challis what happened while Paul views his brother's body. André drove to the Château Erasmus to pick up Josh, but André and Fillingham-Ausling had a furious row before they headed to St. Julien. On the way, André and Josh stopped at Michelet's bar in Pauillac for a drink. Later, the bar owner called the doctor to tell him to come and collect Josh because he was very drunk. But André was also as drunk as a coot, according to Judd. "Utterly incapable of driving — it astonishes me that he could make even the distance he did. Then, whoosh! The poor bastard comes to a bend, can't see a thing, and over he goes, into the river." Later, they join Paul in the makeshift mortuary at the château. André's body is on a long oaken refectory table and covered with a primrose sheet. "That great whack there on his forehead rather looks as if he banged his head on either the steering wheel or the dashboard," whispers Judd.

After Paul arranges to have André's body moved to Château Cloche-Caque, he and Challis drive back to Cloche-Caque. "I formed the impression that Fillingham-Ausling resented the friendship between your brother and Stowe," says the Professor.

"The blunt truth of the matter is that both André and Stowe were alcoholics, dipsomaniacs, whatever you want to call them," says Paul disgustedly. "They liked each other's company, although liked isn't perhaps the right word; needed is nearer the mark, I think — because they shared a common interest and, in a way, a common hunger for understanding. But it went deeper than that: it wasn't just two drunks weeping on each other's shoulders. They were in the Far East together on military service at roughly the same time. Stowe was in Korea mostly, and André was in Indo-China. Whether they met or not, I don't know."

Challis examines André's old grey Fiat, now smeared and caked with mud after being dragged from the river. Apart from a dented roof and a busted side door, it is undamaged. (**Fig. 34**) Challis also walks to where the accident happened, near where he and Ann were by the river painting earlier. He suspects someone may have murdered André and fears that Paul might be next. Then he remembers he has not yet returned his damaged bicycle to Gosset's

Fig. 34 André's damaged old grey Fiat.

garage and suddenly has a blurry memory of it strapped to Ann's car parked in the shadows at Château Erasmus.

Chapter IV

The next day, Professor Challis is frustrated nothing is happening. So he follows the elderly servant Clothilde, and when she takes Madame Lemaignan her breakfast, he walks into her bedroom, pretending to be lost. Madame Lemaignan is talking to Henri Casteret, the cellar master. "Ah, then you are Professor Challis," says Madame Lemaignan. "Paul spoke to me about you. I wanted very much to meet you and talk to you. I shall have coffee sent in. Casteret is leaving now." The matriarch of Château Cloche-Caque is propped up with pillows, sitting in a huge, canopied bed with an eiderdown across her legs and a black woollen shawl around her shoulders. Madame Lemaignan is unusually tall and grotesquely fat. She has dead-black hair, a small face with brooding features that remind the Professor of a Goya painting, and wrinkled skin leather-brown with age. While her eyelids are crumpled, like old gloves, her eyes are bright and black, like a girl's. Her hands are small and waxlike with long, well-kept fingernails. And Madame Lemaignan speaks in a gentle, soft, sweet voice. Challis starts by telling her he is sorry about her son André's death. "I appreciate your condolences, but since André is dead, he is dead," says Madame Lemaignan. "Nothing more is to be done. With Paul, the château will be in better hands."

When the Professor tells Madame Lemaignan he plans to walk to Château Erasmus, she cannot hide her dislike for Doctor Talbot Fillingham-Ausling. "His grandmother was my aunt," she says.

> She owned Château Erasmus, which was very small then and poor and called only Gaudet's Vineyard. It was he who made it a château and gave it another name. Because of his grandmother, he thinks there

is a family link to us. But he will believe anything, like that the blood of the Plantagenet kings of England flowed in his veins, which is why he is obsessed with the idea of owning Cloche-Caque because the Plantagenet kings did stay here — three of them: King John first, then Edward I, and Edward II. Bah! We waste our time talking of this pretentious fool who dreams of Aquitaine. I think you waste your time Professor Challis visiting his — his château.

Challis also tells Madame Lemaignan he needs to go to Pauillac to return his rented bicycle. "Jaquiline will drive you in," she insists. "Go with her. She is a rather pathetic creature. She might enjoy a little company."

"Why is she pathetic?" asks Challis.

"She is a stupid, weak girl — the sort of person who thrives only on subjugation," says Madame Lemaignan.

It is a trait I particularly despise in women. She is an only child, the daughter of my brother-in-law Jean, who died in an aeroplane disaster in Switzerland. She came here as my ward afterward. She is passionately devoted to poor Peter Judd. The child has nothing to offer, yet she plagues him unbearably with her attention. Those sad, tawny eyes of hers! He is a gentleman, of course, and treats the poor wretch with kindliness, but he is far too intelligent to be more than considerate. Do you realise that if I should lose Paul, she will become the mistress of Cloche-Caque!

While Jaquiline Lemaignan is sweet on Peter Judd, according to Madame Lemaignan, he is keen on Ann Gideon.

Jaquiline Lemaignan drops Professor Challis at Pauillac on her way to Cussac, arranging to pick him up in an hour on her way back. He returns the bicycle to the garage and sees Josh Stowe across the road, who invites him for a drink at Michelet's bar. The bar owner is angry with Stowe because the authorities might give him trouble after yesterday's accident. "The police will be around asking a lot of questions because they're strict on a bar giving liquor to a man who isn't fit to handle a car," says Michelet. "I only took over this bar two months ago, and people don't know me yet, and they can make a lot of trouble for a man in a small place like this. Listen, Mister Stowe, you and André Lemaignan were in good shape when you left here last night. I wouldn't like anyone to make trouble for me."

Challis and Stowe finish their drinks and head to Gosset's garage. André Lemaignan's car is there, propped up on jacks. "Well, what do you say we stick around until this grease monkey gets out from under there and stops throwing goo all over the evidence?" says Stowe. "Then maybe I can show you something." Stowe points out a couple of brand-new nuts and washers on the steering column. "They blame drunks for things they do — and that's all right — and sometimes they don't," he tells the Professor. "I guess they ask for that sort of deal — people like André and me — but a drunk's always got plenty of troubles without them pinning all the extras on him."

Chapter V

At four p.m., the Lemaignan family gathers in Cloche-Caque's impressive banquet hall, decorated to simulate a Medieval feudal hall, complete with a *trompe l'oeil* rush-strewn floor, to receive the condolences of employees, neighbours, and villagers, standing like a frightened flock of sheep on the far side of the room. André Lemaignan's body lies in a highly polished black coffin with silver handles, his face surrounded by a sort of coif of white linen to cover the ugly wound on his forehead. Madame Lemaignan sits in a high-backed chair, presiding like some gigantic black symbol of death over the cold body of her son, flanked by Paul Lemaignan and Ann Gideon. Following a few awkward words about the deceased from the local priest, Madame Lemaignan slowly rises to thank everyone for attending. "I am grateful for the respect you have paid André and the sympathy you have shown me," she says.

> But death is not a new thing to any of us. I have known it before and have suffered from it, and I am now an old woman and close to my own time. The continuity of things is of more importance than the death of things, and here at Cloche-Caque, we are the custodians of continuities that have lasted a very long time. André's funeral will be tomorrow at three in the chapel of Saint Vincent. I do not propose mourning beyond this week, and it will not interfere with the marriage of my son Paul and Miss Gideon on the thirtieth of this month.

The news about Paul and Ann's wedding comes as a surprise to everyone, including them. So, after most people have left and Madame Lemaignan has returned to her room, Paul, Ann, Doctor Talbot Fillingham-Ausling, Peter Judd, Josh Stowe, and Professor Challis try to ease the tension with small talk. Professor Challis asks Fillingham-Ausling's permission to see the documents found with the portrait of the Saracen. However, as they are in a mess, it will take Judd a couple of days to put them in order. So Paul invites Challis to remain at Cloche-Caque until they are ready. "On Friday, I must travel along the Dordogne to Montignac: they have opened a new cave there, and I have promised to look at it," says Challis. "But I could be back on Friday night or Saturday morning, and perhaps by then, you may have got things into order?" he asks Judd.

"Yes, I suppose that would be all right," says Judd unenthusiastically. Feeling like he is on a roll, Challis finally asks Paul to see the painting of the Saracen. "Whenever it suits you," Paul agrees. "Tonight if you like. After dinner."

While sitting alone on the terrace, Professor Challis reviews the chief suspects of murdering André Lemaignan — Paul Lemaignan, Ann Gideon, Josh Stowe, Doctor Talbot Fillingham-Ausling, Madame Lemaignan, and Jaquiline Lemaignan. However, he cannot rule anyone in or out. Jaquiline apologises to the Professor for leaving him alone and tells him that Paul and Ann have walked to the river. "If you would like to go and join them, the path to take is there, leading down from that corner of the rose garden." Despite having driven to Pauillac and back with Jaquiline, this is the first time Challis notices her. She was no more than twenty-three but already had many traits associated with middle age and spinsterhood. An air of patient yet unaccepted suffering. A shyness that told of frustrations too long endured yet never conquered. And a primness that revealed uncertainty and fear. Even her complexion already had the faint cloudiness, and her dark eyes the haunted look of forbearance that generally came from martyrdoms endured longer than they should. Yet she was far from unattractive. She had lovely, soft, brown hair, fine eyes, a well-shaped face, and a pretty mouth. Her figure was good, and her hands were well-kept for all the tan flecks upon the skin. The Professor believed there was something about hands that portrayed more of a person's true character than the receptive mirrors of the features.

After Jaquiline goes to organise dinner, Challis looks for Paul and Ann. When he hears them arguing about their wedding, he takes cover behind a clump of azaleas to listen. "Does it matter whether it is now? Or next week? Or at the end of the autumn?" asks Paul.

"It matters to me!" says Ann angrily. "It matters very much to me. I will marry you, yes — I want to marry you — but I will do it in my time as we had arranged, and not just because it is her whim."

Fig. 35 Vincent of Saragossa.

Embarrassed, Challis silently retreats and waits for them. "They told me you had gone down to the river," he says. "I went down and looked for you. Probably, I took the wrong pathway. I hope I'm not intruding; perhaps you were talking privately." When they all reach the edge of the rose garden, Challis sees someone moving on the terrace. Then, two pistol shots ring out. The Professor finds Jaquiline holding a smoking gun and listening to something only she can hear. The only casualty is the nose of the garden statue of Vincent of Saragossa, the patron saint of wine-makers. (**Fig. 35**)

Chapter VI

Jaquiline Lemaignan tells Ann Gideon she went to see if André Lemaignan's study was tidy before Professor Challis looked at the painting of the Saracen and discovered it was missing. She thought a burglar was inside the house and took the pistol from André's antique desk. Outside on the terrace, Jaquiline thought someone was lurking in the garden and fired two shots. "And if she hadn't hit that statue of Saint Vincent, she could quite easily have got one of us," says Paul Lemaignan.

"If she had got you, the Saracen Shadow would have fulfilled its obligations for another century," says Challis, even though he does not believe in curses or superstitious humbug. But the Professor is surprised that, knowing they might return from the river and go through the garden, Jaquiline would take potshots at the first figure she sees moving in the darkness. After dinner, Paul, Challis, and Peter Judd visit André Lemaignan's study. Nothing else seems to be missing, according to Paul. They stare at the space on the wall where the painting used to hang. Paul believes it is genuine, Challis suspects it might be a fake, and Judd is uncertain.

As Professor Challis prepares for bed, Madame Lemaignan knocks on his door. She wants him to tell her what is happening because nobody else will. The Professor says he suspects someone murdered André and wishes to murder Paul — and not a neurotic girl — but someone stranger and darker. Challis wants to protect him but needs his mother's help. "For example, you might tell me how you and André became estranged, what completely changed him, sent him to Indo-China, and turned him into a drunkard," says Challis.

"Leave it alone, Professor," says Madame Lemaignan. "There has been enough evil and tragedy here. Do not add to it."

"Someone murdered André, you know," says Challis quietly. "And I think you might know who it was." But she leaves without saying a word.

The next day, Professor Challis visits the bottling room where the cellar master, Henri Casteret, found the painting of the Saracen. "Down there," says Casteret, indicating the old vault. "We had to pull it down to rebuild." Challis is surprised to find the bar owner, Michelet, sitting on the edge of a pallet in the bottling room, eating bread and cheese. Later, the Professor attends the funeral of André Lemaignan, although he has nothing black to wear since he is on holiday.

Chapter VII

Professor Challis invites Ann Gideon, Jaquiline Lemaignan, Doctor Talbot Fillingham-Ausling, Peter Judd, and Josh Stowe to join him to see the newly opened Gottingen cave in the Dordogne, which has one or two rather fascinating but dangerous features. (**Fig. 36**) Challis assumes Paul Lemaignan will not come since his brother's funeral was only yesterday, but he joins them at the last minute. By getting all the suspects together, Challis hopes to discover who murdered André. They set off in three cars. Paul and Ann in the first, Judd and Fillingham-Ausling in the second, and Jaquiline, Stowe, and Challis in the third. The Doctor brings a hamper of food and a dozen bottles of *vin rosé* grown on the Château Erasmus, which he is anxious for the Professor to try. In

Fig. 36 One of the Lascaux caves near
Montignac (recent photograph).

the car, Challis asks Stowe what happened to André in Indo-China and why he became a drunkard. But the Professor learns nothing new. So he changes tack and asks how Henri Casteret fits in. "All I know is that whenever André got drunk — got really drunk, I mean — he'd always get around to talking about Casteret," says Stowe. Best you ask him." Then Stowe takes a rusty, hexagonal steel nut with a shiny thread out of his pocket and shows it to Challis.

> Yesterday morning, I walked along the road by the river where the car went in. That's what I found in the grass, about seventy yards back from the corner. Maybe there's another one lying along the roadside somewhere, but I just found the one. The nut could have dropped off a truck, or perhaps someone tossed it away. However, I think someone worked on the thread with one of those three-cornered files, but you never can tell. I thought you might be interested after what I said to you in Gosset's garage the day before yesterday.

They meet their guide, Doctor Achille Brion, an archaeologist, and friend of Professor Challis, outside the café beneath the beetling rock cliff upon which the great stone statue of Cro-Magnon Man brooded over the valley in the picturesque village of Les Eyzies. (**Fig. 37**) They bring two acetylene lanterns, a powerful flashlight, and some candles to illuminate the cave. "Now, I want you to leave the acetylene lanterns inside the entrance as markers," Challis tells Brion quietly. "And for the deeper penetration, we shall make with only the electric flashlight — which I should like to carry."

"Don't be absurd," protests Brion. "With only the one light, we shall scarcely be able to see anything," but reluctantly agrees before they walk for about twenty minutes to the entrance of the cave —

Fig. 37 Les Eyzies (left) and the Cro-Magnon Man statue (recent photograph).

a twisted cleft in the pale limestone containing a dark aperture, almost a slot, so narrow that the overweight Fillingham-Ausling was able to squirm through only at the cost of immense effort and two leather buttons off his Donegal jacket. Inside, a dark tunnel twists down through a mass of fallen boulders. It turns behind a great shaft of stone, like the flying buttress of some medieval cathedral, and opens out into an impressive chamber where they gather in impenetrable blackness. Brion leaves the two acetylene lanterns inside the entrance, and he and Challis lead Stowe, Judd, Jaquiline, Paul, Ann, and Fillingham-Ausling along a narrow ledge, thirty-five metres long, lit solely by the flashlight. But about halfway across, it goes out, engulfing them in complete darkness. "Challis, you haven't been fiddling with this thing, have you?" asks Brion sternly. A strong draught prevents them from lighting their candles, and they panic. Jaquiline screams. Challis feels a hand seize his sleeve, but whether to hold or push him, he cannot say. There is a shower of falling pebbles. They hear something heavy thud onto the rocks below. Then the torch comes on again. Judd, Jacqueline, Paul, and Ann are crouching against the wall. Fillingham-Ausling is lying spread-eagled on the ledge. And Stowe is missing.

Professor Challis and Doctor Brion send the others home before telling the local *gendarmerie*, which accepts the death of Josh Stowe as a caving accident. While waiting for a car to take him back to Pauillac, Challis tells Brion over a cup of coffee what he hoped to achieve but failed miserably to do, with tragic consequences. "The recent death in the Lemaignan family stressed the six people I brought with me, and over the last few days, I have been trying to find out what is behind their fears and frictions," says the Professor.

When I met you at Les Eyzies, I thought the cave we intended to explore might present that opportunity. As you know, Brion, the underground world is oddly morbid and atavistic, which can have the most extraordinary effect on a person who is acutely nervous, highly strung, hypersensitive, or even morbidly inclined. One of those six people is a murderer, and I am anxious to find out which one it is — or was.

Challis asks his driver to drop him at Michelet's bar in Pauillac. After the Professor tells Michelet that Josh Stowe is dead, he says that around eight p.m. on Tuesday, André Lemaignan and Stowe argued. Then André left, Peter Judd arrived, Stowe left, and Judd telephoned Ann Gideon. Michelet did not see Doctor Talbot Fillingham-Ausling in the bar that day. Finally, Michelet confesses that he buys wine from Henri Casteret on the side. "For the most part, you have been very frank with me, and I appreciate it," says Challis. "And now, if it would not be too much of a nuisance, perhaps you would be kind enough to direct me to this path through the vines which you say will take me to the Château Erasmus."

Challis watches Judd leave Château Erasmus and drive away while hiding in the shadows. He knocks on the front door, and the cleaner shows him to Fillingham-Ausling's bedroom, where the Doctor is heavily sedated and fast asleep. So, left to his own devices, Challis searches for the documents Judd promised to show him and finds a folder marked "THE CLOCHE-CAQUE PAPERS." In the lower right-hand corner, written in a small and precise hand, was a sort of index of the contents, and midway down the list was "Berber Legend, xvii-xxi. For verification to 19th Cent., see Folios 5, 7, 8, 8a." Taking the folder, he tells the cleaner on his way out, "Thank you very much, I have what I came for."

Chapter VIII

Professor Challis arrives back at Château Cloche-Caque a few minutes after eleven p.m. He notices Peter Judd's car parked discreetly by the side of the road, away from the château's main gate. Clothilde tells him that Paul Lemaignan and Ann Gideon are waiting for him on the terrace, so he gives her the folder and tells her to put it in his room. Paul greets the Professor first and tells him that Achille Brion telephoned to say they found Josh Stowe's body in the river. The Professor asks how Judd took the news, but nobody at Cloche-Caque has seen him since they returned from Les Eyzies. Then Paul goes inside, leaving Challis and Ann alone on the terrace. "How deeply were you attached to Stowe?" he asks her.

"I liked Josh," she says. "I liked him very much, but I was never in love with him if that's what you mean. Paul thought I was. because he is jealous and reads too much into things. But it's Paul I love." However, Ann admits they had a 'flirtation' in the past, which began again a few weeks ago, when she grew concerned his drinking was because of her. But she dismisses the idea that Paul's jealousy might lead to violence. "Paul couldn't be violent," says Ann. "That just isn't the way he is."

"Have you ever had a flirtation with Peter Judd?" asks Challis.

"With Peter!" says Ann indignantly. "Good heavens, no!"

Even though it is almost midnight, Challis asks Paul to see André's study. They unlock the desk, and the Professor rummages through the disorder of loose papers, crumpled letters and envelopes, dogeared account books and brochures, and the donkey's breakfast of heterogeneous litter in the drawer. "Hallo!" says Challis. "The gun is still here."

Fig. 38 André's "squat, black, ugly little Mauser."

"I don't understand," says Paul in disbelief. "I took it from here and ...."

"And someone decided they preferred it to be left where it was," says Challis, removing the bullets and leaving it there. (**Fig. 38**) "Now you must go to bed," he tells him since he wants to soak up the atmosphere and think alone. "I always feel there is something in the atmosphere ... a stimulus that comes from the middle-night silence of a sleeping house." Challis takes a file from André's desk drawer and returns to his room. He is about to start reading it when he notices someone is working in the bottling room. It is one a.m. So Challis postpones reading the file until he investigates who is still up.

Chapter IX

At ten-thirty a.m. the next day, Professor Challis arrives at Château Erasmus to return the folder he took the night before. Doctor Talbot Fillingham-Ausling reluctantly shows him in because he is about to go to Montignac to arrange Josh Stowe's funeral. The Professor then tells him that Peter Judd faked the painting of the Saracen to stay in his good books. "You mean this was all a hoax on Judd's part?" says Fillingham-Ausling in disbelief.

"A good deal of it, I imagine," says Challis. "I might be more definite if I could see this portrait of the sinister Saracen. It is no more than some early unwanted portrait discarded into the Cloche-Caque cellars during a general spring cleaning long ago. Perhaps it was later, shall we say, 'restored' by Judd — possibly as no more than a witty exercise — to resemble an example of Saracen art. But don't you feel it is significant that the moment somebody with some knowledge of Saracenic art appeared on the scene, the picture vanished?" Fillingham-Ausling cannot believe Judd would do that, but Challis assures him he did. "He must have been extremely intrigued, surely, by the fact that while the ownership of Cloche-Caque changed on numerous occasions in the centuries preceding the Revolution, the name Lemaignan never occurs once," says Challis. "I think I should also have been extremely intrigued by the fact that the owner of Cloche-Caque at the time of the Revolution was a man named Jean-Jaques Casteret."

Professor Challis has arranged a tour of the château's winemaking facilities at five p.m. and anticipates trouble. "You won't think I am being old-womanish, will you, if I ask you to stay close beside me?" Challis asks Paul Lemaignan before they meet Henri Casteret in the cellar, but he is nowhere to be found. When the Professor hears a sound like a mouse squeaking, he knows what is about to happen and pushes Paul out of the way and takes cover to avoid three barrels of wine crashing down on top of them. "Come," orders Challis. "We must get up on that shelf above. That's where I saw them getting the trap ready last night."

"Saw who?" says Paul, the wine clotting his hair and dribbling down his cheeks.

From higher up, they see Casteret hanging from a rope over a cross-beam. "Judging by the colour of his skin, he's been dead an hour or more," says the Professor. "So it wasn't him who tried to drop those barrels on top of us."

"Come out of there, or by God, I'll drag you out!" Paul yells at their unseen attacker. Then, in a violent rush, Peter Judd leaps, stumbles, falls, and lies dead on the cellar floor. By now, the commotion has woken almost everyone at the château. Among the first to enter the cellar is Jaquiline Lemaignan, who kneels beside Judd, taking his stained and crumpled body in her arms.

Peter Judd masterminded the entire affair and almost pulled it off. If everything had gone to plan, which it nearly did, everyone would have viewed the death of André Lemaignan as a car accident, Josh Stowe's death as a caving accident, and the deaths of Paul Lemaignan and the Professor as a cellar accident. Then Jaquiline Lemaignan would have inherited Château Cloche-Caque, and Judd would have married her. Even Henri Casteret's unexpected suicide played into Judd's hands because everyone would assume he hanged himself after witnessing the terrible result of his incompetence. And what happened to the painting of the Saracen? Challis suspects Judd persuaded Casteret to steal it from André's study and hide it somewhere, possibly Michelet's bar.

Chapter X

Professor Challis visits Jaquiline Lemaignan because he is concerned that she might have taken André Lemaignan's gun from his desk. "I looked in the drawer a few minutes ago, and it wasn't there," says the Professor. "I thought you might have it."

"It's beneath my pillow," says Jaquiline in an absent, flat tone. "Take it if you want it."

"I don't want it, no," says Challis. "As long as I know where it is. As long as you know that it isn't the answer." Jaquiline is particularly troubled that Judd thought she murdered André by tampering with his car. "Jaquiline, listen to me," says Challis. "He didn't think you killed André. He knew you had nothing at all to do with it. I can explain it all to you, but —"

"He did, I tell you!" Jaquiline protests. "I told him I hadn't but he didn't seem to understand."

After repeatedly failing to convince her, Challis finally tells Jaquiline the harsh truth about Judd. "He did not wish to understand because he murdered André Lemaignan," says the Professor. "Deliberately and calculatingly — so calculatingly that if anybody ever became suspicious of his victim's death, the focus would be on you, not him. So when the time came for his plans, there would be no way you could escape the wall of deceit he built from when you came here five years ago."

Chapter XI

Finally, Professor Challis sees Madame Lemaignan in her bedroom to tell her, "Henri Casteret hanged himself this afternoon in the big cellar. He is dead, André is dead, and Peter Judd is dead, too. I know you liked Judd, but he killed them all. He also tried to kill Paul."

"Why did Henri hang himself?" asks Madame Lemaignan.

"I think he was pressed too far," replies Challis.

"Henri could have waited," says Lemaignan.

"Perhaps he felt he had waited long enough," says Challis.

Madame Lemaignan tells Challis that Henri's father was her brother-in-law Jean Lemaignan, and that she was his mother. But the Professor had already guessed that. Madame Lemaignan gave birth to Henri secretly in a Bordeaux nursing home in July 1912, registering him under her maiden name, Casteret, and thus denying him his birthright — a share of Château Cloche-Caque. Finally, Challis convinces Madame Lemaignan to reveal all, especially to Jaquiline, who he believes she has treated particularly cruelly.

THE END.

Comments, Opinions, Reviews

You Can't Tell A Book By Its Cover

Collins published **The Saracen Shadow** in Great Britain. Since William Randell had designed the dust jacket for the first Professor Challis novel, **Twelve Girls in the Garden** (1957), they hired him to do one for the second novel, too. It showed the scene where Jaquiline Lemaignan followed someone, possibly a burglar, onto the terrace of Château Cloche-Caque and nervously fired her dead cousin's Mauser at a shadow in the garden, narrowly missing Paul Lemaignan, Ann Gideon, and Professor Challis, with him in the distance over Jaqueline's right shoulder, which was the first time anyone had depicted him. While Randell successfully captured his unruly white hair, he is not quite pixie-like enough for me. (**Fig. 39**) However, the crime novelist Frances Iles (aka Anthony Berkeley Cox, 1893-

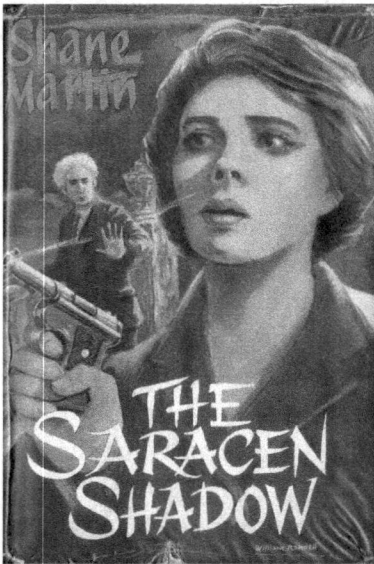

Fig. 39 Dust jacket for **The Saracen Shadow** by William Randell.

1971), who reviewed crime fiction for the **Guardian** in London, was even unhappier than me, taking umbrage to Randell's choice of scene, saying it was "a pity that the jacket should show a girl holding a smoking revolver, even though the incident does occur (quite unimportantly) in the book, for this has now become almost the hallmark of the very cheapest kind of thriller."[1] But, since the scene happened and demonstrated Jaquiline's emotional fragility, I think it was rather unfair and wrong of him to say that. What was Randell supposed to do? Give the game away on the front cover?

While George Johnston was happy with **The Saracen Shadow** enough to dedicate it to his wife and fellow writer, Charmain Clift,[2] his American agent Harold Ober did not like the novel.[3] Consequently, William Morrow did not publish it in the USA, denying Johnston access to the lucrative American market.[4] Nor was **The Saracen Shadow** published in Australia. Surprisingly, Collins did not try to sell more copies in Australia, if only for Johnston's sake, but it seems they did not because I found no reviews of **The Saracen Shadow** in the local newspapers. Furthermore, I found only three in the British press. The **Times Literary Supplement** thought Shane Martin/George Johnston "packed too many characters and too much plot into too little space."[5] The **Birmingham Mail** said, "A story of villainy in a forbidding old French château enables Professor Challis to test his theory that archaeology and crime detection call for similar treatment. Shane Martin makes it tense and credible."[6] The third was in the **Guardian** by Illes, already mentioned. It seems he got up on the wrong side of the bed that morning since he was also unhappy because the characters were "large-size oddities," the plot was "highly complicated" and Johnston's English was "far from perfect." Regarding the latter, Illes criticised him for saying 'inference' instead of 'implication,' and using the expression, 'sensible to,' which was "a new one even to me," he said. Although, overall, he thought it was "a pleasure to read because it is the work of an educated man with widely diverse interests from claret to speleology."[7] I find it ironic that he should have praised **The Saracen Shadow** for its speleology because, if he was going to criticise it for anything, it might have been for the crazy stunt in the cave arranged by Professor Challis, which led to the death of Josh Stowe and almost himself while failing to flush out the murderer.

The Saracen Shadow was the first of three Challis novels that featured cave scenes — **The Man Made of Tin** (1958) and **The Myth is Murder** (1959) were the others. In Johnston's autobiographical novel, **My Brother Jack** (1964), David Meredith said, "In recent years, several critics have wondered why in all my books there is invariably some more-or-less, symbolic cave scene."[8] According to Meredith, they were a later-in-life, Freudian manifestation of the claustrophobic front room at 11 Buxton Street, Elsternwick, where most of the formal Meredith — and Johnston — family gatherings occurred. These ranged from entertaining stiffly-seated Sunday afternoon visitors to paying final respects to deceased relatives lying in their coffins on the big, central dining table.[9] Perhaps this also explains why in **The Saracen Shadow**, Challis believed that caves were "the stuff of childhood's mysteries and magics and terrors."[10]

A Rue By Any Other Name …

George Johnston wanted to call his second Challis novel, **Press the Rue for Wine**, which is a line from "The Rover's Adieu" (1813) by Sir Walter Scott (1771-1832) that Professor Challis recites to himself when he smells Cloche-Caque's fragrant herb garden wafting through his bedroom window:

> A weary lot is thine, fair maid,
> A weary lot is thine!
> To pull the thorn thy brow to braid,
> And press the rue for wine![11]

Johnston changed the title to **The Saracen Shadow** at the request of Collins. Maybe they thought that because the setting was France, readers might presume the rue in the title was French for street instead of the herb rue. (**Fig. 40**) But in his biography of Johnston, Garry Kinnane said it was "awful,"[12] without providing

Fig. 40 The herb, rue *(ruta gravelons)*.

any context whatsoever, which was yet another example of how he unfairly criticised the Challis novels, in my view. Johnston's preferred title might have been confusing, but it was not awful!

So, where did **The Saracen Sword** come from? Perhaps the new title — and even the idea of having the portrait of a Saracen at the heart of the mystery — was inspired by the Saracen's Head Hotel at 389 Bourke Street in Melbourne, which had the head of a Saracen and the name of the hotel prominently displayed on the façade of the building. (**Fig. 41**) Johnston knew this pub very well since it was only a few minutes' walk from his office in the Argus Building on the corner of Bourke and Elizabeth streets. Furthermore, in **My Brother Jack** his alter ego David Meredith tells how his Uncle Davy had been a successful journalist until "he made the mistake of falling in love with a red-haired barmaid at the Saracen's Head Hotel, drank to excess just to be with her, lost his job, lost the barmaid also, and sank into obscure poverty."[13] I can imagine Johnston sitting in

Fig. 41 The Saracen's Head Hotel in the 1950s.

front of his typewriter on Hydra, raking through his past for inspiration. Then, bingo! He remembers the Saracen's Head Hotel in Melbourne.

Chateau Cloche-Caque

George Johnston was the London correspondent of the **Sun** when he and Charmian Clift accepted a two-week junket paid for by the French Government to the Dordogne River region of southwest France in April 1953. If what he wrote after returning to work is anything to go by, they enjoyed their free holiday:

> The atmosphere was dream-like enough, coming back to London after two weeks of French sunshine, steaks Chateaubriand and the nectar-like wines of Lafite, Latour, and Yquem. There was the contrast of the pastel tints of the Loire in springtime and the greyness of Fleet Street, the faded paint and peeling stucco of France and the gilded crowns, puttering banners, Tudor roses and pretty painted lampposts of the Coronation city.[14]

The places they visited in France provided Johnston with background material for **The Saracen Shadow**, set in the Lemaignan family estate Château Cloche-Caque ('Bell-Barrel' in English), which was "very old and very beautiful with long windows with faded tan shutters running like music around the spacious quadrangle and round turrets at each corner like illustrations from a fairy-tale, the old stones which seemed to have been soaking for centuries in sunlight and dew, the high-pitched slate roof gleaming like bronze against the unclouded sky,"[15] said Professor Challis. In a note at the start of **The Saracen Shadow**, Johnson declared that "Cloche-Caque is entirely a château of the imagination, as this story is entirely a fiction."[16] While that may have been true of the

134

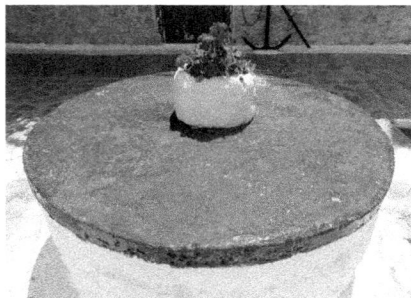

Fig. 42 The covered well in front of the Johnstons' house on Hydra (2018).

chateau, as a whole, it seems to have comprised architectural elements familiar to him. For example, when Ann Gideon parked her car in front of the chateaux, Challis observed a boy sleeping against "an old covered well,"[17] which sounded very much like the one in front of the Johnstons' house on Hydra, which also pops up in **Twelve Girls in the Garden**[18] and **Clean Straw for Nothing** (1969).[19] It seems to have been a new book, a different country, but the same well. (**Fig. 42**)

Identifying other architectural sources for Château Cloche-Caque was trickier, although Johnston inadvertently gave some hints. By noting at the start of **The Saracen Shadow** that "Any vague resemblance to such châteaux as Beychevelle, Lafite-Rothschild, Calon-Segur, F'Yquem, or Auzone, can be attributed to the author's wistful memories of warm hours spent there,"[20] he was also saying they were on his mind when he imagined Cloche-Caque, otherwise, why did he mention them? So, based on the description of Cloche-Caque by Professor Challis, Johnston might have combined the shuttered windows and spacious quadrangle of Beyche-velle (**Fig. 43**) with the round turrets and high-pitched roof of F'Yquem (**Fig. 44**). The

Fig. 43 Château Beychevelle (recent photograph).

Fig. 44 Château F'Yquem (recent photograph).

135

Johnstons used **Three Rivers of France: Dordogne, Lot, Tarn** (1952) by Freda White (1894-1971) as their vacation guidebook on this holiday, according to Kinnane. However, surprisingly, she did not mention any of the five châteaux Johnston identified.

Once again, this time with Cloche-Caque, George Johnston demonstrated his descriptive mastery and sense of place. "The bewildering transit through the fantastic rooms of the château [was] like Alice's journey down the rabbit hole,"[21] said Professor Challis. It was "like a dream, half seen, out of perspective, the strange unexpectedness of gloom after sunlight."[22] Some parts of the château were so impenetrably dark the professor could not tell whether they were "passageways or other doors or the mouths of caves or the lairs of wild beasts."[23] The most impressive and unique room was undoubtedly the banqueting hall, "the elaborate whim of some ancestor, living perhaps at the decayed end of the Renaissance, who had succumbed utterly to the novel appeal of *trompe l'oeil*."

> Every square inch of walls and ceiling had become a cunningly devised optical illusion of colour and perspective planned to simulate a rafted feudal hall of the Middle Ages, even to the pretence of a rush-strewn floor stretching to distant apartments. No trick that could artfully employ a union of painting and skill and an uncanny knowledge of perspective had been neglected. A door ajar enclosed an armoury within, with racked pikes, and crossbows, and visored helmets; through a painted window, which seemed fifty yards away, bright tents and

pennons waited forever for the tournament to begin. But time and the shuttered darkness of Cloche-Caque had laid a gloomy patina across the once-gay pigments: they would have to hurry with the tournament, the Professor reflected, for dusk had come and nightfall was at hand."[24]

Memorable for totally different reasons was Jaquiline Lemaignan's bedroom in Cloche-Caque. Just as the sitting room at 221B Baker Street displayed the eccentricities of Sherlock Holmes, it exposed her insecurities:

It was a pretty room, all in white and a very pale dove-grey: clearly, [Jaquiline] had spent much time and thought in making it pretty. The edge of lace on the curtains, the finely worked mats on the dressing table, the embroidered pillow-cases, the *petit-point* and *appliqué*, the crocheted shawl around her shoulders: all these were clearly the painstaking work of her own hands. So meticulously neat and tidy and pretty, so feminine ... the dainty little pin trays and candlesticks, the carefully ordered sets of Racine and Dumas in grey Morocco between porcelain bookends, the combs and brushes and mirrors, the pins in an embroidered sachet in the shape of a heart ... her own pathetic little citadel in dove-grey and white, her oasis of prettiness to which she had felt herself able to retreat from loneliness and fear and shame.[25]

Doctor Talbot Fillingham-Ausling

The Lemaignans' neighbour was the art historian Doctor Talbot Fillingham-Ausling, who the American actor Sydney Greenstreet (1879-1954) — best known for the movies, **The Maltese Falcon**

(1941), **Casablanca** (1942), and **Passage to Marseille** (1942) —
might easily have played. (**Fig. 45**) Fillingham-Ausling's place,
Château Erasmus, was newer and smaller than Château Cloche-
Caque next door. In addition, it had *nouveau riche* pretensions
disapproved of by Madame Lemaignan and Professor Challis,
echoing George Johnston's snobbish views of architecture.

> If the building was not quite Stockbroker's
> Renaissance it fell short of the mark, or kept above
> it, only because the architect had managed to retain
> some sense of proportion even in the bogus spires
> and twisted chimneys. It still did not quite come off.
> It had much of good taste and a pleasing enough
> appearance, but in striving to appear as a survival
> from the grand days of the *ancien régime* it could
> not quite get rid of the smell of new cement.[26]

Fig. 45 Sidney Greenstreet could have played Fillingham-Ausling.

138

In **Twelve Girls in the Garden**, George Johnston used subtle innuendo to establish that Professor Challis's landlord, Mr. Valentine, was gay. In **The Saracen Shadow**, Doctor Fillingham-Ausling is also gay, but this time Johnston is more direct about it while still not saying it. For example, the Doctor "doesn't care for women," said Ann Gideon, and gave her "the creeps!"[27] He was an "effeminate old popinjay"[28] with "a pursed effeminate mouth"[29] and an affected lisp.[30] Fillingham-Ausling had "old-womanish concerns,"[31] wrung "his chubby hands together like a woman,"[32] put rouge on his cheeks,[33] dyed his hair with henna,[34] and in bed at night, wore "three arched aluminium hair-grips and a fine-mesh net"[35] to keep his hairdo in place.

While Fillingham-Ausling shared a love of antiques with Mr. Valentine, he went further and was more over the top.[36] Thus when Challis visited him at Château Erasmus, he found him in his "pink and white drawing room," lying on a "velvet-covered *chaise lounge,* beneath a ceiling of gilt bosses and painted cherubs," wearing a "brocade smoking jacket over pale shantung pyjamas," and rubbing a "cologne stick" on his forehead.[37]

It was no coincidence that Fillingham-Ausling reminded Challis of the portrait by Henri Toulouse-Lautrec (1864-1901) of arguably the most notoriously gay man in history — the Irish poet and playwright Oscar Wilde (1854-1900). "Except for the startling coils of his eyebrows, he looked exactly like Toulouse-Lautrec's drawing of Oscar Wilde,"[38] said the Professor. (**Fig. 46**) Johnston occasionally recycled things he wrote in the Challis novels, including this reference to Wilde. In **Closer to the Sun** (1960), Johnston's surrogate David Meredith said the artist Feodor Janecek had a "startling resemblance to the Toulouse-Lautrec drawing of Oscar Wilde."[39] Like Fillingham-Ausling, Janecek was also gay.

Fig. 46 *Oscar Wilde* (1895) by Henri Toulouse-Lautrec.

Fillingham-Ausling had two house guests — the English writer Peter Judd and the American artist Josh Stowe. When Professor Challis asked Ann Gideon how Stowe fitted into "this queer masculine ménage at Château Erasmus,"[40] her answer almost made him sound like a rent boy. "The Doctor brought him back from Paris around Christmas."[41] But whether Gideon meant that or not, Fillingham-Ausling and Stowe appear to have had a relationship because when the Doctor was leaving to arrange Stowe's funeral, Challis told him, "I am sorry, you know. I do understand how you feel. I liked him. I liked him too."[42] This tender exchange between them made me wonder whether the Professor was gay, too. He may have been because, apart from one close call with a young woman from Vassar while studying law at Harvard,[43] he never married and was a sixty-six-year-old confirmed bachelor. Maybe Johnston was amused by the perpetual debate over whether or not Sherlock Holmes and Doctor Watson were gay, so he was also ambiguous about the sexuality of Challis.

Lastly, and perhaps most subtly, Fillingham-Ausling

Fig. 47 The Dutch philosopher and theologian Erasmus.

named his château after the Dutch philosopher and theologian Erasmus (1469-1466) because he believed he had stayed nearby on his travels.[44] (**Fig. 47**) But since Erasmus was gay — or so many people believe, writing passionate love letters to Servatius Rogerius (b. 1466) and making advances to Thomas Grey (1455-1501) — perhaps Johnston named Fillingham-Ausling's château after him to further hint at the Doctor's homosexuality. After all, Johnston had a sharp eye for details.

Miss Marple, Maigret, Holmes, and Johnston

Professor Challis told Ann Gideon that unearthing an ancient city was akin to unravelling a crime. "In a sense, that is my profession [...] piecing things together,"[45] he said. Indeed, Challis is an archaeologist, not a consulting detective like Sherlock Holmes by Sir Arthur Conan Doyle or a policeman like Paris Chief Inspector Jules Maigret by George Simenon. Therefore, the Professor has to find the mysteries himself; they do not automatically find him. He also said he was "an interfering old busybody who keeps asking far too many questions" and that murder was his hobby.[46] In these respects, Challis resembled Miss Jane Marple by Dame Agatha Christie. But the big difference was that Marple belonged to the

Fig. 48 (L-R) Miss Jane Marple, Chief Inspector Jules Maigret, Sherlock Holmes, and Professor Ronald Challis.

quaint English village community of Saint Mary Mead, whereas Challis was a world traveller and comparatively centreless. (**Fig. 48**) Consequently, George Johnston sometimes struggled to introduce Challis into the mystery naturally, but never more so than in **The Saracen Shadow**, which seemed very staged: Chasing after a young woman he had never met, only having seen her photograph in the wallet of her fiancé whom he had met only once, seemed like a rather implausible beginning. But once Johnston had Challis in the thick of things, events usually proceeded more smoothly.

At his best, George Johnston was the equal of those crime novelists acclaimed for their strong sense of place, such as Sir Arthur Conan Doyle, Dame Agatha Christie, and Georges Simenon, which is high praise, but justifiably so, I believe. Since the setting for **The Saracen Shadow** is France, let's compare apples to apples. Chief Inspector Jules Maigret would happily have a tipple at the drop of a hat; therefore, Simenon described many French bars throughout the seventy-five Maigret books he wrote. But none quite so vividly, in my view, as Michelet's bar in **The Saracen Shadow**:

> There was nothing particular about Michelet's bar: a long counter covered with damp brown linoleum with a big, nickel-plated cash register at the end, high metal stools, a constricted row of small booths coated with aged, scratched varnish, [and] on the rather grubby walls a tattered calendar with every date until two months before meticulously crossed out with blue pencil; the plaster of brightly-lettered advertisements — Dubonnet, Remy-

Martin, Noilly-Prat, Corsica for Sunshine — [and] a big roadmap, fly-spotted and peeling which said, *Les Vins de Bordeaux — Route des Grands Crus*. Michelet himself, although a young man, had already acquired the reticent, hooded eyes of the professional bartender.[47] [...] The bar had a cheerless Friday evening emptiness, and Michelet was leaning his elbows on a corner table, reading a day-old copy of **France-Soir**. He looked up quickly at the Professor's entrance, gave a polite greeting, stubbed his cigarette in a tin ashtray, and walked slowly behind the bar, automatically picking up the wash-cloth on the way and rubbing a broad swath of gloss along the dull brown of the linoleum."[48] [...] On the wall, a clock with a mustard-coloured face ticked on impassively. Michelet went to the big, nickel-plated cash register and wrote something down on a block. The Professor glanced up at the tattered calendar. Since his last visit with Josh Stowe, no more dates had been crossed out.[49]

In **The Saracen Shadow**, George Johnson alluded to the most famous Sherlock Holmes short stories, 'The Speckled Band' (1892) by Sir Arthur Conan Doyle, which is about how a deadly snake — the speckled band — enters the bedroom of its unsuspecting victim by "a thick bell-rope, which hung down beside the bed, the tassel actually lying on the pillow"[50] and kills her. This story is so iconic that the merest mention of a bell-rope in a crime thriller will make people think of it, Pavlov's dog-style. Accordingly, Professor

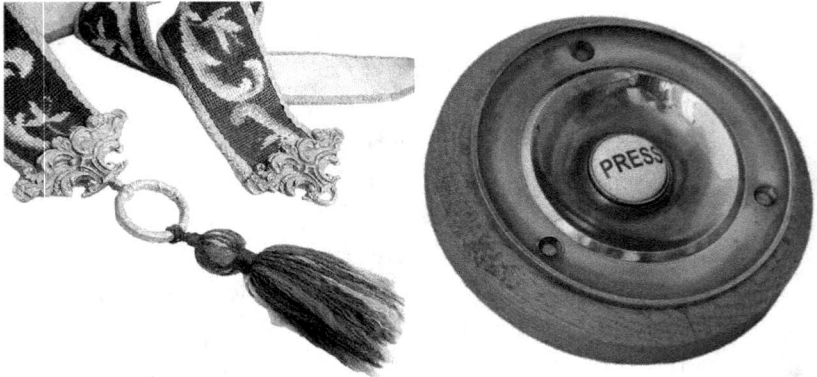

Fig. 49 Bell-rope versus push-button.

Challis channelled 'The Speckled Band' when he imagined Madame Lemaignan summoning her niece to her bedroom by wondering "Was the bell by which she permitted life to enter operated by a press-button or — surely it must be — a great pull-rope of velvet, corded and tasselled?"[51] When he finally met the matriarch of Château Cloche-Caque in her bedroom, "He was disappointed to see, mounted on a porcelain panel beside the bed, a push-button for a bell."[52] (**Fig. 49**)

According to Charmian Clift, George Johnston, "shied away from any written expression of his own emotional reactions to things and settled instead for what he thought his reactions should have been if he had been in the skin of an elderly professor of archaeology, or however he was disguising himself for that particular novel."[53] That was very easy for him to do in the case of Professor Challis because, to a large extent, Johnston was Challis.

For example, take the little quirk shared by the mothers of the Professor and David Meredith.

In **The Saracen Shadow**, while searching André Lemaignan's desk for clues, apropos of nothing, Challis tells Paul Lemaignan:

> When I was a boy, my mother always insisted on our clock being twenty minutes fast. Always. She was absolutely rigid about it. It was supposed to ensure that we were always on time for things, never late. I've often tried to work out her logic since everybody knew [...] you had to allow twenty minutes for the clock. Perhaps it worked ... I don't remember.[54]

Likewise, in **My Brother Jack**, Meredith says his mother, Minnie, always set the alarm clock on the kitchen shelf twenty minutes fast so that whenever his father complained at breakfast, "Get a move on, Min, for God's sake!" his mother could reply, "You're all right, that clock's twenty minutes fast."[55]

Johnston's story about Challis's/Meredith's/his? Mum setting the clock twenty minutes fast sounds too authentic to have been made up to me. Significantly, it shows the close links between Johnston and Challis and Challis and Meredith. It indicates, yet again, that Johnston was plumbing his past for material well before he wrote **My Brother Jack**. And it is yet another instance of Johnston trying something out in a Challis novel first and then using it in another book later. All this makes the Challis novels even more significant, in my view, and the fact that most Johnston scholars have ignored or dismissed them is even more baffling.

For all of George Johnston's drinking, illness, misfortune, and socialising on Hydra, no one could fault his work ethic or literary output. As he told his American agent Harold Ober when **The Saracen Shadow** was ready for publication, his next Professor Challis novel, **The Man Made of Tin** (1958), was almost finished.[56] — bang, bang, bang, three done in less than two years.

Endnotes

[1] Francis Iles, 'Criminal Records,' **The Guardian** (London, UK), 1 November 1957, p. 6.

[2] Shane Martin (George Johnston), **The Saracen Shadow**, London: Collins, 1958, dedication, unpaged.

[3] Garry Kinnane, **George Johnston: A Biography**, Melbourne, Australia: Nelson Publishers, 1986, p. 163.

[4] Peter Armenti (Library of Congress), Email to Derham Groves, 14 April 2023.

[5] 'Dirty Deeds,' **Times Literary Supplement**, 20 December 1957, p. 769.

[6] 'Books,' **The Birmingham Mail** (Birmingham, UK), 27 November 1957, p. 8.

[7] Ibid.

[8] George Johnston, **My Brother Jack**, London: Collins, 1964, p.47.

[9] Ibid., p. 46.

[10] Shane Martin, **The Saracen Shadow**, London: Collins, 1957, p. 150.

[11] Ibid., p. 236.

[12] Garry Kinnane, p. 162.

[13] George Johnston, 1964, p. 30.

[14] George Johnston, 'Gentlemen Will Look Gay in Coronation Rig,' **Sun** (Sydney, Australia), 13 May 1953, p. 19.

[15] Ibid., pp. 17-18.

[16] Shane Martin, **The Saracen Shadow**, 'Note,' unpaged.

[17] Ibid., p. 17.
[18] Shane Martin, **Twelve Girls in the Garden**, New York: William Morrow and Company, 1957, p. 202.
[19] George Johnston, **Clean Straw for Nothing**, London: Collins, 1969, p. 53.
[20] Shane Martin, **The Saracen Shadow**, 'Note,' unpaged.
[21] Ibid., p. 20.
[22] Ibid., p. 18.
[23] Ibid.
[24] Ibid., pp. 86-87.
[25] Ibid., p. 221-222.
[26] Ibid., p. 46.
[27] Ibid., p.32.
[28] Ibid., p. 102.
[29] Ibid., p. 21.
[30] Ibid., p.22.
[31] Ibid., p. 100.
[32] Ibid., p. 50.
[33] Ibid., p. 91.
[34] Ibid., p. 22.
[35] Ibid., p. 176.
[36] Ibid. p. 21.
[37] Ibid. pp. 49-50.
[38] Ibid., p. 50.
[39] George Johnston, **Closer to the Sun**, London: Collins, 1960, p. 73.
[40] Shane Martin, **The Saracen Shadow**, p. 50.
[41] Ibid., pp. 32-33.
[42] Ibid., p. 201.
[43] Shane Martin, **Twelve Girls in the Garden**, pp. 171-172.
[44] Shane Martin, **The Saracen Shadow**, p. 46.
[45] Ibid., pp. 16-17
[46] Ibid., p.125.
[47] Ibid., p. 80.
[48] Ibid., p.1 63.
[49] Ibid., p. 165.

50 Sir Arthur Conan Doyle (1892), 'The Speckled Band,' in William S. Baring-Gould (ed.) (1968), **The Annotated Sherlock Holmes**, London: John Murray, 1973, vol. I p. 254.

51 Shane Martin, **The Saracen Shadow**, p. 65.

52 Ibid., p. 71.

53 Charmian Clift (1969), 'On **Clean Straw for Nothing**' in Nadia Wheatley (ed.), **Sneaky Little Revolutions**, Sydney: NewSouth Publishing, 2022, p. 401.

54 Shane Martin, **The Saracen Shadow**, p. 186.

55 George Johnston, 1964, pp. 138-139.

56 Garry Kinnane, p. 163.

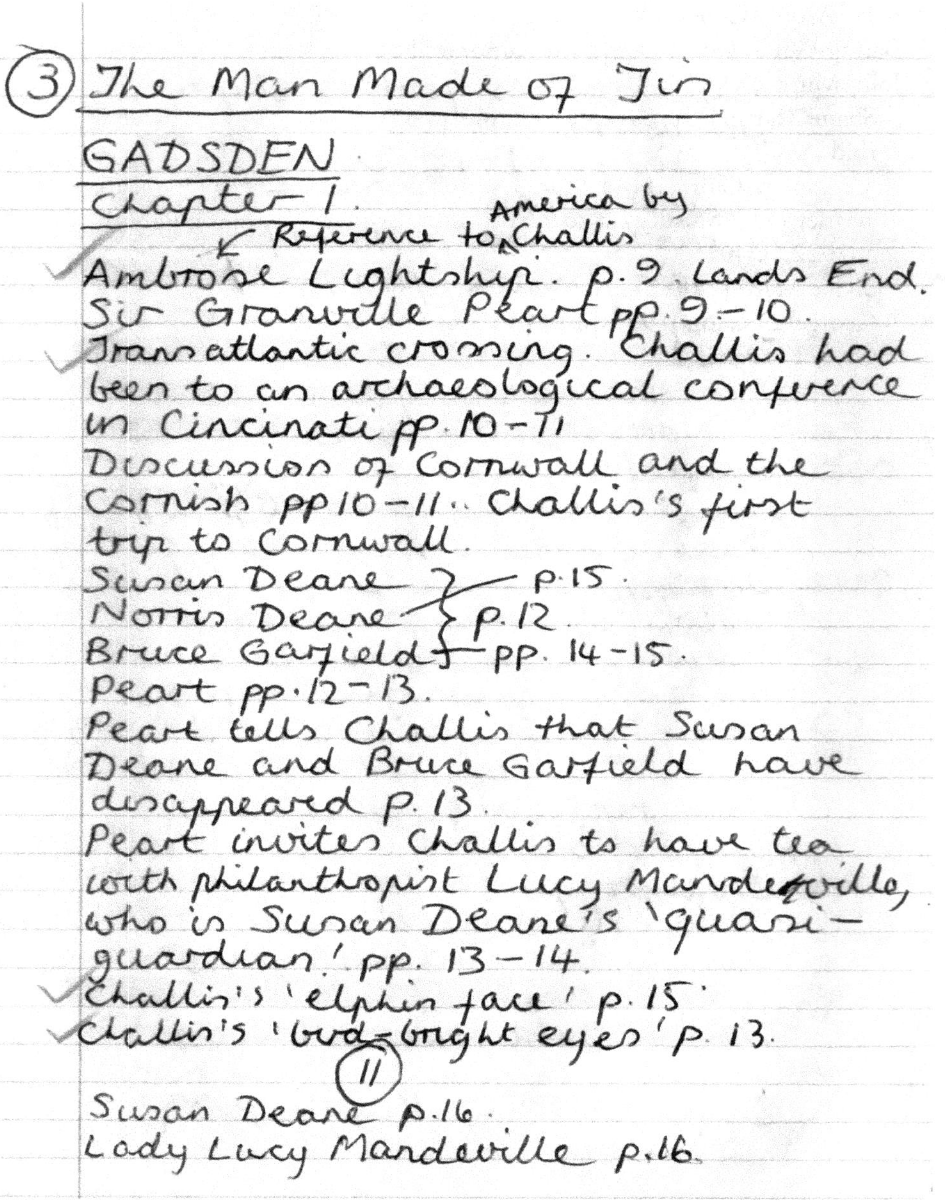

③ The Man Made of Tin

GADSDEN.
Chapter 1.
✓ Reference to Challis America by
✓ Ambrose Lightship. p.9 Lands End.
Sir Granville Peart pp.9-10.
✓ Transatlantic crossing. Challis had
been to an archaeological conference
in Cincinati pp. 10-11
Discussion of Cornwall and the
Cornish pp 10-11. Challis's first
trip to Cornwall.
Susan Deane ⎱ ─ p.15.
Norris Deane ⎰ p.12.
Bruce Garfield ⎰ pp. 14-15.
Peart pp. 12-13.
Peart tells Challis that Susan
Deane and Bruce Garfield have
disappeared p.13.
Peart invites Challis to have tea
with philanthropist Lucy Mandeville,
who is Susan Deane's 'quasi-
guardian'. pp. 13-14.
✓ Challis's 'elphin face' p.15.
✓ Challis's 'bird-bright eyes' p.13.
⑪
Susan Deane p.16.
Lady Lucy Mandeville p.16.

Plate 4 Page from Derham Groves' notebook.

3. The Man Made of Tin

The Man Made of Tin *(1958) is the third Professor Ronald Challis novel by George Johnston/Shane Martin. It takes place in Cornwall over a week in early September 1955. Like its predecessor,* The Saracen Shadow *(1957), Collins published* The Man Made of Tin *in Great Britain, but no American or Australian editions were published. It has been out of print for years, and second-hand copies are difficult to find. Following is a summary of* The Man Made of Tin *with comments, opinions, and reviews.*

Dramatis Personae

Professor Ronald Challis	Archaeologist and amateur detective.
Sir Granville Peart	Archaeologist and friend of the Professor.
Sam Jackett	The Professor's landlord in Gadsden.
Mrs. Jackett	Jackett's bedridden wife.
Susan Deane	Young socialite who goes missing.
Norris Deane	Archaeologist and Susan's husband.
Lady Lucy Mandeville	Wealthy philanthropist and Susan's guardian.
Bruce Garfield	American amateur archaeologist.
Ruth Cadell	Garfield's American fiancé.
Galloway	Dairy farmer and Garfield's landlord in Gadsden.
Crosbie Dahl	Owner of the Tyrian Traveller.
Freda Dahl	Dahl's wife and cook at the Tyrian Traveller.
Peggy	Bartender at the Tyrian Traveller.
Charlie Fallenden	Gadsden's well-liked spiv.
Mad Jolly	A crazy old tin miner who died years ago.

Gadsden

Professor Ronald Challis and his friend, the English archaeologist Sir Granville Peart, are returning to England by ship after attending a conference in Cincinnati, USA. The coastline of Cornwall looms large on the horizon. Since Challis has never been there, Peart tells him how gloomy, uncivilised, and forbidding it is before asking, "Did you ever know Susan Deane? Got herself married to Bob Deane's son, Norris, who's by way of being an archaeologist of sorts." During the summer, the Deanes went to Gadsden in Cornwall with a wealthy, handsome American named Bruce Garside, who dabbled in archaeological projects. But on the second of August — about six weeks ago — Susan and Garside disappeared, and Norris subsequently suffered a complete nervous collapse.

A steward hands Peart a cablegram, "EXPECTING YOU TEA FIVE TOMORROW — LUCY." Lady Lucy Mandeville is Susan Deane's eighty-six-year-old 'quasi-guardian' who asked him to inquire about Garfield while visiting America. "Absolute waste of time, of course," says Peart. "I found out precisely nothing." Then he has an idea. "You're at a loose end until the December lectures. What's stopping you from going down to Cornwall and rummaging around for a while?" You are curious and have deductive skills.

The next day, they visit Mandeville, who, while worried about Susan, is reluctant to cause a scandal by calling in those soft-spoken young men with their Balliol accents and mackintoshes from Scotland Yard. "Susan has always been very erratic," says Mandeville. "Given the appropriate circumstances, she might run off with some other man — I have always suspected that neither she nor Norris has ever been altogether happy with each other — yet one is left with the misgiving that the solution falls too pat."

Fig. 50 Excavations at Boyne Valley, Ireland (2007).

Peart knows Deane and Garfield professionally, so Challis asks him about them. "At Oxford, Deane was good but not good enough," says Peart. "Then he made some fluky Irish discoveries near the Boyne excavations, which gave him a reputation out of proportion, and ever since, he has tried to bring it off again but lacks the imagination and luck. By contrast, Garfield has both in spades." (**Fig. 50**)

Mandeville shows Challis the last postcard she received from Susan, postmarked the thirtieth of July — three days before Norris left Cornwall for a big book-worming session at Oxford. Susan told Mandeville she would not miss Deane since she had seen almost nothing of him since his new friend Bruce Garfield came down. "They are thick as thieves and tramping the moors together," wrote Susan. "Garfield is very handsome and quite interesting, but there is something odd and creepy about him. I will see you in a fortnight when I come up for Clarissa's do. Much love, Susan."

Since Mandeville believes Susan would never miss a fashion show by her friend, the West End couturière Clarissa Bell, Challis alarmingly suggests there is a possibility someone murdered her. So, he decides to go to Gadsden the following day and investigate.

The bus from St. Ives drops Professor Challis opposite a small church in Gadsden. Inside, a man is busily sweeping the floor. Just as Challis is about to interrupt him, a sudden gust of laughter, followed almost immediately by a bellowing roar of song, comes from the inn next door, so Challis heads there instead.

The landlord of the Tyrian Traveller, Crosbie Dahl, introduces himself and takes the Professor's order. "One cognac. The best," Dahl tells the barman he calls Peggy, whose face is a mask of skin, unnaturally pale and mottled in queer patches and puckered around the nose and mouth like a piece of cloth. It was a miracle of plastic surgery that had not been miraculous enough.

As the Tyrian Traveller does not take guests, Dahl recommends Laurel Cottage, Sam Jackett's bed-and-breakfast, which is the best in Gadsden. "That's right," agrees Jackett, popping up from behind his beer glass, who turns out to be the man the Professor saw sweeping the church. Challis buys him a drink and asks about Bruce Garfield. "Queer sort of codger," says Jackett. "Rented that old cottage at Galloway's Farm. Some sort of foreigner, wasn't he? Well, he went away."

"So I understand," says Challis. "What I am trying to find out is when."

"Gentleman here is inquiring after that Mr. Garfield who was here midsummer and took the Galloway cottage. Six weeks or so since he was here, wouldn't it be?" Jackett asks those in the bar. The question produces odd looks from Dahl, his wife Freda, Peggy, and Gadsden's loveable spiv, Charlie Fallenden. The Professor has been in Gadsden for less than an hour, and already, here are four people who possibly know something about the disappearance of Garfield and Susan Deane.

While getting the best room ready for Professor Challis, Sam Jackett tells him that Crosbie Dahl said nothing about Susan Deane because he, Peggy, and Bruce Garfield were all chasing after her.

"I did hear a rumour that Garfield had gone away with this woman," says Challis leading him on.

"It's what they say," Jackett replies. "Well, none of them can say I ever spoke a word against her." It turns out Susan lived next door at Heather Rest Cottage. "I always found her a nice young lady," says Jackett. "Always friendly and liked a joke, a laugh, and a drink. A good sport, she was, but I never saw any of this funny business everyone spoke about later."

Challis is surprised to find the cottage next door occupied. "Woman by the name of Cadell," says Jackett. "She rented it the week before last from the agent in St. Ives. A funny sort who keeps to herself all the time."

The next day, a sudden downpour drenches Professor Challis while walking around Gadsden, so he uses it as a ruse to call next door at Heather Rest Cottage, telling the slim young woman who answers the door, "I was trying to find my way to an address and got caught in this wretched downpour."

The woman is writing a thesis on the Etruscans and recognises Challis from the photographs in his books, so she invites him inside out of the rain, telling him, "You have the sort of face not easily forgotten. I'm Ruth Cadell."

The Professor explains he is looking for the Deanes.

"They lived here! They had this cottage!" says Cadell. Continuing with the ruse, Challis tells her he hoped to look at the archaeological artefacts they had collected and suggest how best they might be packed up and removed. "Go ahead," says Cadell. "It's all in the next room, a sort of little museum they'd arranged. I don't think you'll find it all that interesting."

> There were the inevitable collections of flints and eoliths, all drearily brown and saddeningly alike; monstrous chunks of granite that appeared to be the fragments of Saxon querns; a whole shelf of meaningless scraps of undercoated terra-cotta pottery; innumerable bone needles and arrow heads; and a group of what appeared to be unclassified stones. There were also two iron man-traps (doubtless representing a much later development of civilisation), a millstone five feet in diameter and cracked across the centre. And a group of primitive ploughshares and farm implements, half of a human shin bone, two fractured skulls, a tray of beads and unidentifiable coins, and several picks made of antlers.

The only thing of interest is a crude, black, metal figure about nine inches high of a Greek soldier wearing a plumed helmet and body armour and carrying a shield. (**Fig. 51**) Challis notices its label, "THE MAN MADE OF TIN," is written on the back of Bruce Garfield's business card, so he quietly puts it in his pocket.

Fig. 51 The Man Made of Tin (dust jacket).

Professor Challis visits the Tyrian Traveller to ask Crosbie Dahl why he changed the pub's name from the Farmer's Arms. He named it after a Phoenician trader who came to Cornwall and fell in love with a local girl, leaving his wife and children in Tyre. He sent a ship back to retrieve his fortune, but it sank off the Cornish coast on its return. The Phoenician drowned himself in despair at losing his wealth, or according to another version of the story, drowned trying to rescue the captain. In either case, his sweetheart died of a broken heart soon after. "It's a pleasant tale, and like so many of those stories, it could have a considerable basis of historical truth," says Challis.

When Peggy, the barman, gets sawdust for the floor, Dahl tells the Professor how the former World War Two bomber pilot was injured.

> One night, flying over Bremen, they got mixed up with some flak. Somehow, he managed to get the aircraft back over the Channel, then made the crew bale out over Kent while he took it in on his own and tried to land it. He did bring it in on its belly, but it burst into flames. For his effort, they gave him a bar to his DFC. But it's hardly

compensation. Is it? Surgically, there was nothing more the doctors could do for him — you've only seen the poor devil's face, not his arms, chest, and shoulders. They must have used an acre of skin graft! But that still left him with a shattering case history of war neurosis.

A farmer named Galloway is drinking at the Tyrian Traveller. (**Fig. 52**) He rented a room to Bruce Garfield. "Galloway, this gentleman here was inquiring last night about that chap you

Fig. 52 The Tinner's Arms – the model for the Tyrian Traveller (recent photo).

had staying with you in the summer," says Dahl. "He is simply interested in knowing when his friend left Gadsden."

"Round second week in August," says Galloway before draining his glass of beer and leaving immediately.

"That's a detestable bastard if ever there was one," says Dahl. "Lives up there all alone in his pigsty of a farm."

"How far away from here is Galloway's Farm," asks Challis.

"A mile or so," says Dahl. "I should warn you that you won't find welcome on the mat."

Returning to Laurel Cottage, Professor Challis wishes to pay his respects to Mrs. Jackett, Sam's bedridden wife who lives upstairs, whom he has yet to meet. "Why, there's nothing the old lady would not like more," says Jackett. "Well, you know how it is, stuck up there on her own most of the time … she's always ready for a natter with someone." However, the Professor believes Mrs. Jackett may be helpful since a bedridden woman, segregated from village life yet poised above it in Olympian detachment at a commanding window, might well have a particular omniscience denied to the more peripatetic of her fellows.

After they discuss her earlier missionary work in China, Challis asks about her former next-door neighbour, Susan Deane. "She had men hanging around that cottage all the time, night and day, whenever her husband was away," says Mrs. Jackett.

> There was Crosbie Dahl, Peggy, even my Sam, until I spoke with him. There was young Ken Polkinghorne from Cromer Farm and his cousin Jeff from Gurnard's. There was that man Fallendon

— of course, there's nothing his nose isn't into! And Gablock, the Customs officer, and that artist Jenkins from St. Ives, and he's been divorced three times as if that isn't enough! Why, even the vicar was in there more than he had the need or the right to be. Him a man of God, mark you, and in there with her sprawling around in those shorts!

"Among Mrs. Deane's callers, was there a man named Garfield?" asks Challis cautiously. "He was a visitor here during the summer, a tall and very well-built man."

Mrs. Jackett recognises him as the man in the checked shirt who used to call quite often at the cottage. "He was a friend of Mr. Deane's. But he only came when he was here, never when he was away." She says emphatically.

While Professor Challis has lunch, someone knocks at the door. "I'm sorry to interrupt," says Ruth Cadell. "But I'd like to know why you took that card from my cottage."

"It's Bruce Garfield's, and I am rather interested in him," says Challis.

"So am I," says Cadell. "He happens to be my fiancé." Later, next door, they discuss the disappearance of Garfield and Susan Deane. Challis suspected Cadell was connected to Garfield since they were both American, of a similar age, and interested in pre-classical Mediterranean archaeology. He tells her he is looking for Susan, not Bruce, but perhaps they could help each other.

"I would help you if I could, Professor Challis," says Cadell. "But I have found out absolutely nothing."

Challis tells Cadell that based on Mrs. Jackett's observations, he does not think Garfield ran off with Susan, although their disappearances are probably somehow linked. "I think I should begin with that little man made of tin," he says. "What is it supposed to represent? Where did it come from? Why did it have a particular interest to your fiancé?"

Galloways

Sam Jackett agrees to take Professor Challis to Galloway's farm at Hammer Cove. After walking through waist-high bracken and ling for about half an hour, they see several abandoned stone cottages and tin mines in the distance. "When we get along further, there's the Red Bird Mine, right alongside Galloway's place," says Jackett.

> They took eighty million pounds out of tin and copper before they closed it down," says Jackett. "Only a shallow shaft — not two hundred feet, I reckon — but they ran a tunnel a mile long out under the sea. Then, one day, the workings flooded, and they closed it down. ... There it is, Galloway's Farm. You see up there, at the far end, on that rise just a little to the left of the mine — a smallish stone shack. Well, that's the cottage where your friend, Mr. Garfield, stayed.

"I would like to take a closer look," says Challis. As they approach the entrance to the farm, they read a crudely painted sign nailed to the gatepost, "PRIVATE PROPERTY. TRESPASSERS ARE STRICTLY PROHIBITED. KEEP OUT."

"What the hell do you want," bellows Galloway. "I don't want people snoopin' around my land. If you're not out of here in two minutes, I'll loosen the dogs!"

Later, Professor Challis meets Ruth Cadell at the Tyrian Traveller to show her two newspaper articles he found that may help to explain the disappearance of Susan Deane and Bruce Garfield. The first is about the *Thekla,* a cargo ship that ran aground on rocks in Hammer Cove between eight-thirty and nine p.m. on the second of August. (**Fig. 53**) "The report says that all hands were safely brought ashore by breeches-buoy and that local farmers and villagers were assisting with salvage operations," says Challis, or in other words, looting the ship's cargo. The second article, 'Dead in Cliff Accident,' says, "Kenneth Ronald Polkinghorne, twenty-three-year-old farm labourer of Cromer Farm, near Gadsden, died

Fig. 53 The *Traute Sarnow* – the model for the *Thekla* (1954).

last night in an accidental fall from the cliffs near his home during rescue and salvage operations at the stranded motor-ship, *Thekla*."

Challis says the last time anyone saw Susan Deane was on the second of August, and Bruce Garfield was staying at Galloway's at Hammer Cover. But Cadell doubts they are concerned with their disappearance.

Cadell shows Challis a letter that Garfield wrote her at the end of July when she was in Paris, telling her something big and rather exciting and not without a spice of real danger has come up, asking her to delay her visit by a week, and saying he will meet her in London without fail on the twentieth of August. But he never came, which was out of character. "Tell me a little about him," says Challis.

"It is as if there are two Bruce Garfields," says Cadell. "The normal one whom you can know and understand and admire and love; and another man altogether — a strange, lonely, haunted person, driven by some obsessive compulsion, as if there is some part of him that belongs to a long-lost thing of the past — it's always the past that obsesses him — and he has to go back, quite alone, in search of it."

"Your fiancé and Mrs. Deane did not run away together," Challis tells Cadell, predicting to find Bruce within twenty-four hours. Since it is only nine p.m. and a moonlit night, the Professor suggests they investigate Galloway's Farm instead of returning to their cottages. As they get nearer the farm, Challis advises cutting through the bracken and coming out behind the Red Bird Mine to avoid rousing the dogs. While the Red Bird Mine is a ruin, the ominous-looking mine shaft is still open. They follow a path to the cottage Garfield rented. Suddenly, Charlie Fallenden appears from nowhere. "It is dangerous hereabouts," he warns, offering to drive them back to Gadsden and dropping off Cadell first. "There are fine walks around here and plenty of handsome rare places to see without that sort of tramping around," Fallenden tells Challis before offering to take

Fig. 54 Trencrom Hill, Cornwall (recent photo).

him to see the view from Trencrom Hill tomorrow. "I'll call for ye sharp at nine-thirty," he says. (**Fig. 54**)

Charlie Fallenden picks up Professor Challis and drives him to Trencrom Hill. A dark-complexioned man wearing a soft felt hat, a grey gabardine raincoat, and dark sunglasses of the pattern favoured by American airmen during the war is also there, introducing himself as Jacob Tufts from Baltimore.

After Fallenden drops him at Laurel Cottage, Challis goes next door to Heather Rest Cottage. "I have just been talking to your fiancé," he tells Ruth Cadell. When the Professor started snooping around, Galloway and Fallenden must have warned Garfield. Knowing that Challis would be at Trencrom Hill, Garfield disguised himself as Tufts and met the Professor out of curiosity. "First, I think we should chat to our Cornish friend Mr. Fallenden," Challis tells Cadell.

> We must do a little diligent exploring in the vicinity of Hammer Cove. I should find out a whole lot more about poor Peggy. We must discover what this highly secret project is that has so utterly absorbed your fiancé for the last two months or so. But where is Susan Deane? We still haven't any idea what has happened to her!

Professor Challis asks Sam Jackett to send Sir Granville Peart a telegram telling him to arrange a meeting on his behalf with Norris Deane at his nursing home. The Professor also asks Jackett where he might find Charlie Fallenden. "He'll be down at his shed," he says. "See that red iron roof just behind Trevelyan's haystack. That's it."

Challis finds Fallenden in his shed, an Aladdin's cave of ill-gotten goods from ships wrecked off the coast, the rewards of many nights of reckless cliff-climbing and stealthy forays through the lonely moors. "What happened immediately after the *Thekla* ran aground in Hammer Cove?" asks the Professor.

> How was young Ken Polkinghorne killed? What occurred at Hammer Cove that caused Mr. Garfield to hide? What happened to Mrs. Deane? And what is the connection between the grounding of the

Thekla and the tunnel of the old Red Mine? You see, Mr. Fallenden, you can hardly charge me with idle curiosity!

"Ken Polkinghorne thought he knew better than those wiser than himself and went ferreting around the cliffs at night," says Fallenden over a glass of his best-looted cognac with the Professor. "Rest of us, we didn't know he was there that night until we came across his body all champed up. 'Tis a place to take care in, Hammer Cove." In the hope that Fallenden will relay the information to Bruce Garfield, Challis tells him that he and Ruth Cadell will be at Hammer Cove between three and five p.m. tomorrow.

"Here we are," says Ruth Cadell. "And now, what do we do?"
"We just wait," says Professor Challis.
"Yes, but what are we waiting for?" says Ruth.
"I hope we are waiting for Bruce Garfield," says Challis. In the meantime, the Professor explores Hammer Cove and discovers a partially hidden cave leading to the old tin-mining tunnel that Sam Jackett told him about, which runs out under the sea from the Red Bird Mine. "Come up here!" Challis tells Cadell. "I want to show you something. It explains why your fiancé was so anxious to stay at Galloway's Farm. There is only one way we can find out if it is true. To do a little cave exploration ourselves." But as it is getting late and they are ill-equipped for cave exploring, they decide to return another day.

As they scramble up the rocks to get back on the path, they see Peggy holding a shotgun and sitting on a rock. "Sometimes I come to places like this to shoot at the birds," says Peggy.

As it is unlikely that Garfield will show up now, the Professor turns his attention to Peggy. "On the night the ship went ashore when everyone for miles around was down here, was Susan Deane among then?" asks Challis.

"She was here somewhere," answers Peggy. "I don't know whether she came down here with the others. I saw her when I was up top. Just for a few minutes, and then she went away."

Professor Challis took the Man Made of Tin from Norris Deane's little museum to show Sam Jackett. "Could be one of Mad Jolly's things, that could," says Jackett.

> He has been dead for years and years. Barmy he was, right off his rocker. He was an old tinner who worked in the mines about here. He was always talking about the Old Ones who lived in these parts in the old days, centuries ago, before even the saints came here. Well, he was working down one of the mines and dug into a sort of grave or something like that, and it was chock-a-block with things the Old Ones had left there, just like a bleeding Aladdin's cave, according to him. He used to make figures like that to show everyone how the Old Ones looked.

Jackett and Challis are interrupted by the doorbell. It is a telegram from Sir Granville Peart, "NORRIS DEANE DIED DURING NIGHT OVERDOSE DRUGS PRESUMABLY SELF-ADMINISTERED STOP DRIVING DOWN TODAY EXPECT ME GADSDEN EIGHTISH – PEART."

Norris Deane agreed to meet Challis any time but overdosed on sleeping pills that night. Peart believes it was because Deane was neurotic, while Challis believes it was because he was investigating his wife's disappearance and wanted to ask him some questions.

The next day, Professor Challis, Ruth Cadell, and Sir Granville Peart discuss events by the fire at the Tyrian Traveller. Challis suspects that Norris Deane showed Bruce Garfield the Man Made of Tin without realising its significance. But as Garfield had worked with Herschel, he knew about pre-Christian mercantile activities connected with the tin and amber trade and even may have seen a reference to the tomb of the Tyrian traveller found by Mad Jolly carved on an ancient stele. While this makes sense to Cadell, she does not believe Garfield is the sort of person to wheedle some confidence out of Deane and use it to benefit himself. And Peart is concerned that all the focus is now on Garfield. "I still want very much to know what has happened to Susan Deane," he says. "Is she dead? Is she alive? If she is, then where the devil is she?"

Garfield

Professor Challis and Sir Granville Peart explore the Red Bird Mine the following day. They cautiously proceed until rocks are blocking the tunnel, but the Professor sees a small opening high up on the left, and they manage to squeeze through to the other side. "Nothing but a damned labyrinth, Challis!" exclaims Peart. "My God, man, it would take six months to examine all this!"

"Exactly!" says Challis. "No wonder Garfield has been busy. Any of these tunnels might lead to the tomb that Mad Jolly found and then lost. The needle in a haystack has nothing on this!" They see signs of life — a pair of muddy boots, a rock hammer, and a lunchbox. After a hundred yards, the tunnel widens into a chamber with three more tunnels off it. "Let's try the one in the middle," says Challis. However, a rockfall has sealed it about two hundred yards in. They can hear waves splashing above them and realise they are underwater. Challis wonders whether an eight-hundred-ton ship pounding on the rocks in a westerly gale might have caused the rockfall. That could explain why Garfield has been flat out since the *Thekla* foundered. It suddenly dawns on them that the mine might flood any moment, so they hastily retreat, only to be confronted by a bright light coming toward them.

"If it is Mr. Garfield who you're anxious to see, you'll find him back along the working a bit," says Charlie Fallenden. "He's waiting for you there."

"How is Ruth?" asks Bruce Garfield.

"She's well," says Professor Challis. "We came here because we thought we might be able to help you."

"Thanks," says Garfield. "There's no help I need right now."

"Oh, let's stop this nonsense," says Sir Granville Peart. "Do you think we came down here to indulge in small talk? We'd very much like to know what happened to Susan Deane."

"What has she got to do with it?" asks Garfield.

"Are you completely ignorant that your names are linked?" says Peart.

"I've heard about that," says Garfield. "It isn't true, just something that goes back to those crazy ideas her husband had. Have you asked Norris about it?"

"We can't ask him," says Peart. "He's dead."

"She made a nuisance with me towards the end," says Garfield. "Then she went away. That's all I can tell you. Now leave me alone."

Professor Challis wants Ruth Cadell to see Bruce Garfield and ask him to leave the Red Bird Mine. "He is very nearly at the end of his tether — mentally as well as physically — and down in that place, anything could happen," says Challis.

Cadell agrees and while waiting for Charlie Fallenden to take her to Garfield tells Challis she has been talking to Freda Dahl, the wife of Crosbie Dahl, the publican at the Tyrian Traveller, who told her they were planning to fire Peggy.

> He drinks too much. He insults the customers. He behaves badly when women are around. He's never there when he's wanted. And he's taken to stealing. It's been going on for some time — silly, rather pointless little thefts — food and so on. Not money, or anything like that, although they think he has some place where he sells the things and then spends the money on liquor.

"Well, that gives me something with which to occupy myself while you're away," says Challis. "I shall find Peggy and talk to him."

Professor Challis suspects he will find Peggy if he heads to the abandoned cottages near the Red Bird Mine, and sure enough, he does. "Peggy, I came here because I wanted to talk to you away from other people," says the Professor. "I'm just about the only person who can help you because I don't belong here and am not part of it. Since Norris Deane is dead, we can talk about it now."

"If he'd come back here, I would have killed him," says Peggy. On the day Deane was supposed to go to London, he left the train at St. Erth, and Peggy spotted him skulking around Cromer Farm. "I knew what Deane was up to then," explains Peggy.

> He was jealous of everyone, but Crosbie Dahl didn't help by telling Deane to watch his wife since women go for men like Garfield. Deane waited until dark before sneaking behind the old mines, catching Susan crossing the moors, and throwing her down an old quarry pit. (**Fig. 55**) I might have been able to stop him had I not gotten into a fight

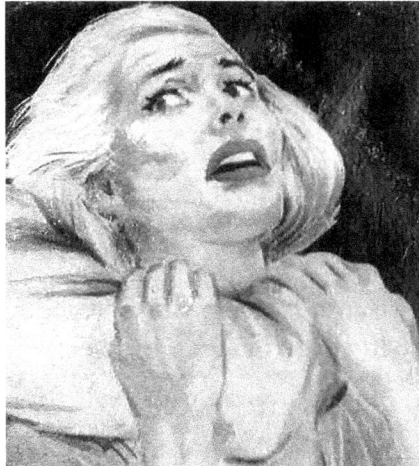

Fig. 55 Susan Deane by William Randell (dustjacket).

with Ken Polkinghorne, who was one of those always chasing after Susan. But I didn't kill him; he fell over a cliff.

"Were Deane's suspicions of Garfield justified?" asks Challis. "Was he and Mrs. Deane having an affair?" But Peggy will not say.

"Do you want to come along with me now?" asks Peggy before he and the Professor enter one of the abandoned cottages. "I've brought someone to see you," Peggy tells Susan.

Peggy has cleaned the cottage, equipped it with a primus cooker, and installed shelves made from packing cases stocked with food he took from the Tyrian Traveller and an array of medical and pharmaceutical supplies. Peggy has cared for Susan since he found her after Norris Deane beat her. She had lost a lot of blood and could not walk, but she is slowly recovering. "I did four years' medicine once," explained Peggy. "I remember a lot."

Professor Challis suggests Susan would be better off in the hospital, but Peggy will not have a bar of it, accusing him of wanting to take her away from him. "Peggy, I'm your friend," says Challis. "I want to help you, but I must tell her friends in London what has happened to her because that was what they sent me to find out. Do you think they will shrug their shoulders and let it go? There'll be inquiries, quite probably a scandal, and newspaper stories. You will be in grave trouble. And then what?"

Professor Challis meets Susan Deane for the first time. She is very different from what he expected. Susan is not the sort of woman seen in expensive contemporary women's magazines but in Victorian steel engravings. Only a plaid shawl is missing to complete the picture of the little invalid wasting away in the miner's cottage. Peggy goes out to get some firewood, leaving them alone. Challis suspects Susan enjoys being in this **Wuthering Heights**-style melodrama. He tells her Norris Deane is dead and asks what he should say to Lady Mandeville and Sir Granville Peart — her 'Uncle Gabby.' But Susan is more concerned about Peggy than them. Challis agrees to let her stay, for now, since she is safe and getting better.

Professor Challis and Ruth Cadell discuss events at the Tyrian Traveller. "I take it that you didn't convince Bruce Garfield to leave the Red Bird Mine," says the Professor.

"He looks terrible and can hardly stand, but he won't budge," says Cadell. "He's scared that if the weather gets worse, he won't be able to go on. He begrudges every wasted minute." Cadell shows the Professor a fifth-century Phoenician/Tyrian coin Garfield found in the tunnel. (**Fig. 56**) "He has seventeen others. And a thin gold fillet stamped with myrtle leaves," says Cadell.

"But, good heavens, this means he found Mad Jolly's treasure!" says Challis excitedly.

"He hasn't found it, but he's very close," says Cadell. "What Bruce found is a steep tunnel about one hundred and twenty feet long that ends abruptly against a layer of granite. That was where he found the coins and the gold fillet. Along either side are twenty-three smaller tunnels sealed with earth and rock. Bruce believes the tomb of the Tyrian traveller is in one of them. So far, he has opened fourteen but found nothing."

Sir Granville Peart must leave for London tonight. "Tell me what *we* will say to Lucy Mandeville," Peart asks Professor Challis.

"*You* could tell her that Susan is safe, that she has been severely injured but is recovering steadily, that she is being well cared for by the man who saved her life and gives her the most devoted attention," says the Professor.

"But she can't stay in a tumbledown shack!" protests Peart.

"She can for a little while longer," says the Professor. "There's something Susan and Peggy have to resolve by themselves. Nobody else can help them." However, as she will have to move to London soon, Challis intends to offer Peggy his flat in St. George's Square while he is in Paris until December.

"Why, the mind boggles at the picture of that great ape blundering around among your bric-à-brac!" says Peart, horrified.

"No, I don't think so," says Challis. "And I have no bric-à-brac."

Fig. 56 A fifth century Phoenician/Tyrian coin.

It is one a.m., and the wind is hammering Sam Jackett's cottage. Professor Challis is still awake, wondering if Bruce Garfield has found the tomb of the Tyrian Traveller yet. He hears Jackett making tea downstairs in the kitchen and sees a light in Ruth Cadell's cottage. "I know it's an unusual hour to have guests, Sam, but it might be nice to ask Miss Cadell in from next door," says the Professor. Ten minutes later, Jackett returns with Cadell. At five a.m., they hear a loud commotion outside. "Must be a ship ashore somewhere," says Jackett, looking out the window. "Something is going on down at the pub. Maybe we better go down and see what the fuss is about."

"A ship carrying general cargo up from Buenos Aires has run ashore at the east end of the big beach, right below Sennen," announces Charlie Fallenden to everyone in the Tyrian Traveller, prompting them to head for the door in their gumboots, oilskins, and sou'westers. "I have the car outside if you'd like to come along with me," he tells Challis, Cadell, and Jackett.

"Count me out," says Jackett. "I've been on these bleeding picnics before. Wet tail, no fish, and thistles in your socks! And fall over a cliff and break your bleeding neck as like as not." But Challis and Cadell accept his offer.

"Aren't we going to the wreck?" asks the Professor when they head off in the opposite direction to the others.

"Ah, that would be a waste of time, Mr. Challis," says Fallenden. "The Sennen folk have been at her three hours or more. It wouldn't be much to pick over like. 'Tis the first time Charlie Fallenden's turned his back on a wreck in twenty-two years, so 'tis a good thing it has to be a Peru tramp with nothing in her holds but nitrates from Antofagasta!" he laughs. Instead, they drive to the Red Bird Mine to see how Bruce Garfield has fared in the storm. As the grey-green water is like a cauldron, it looks hopeless until Fallenden spots him sitting on a rock.

"Hello, Honey," Garfield greets Cadell. "From now on, you have my undivided attention. And about time, too! I was whacked and went to fix some coffee laced with brandy when I heard this loud whoosh like Old Faithful in Yellowstone Park. It must have squirted out five hundred tons of water and thrown it clear across the width of the cove against those cliffs on the far side. It's all gone." Garfield had opened all but four tunnels. While he cannot say for sure, he believes the tomb of the Tyrian traveller must have been in one of them. "Maybe it was best it happened the way it did," says Garfield. "You can always think how goddam close you got to it!"

THE END.

Comments, Opinions, Reviews

And Just The Same Can Be Said Of ...

Collins published **A Man Made of Tin** (1958) in Great Britain, but nobody published it in America or Australia. It suffered the same fate as **The Saracen Shadow** (1957), receiving hardly any publicity. The **Manchester Evening News** described **A Man Made of Tin** as "Admirable,"[1] the British crime writer Julian Symons (1912-1994) described it in a Collins ad as "Very lively,"[2] and Francis Iles of the **Guardian** mentioned it in passing: Talking about **Dead Man's Shoes** (1958) by Leo Bruce (aka Rupert Croft-Cooke, 1903-1979), Iles said it was "not so good perhaps as Mr. Bruce's earlier books, but pleasant entertainment for all that. And just the same can be said of Shane Martin's **The Man Made of Tin**."[3] That was it! But, despite its underwhelming reception, **The Man Made of Tin** was an entertaining read nevertheless. It differed from its two predecessors because the Professor was in his element among archaeologists more than artists in **Twelve Girls in the Garden** (1957) and winemakers in **The Saracen Shadow**. Thus, George Johnston introduced him to this mystery through his friend and colleague, Sir Granville Peart, more convincingly and smoothly than in the other two novels.

Collins hired William Randell, once again, to design the dust jacket for **The Man Made of Tin**. He depicted the dramatic scene where Norris Deane threw his wife Susan down an old quarry pit. (**Fig. 57**) "That face [...] swirling out of the fog, all twisted up, hating me! And his hands at my throat — hating me, hating me, hating me!"[4] she told the Professor.

Fig. 57 Dust jacket for **The Man Made of Tin** by William Randell.

Johnston dedicated **The Man Made of Tin** to the Australian artist Cedric Flower (1920-2000) and his English-born wife, the writer Pat née Bullen (1914-1977). The Johnstons and the Flowers were friends in Sydney and later in London after both couples moved there. Significantly, George helped launch Pat's career as a successful crime novelist. In 1954, he sent his literary agent, David Higham, "the MS of a first novel by a friend of mine, Miss Patricia

Bullen. It is a sort of thriller and does have [...] some possibilities," wrote Johnston. "Perhaps one of your readers could [...] look at it to see whether it might be worth submitting to a publisher or two."[5]

Johnston did not mention the title of Flower's manuscript, but it was possibly **Wax Flowers for Gloria** (1958), the first of fifteen crime novels she wrote between 1958 and 1976. She initially intended to write under her maiden name, but, instead, used her married name, thematically liking it to several plots, such as **Goodbye Sweet William** (1959), **A Wreath of Water Lilies** (1960), and **One Rose Less** (1961). Flower killed herself by overdosing on pentobarbitone in 1977, just as Charmian Clift had done in 1969.

Cornwall

While living in London, the Johnstons sometimes holidayed in Cornwall, which reminded George of Australia. "Cornwall's beaches, coastline, and people bear a remarkable resemblance to their Australian counterparts, and if it is not quite as sunny as Australia [...], at least it is the only English county able to boast that it once grew a banana tree," he wrote in his weekly column, 'London Diary,' in August 1953.

> In the days of 'Back-along,' the plinth of Cornish prosperity was 'tin, fish, and copper.' Today, it's 'holiday-makers, bed and breakfast, and Cornish cream teas,' with bearded artists thrown in for good measure. Fortunately, the veneer of tourism is [...] thin around the real Cornwall, which remains almost jingoistically proud of its un-Englishness and accepts tourists almost as foreigners but with good-natured free-and-easy hospitality more reminiscent of the Australian attitude than anything I have so far seen in England. [...] In this place there are

people who still more than half-believe in goblins, mermaids, and giants. [It] is a land shrouded in forgotten Celtic mysteries — 'home of the silent, vanished races,' as one eminent historian puts it. These people, conditioned by countless centuries of sombre superstitions, have found brand new superstition."[6]

Similarly, Sir Granville Peart remarked on the other-worldliness and superstitions of Cornwall in **The Man Made of Tin**. "Queer place that," he told Professor Challis.

All moods and mists. Odd things happening all the time. Odd people, for that matter. Dark, strange. Foreigners, really. Came here thousands and thousands of years ago, and they're still scarcely any more English than your vanished Minoans. [...] Oh, not necessarily all of Cornwall, but that peninsula in particular. Gloomy. Uncivilised. Forbidding. [...] And chock-full of bloody saints of whom nobody has ever heard![7]

Sir Granville Peart was the only recurring character in the Challis novels apart from Challis himself. We learned in **Twelve Girls in the Garden** (1957) that he was married to Erica Barrington, the Greek widow of the Professor's American friend, John Barrington.[8] Peart took no active role in that novel but was almost like the sidekick of Challis in **The Man Made of Tin**. Peart was sixty-six,[9] and Challis was sixty-four,[10] and they had been friends for over thirty years.[11]

The Professor believed there was "always something comfortingly stolid and pompous" about Peart, "something of that granite self-possession which the more volatile Continentals generally found so infuriating in the English."[12] Peart was a distinguished British archaeologist, who — just like Professor Gregory Foster (1878-1931), Provost of University College London (1904-1929) — also had been painted in his academic robes by the Irish artist, Sir William Orpen (1878-1931).[13] (**Fig. 58**) No doubt, George Johnston saw Orpen's painting of Foster and thought "I'll have one of those for Peart, too!"

Fig. 58 *Professor Gregory Foster* by Sir William Orpen.

George Johnston painted a vivid picture of Gadsden, the Cornish setting for **The Man Made of Tin**. "The village had that peculiar air of brooding secrecy that comes mostly from having no supply of electricity," he wrote.

> A fretful wind gusting from the westward carried a smell of gorse and ling and sea-salt and cow barns, a combination of odours that had a wild, outlandish quality yet somehow belonged to the scatter of white-washed farms and cottages dimly visible in the darkness. In a way, everything belonged to the smell coming out of the sea and the moors — the fugitive glow of lamplight behind curtained windows; the bare encircling hills, mysteriously dark against stars which were already smudgy and would grow smudgier as the wind rose; the unlit road and its tributary web of stone-walled lanes which twisted away through kale meadows and fields of growing corn, all climbing up towards the black, uneven lip of the high cliffs, behind which the unseen groaned.[14]

At the beginning of **A Man Made of Tin**, Johnston declares, "Gadsden does not exist in reality."[15] However, I suspect he modelled it on the tiny, legend-haunted hamlet of Zennor situated on the northwest coast of Cornwall. (**Fig. 59**) The Church of St. Senara in Zennor is like the unnamed church in Gadsden. For example, both have a "squat-square Cornish bell tower with four spiky little spires."[16] And both are also next to the village inn. I put these similarities to Gilly Wyatt Smith, the warden of St. Senara's, who agreed they sounded very much alike.[17]

Likewise, Johnston modelled the Tyrian Traveller in Gadsden on the Tinners Arms in Zennor. He spent a raucous Saturday night at the inn in 1953, reporting on the topsy-turvy weather Cornwall was having at the time.[18] The farmers, fishermen, coast guardsmen, and lightkeepers who packed the cosy, thick-walled inn six-deep blamed their warm midwinter and calm, unblustery summer on the atomic bomb! (**Fig. 60**)

With the money his uncle left him, Crosbie Dahl bought the Farmers Arms from old Jeremy Trebena less than a year ago, promptly changing its name to the Tyrian Traveller.

Fig. 59 Old postcard of Zennor (1950s).

Fig. 60 The Tinners Arms – the model for the Tyrian Traveller (recent photo).

The inn, unimpressive when seen from the bus stop, acquired a certain rough charm on closer inspection [...] a straightforward, no-nonsense, lime-washed structure [...] built like a barn [...]. From five identical windows [...] so small and [...] deeply recessed that they were almost embrasures — a cosy light filtered through gingham curtains.[19] [Entering the inn] was like walking into a physical wall of conviviality [...] not of bricks and mortar but of the stuff of surrealism — the thick drift of tobacco smoke, the smell of beer and frying sausages, of men's pipes and wood smoke; of feet stamping in black rubber gumboots and a turquoise-feathered dart flicking through the fug like a tropical bird; of red faces in cloth caps with wide-open mouths, singing [...].[20] The old mahogany bar counter, worn, knife-nicked, pocked black by a thousand cigarette ends, [...] the big ashtray on the bar made from the porthole of a wrecked ship.[21] [...] The great log, fallen away into red coals in the huge open fireplace, the ship's lantern over the door and the aquatint of the Sennen lifeboat bringing back the survivors of the foundered Swedish barquentine *Jenny Lind*, the rubbed black wood of the oaken settles and the Windsor chairs, the pitted cork disc of the dartboard.[22]

Dahl had been a playwright and a Fleet Street critic before becoming a public relations officer in the Royal Air Force during World War II.[23] I feel Johnston put a lot of himself into Dahl, which was rather brave since Dahl was a smart alec, a know-it-all, and not very nice. Johnston and Dahl were both fugitives from Fleet Street. Johnston was an outsider on Hydra, and Dahl was an outsider in Gadsden, where "respect for the non-native stranger would always be both grudging and qualified."[24] Johnston and his wife, Charmian, were often angry and resentful of each other like Dahl and his wife, Freda. Lastly, Johnston felt inadequate compared to his brother Jack, while Dahl felt lacking compared to his barman Peggy.

Bruce Garfield

Sir Granville Peart met Bruce Garfield about ten years ago, in the spring of 1946, shortly after he graduated from Princeton "with a remarkably brilliant scholastic record."[25] According to Peart, he possessed "those two special gifts which make the great archaeologists" — imagination and intuition.[26] Now fortyish, Garfield was "highly civilised," extremely wealthy, and very good-looking. "Tall and strong-bodied, dark-skinned, with the most penetrating eyes I have ever seen. Jet-black, like his hair," said Peart. "A bullocky, husky man who physically might have been an all-American fullback [...] a poet built like a navvy." On the other hand, Garfield was "Not an easy chap to get on with."[27] He was aloof, autocratic, and not very approachable with "no sense of teamwork whatsoever, nothing of *esprit-de-corps*."[28]

But the most intriguing thing about Garfield was his interest in only "the search, the finding, the problem itself. That's why he doesn't much care for our sort of people," Professor Challis told Peart. "In his view, we've taken the fun out of archaeology [and] we've turned it into a Big Business, made capital out of it, shoved the past into museums and filled [...] the gaps with concrete. [...] We're the credit-grabbers, the lecturers, the compilers of monographs, the organisers of conventions, the acceptors of honorary degrees, the authors of scholarly works, the custodians of museums, the scratchers and biters of [our own] scholastic backs. We're not only the prostitutes of the game [but] the panderers as well."[29] So, if Garfield had found the tomb of the Tyrian traveller, he planned "to hand it over to [Norris] Deane lock, stock, and barrel. As far as anybody was concerned, it would have been [his] discovery. Garfield's interest was entirely in the search, the finding, the problem itself."[30]

In this respect, Garfield was like Sherlock Holmes, who loved art for its own sake and often would allow less talented and less worthy participants to take credit for his successes. For example, in 'The Adventure of Black Peter' (1905), Dr. Watson says that "Holmes [...] like all great artists, lived for his art's sake,"[31] giving the credit for solving the murder of Captain Peter Carey to Inspector Stanley Hopkins of Scotland Yard, even though Holmes solved it.

The Man Made of Tin also has another allusion to the Great Detective. We learn that Challis spent "two of the happiest nights of his life [...] in a filthy opium den on the edge of the Gobi Desert, in the villainous company of five professional cut-throats, on the occasion when he had gone to Turkestan in search of poor Respighi." Anyone reading this who was also familiar with the Holmes stories by Sir Arthur Conan Doyle — as George Johnston certainly was — would immediately think of 'The Man with the Twisted Lip' (1891), in which Holmes and Dr. Watson each searched the notorious opium den, the Bar Of Gold, for Neville St. Clair and poor Isa Whitney, respectively.[32] Typically, Johnston borrowed the name of the Italian classical composer Ottorino Respighi (1879-1936) for the Professor's quarry.

The Man Made of Tin starts as a search for two missing persons and ends up as a race against time between Bruce Garfield and the sea, which floods his diggings before he can find the tomb of the Tyrian traveller. George Johnston had a similar central character to Garfield and a similar scenario to **The Man Made of Tin** in his dystopian thriller, **The Darkness Outside** (1959),[33] which is another instance of Johnston trying out an idea in a Challis novel and then using it in something else later. Although, he did not wait very long since he started writing it immediately after **The Man Made of Tin**.

In **The Darkness Outside**, an American archaeologist named Eliot Purcell and his team have been working in isolation for months in Iraq. In the end, they have to race against time to find a lost Mesopotamian city before a river, in this case, floods their diggings. They try to give themselves more time by building a levee higher and higher, eventually to no avail. In addition, Purcell has to deal with the delirious ramblings of a stranger he rescued about a plague in Europe — possibly radiation sickness from an atomic bomb — and a horde of Asians on the march westwards. Indeed, Johnston initially wanted to call the book **The Horde** but his American publisher, William Morrow, convinced him to change it.[34] Johnston's biographer Garry Kinnane compared **The Darkness Outside** to **The Nigger of the *Narcissus*** (1897) by Joseph Conrad (1857-1924) but had nothing to say about **The Man Made of Tin.**

In 1960, **The Darkness Outside** was adapted for television by Eve Martell (1929-2011) and her husband Peter Graham Scott (1923-2007), who also directed the ninety-minute play for **ITV Play of the Week**. Marius Goring (1912-1998) played Eliot Purcell; Jack Hedley (1929-2021), Rudy Levin, an Australian; Virginia Maskell (1936-1968), Grace Adams; Patricia Driscoll (1927-2020), Muriel Turnbull; Frederick Jaeger (1928-2004), Humphrey Bequeville; Anthony Newlands (1925-1995), Ernest Steindorf; and Wilfred Lawson (1900-1966) played the stranger. (**Fig. 61**) Production of **The Darkness Outside** for television raises the question of why nobody has ever adapted the Challis novels for TV, which would make very entertaining ninety-minute television thrillers, in my view. While too late now, the English actor Wilfred Hyde-White (1903-1991) — best known for the movies, **The Third Man** (1949), **Let's Make Love** (1960), and

Fig. 61 Marius Goring played Eliot Purcell on television.

Fig. 62 Wilfred Hyde-White (left) could have
played Professor Challis (right).

My Fair Lady (1964) — would have been ideal to play Professor Challis. (**Fig. 62**)

Peggy

The Tyrian Traveller's barman, Peggy, was the bravest and saddest character in the five Challis novels. He was also the series' most unusual male love interest. Peggy did four years of a medical degree before joining the Royal Airforce during World War II. He flew a Lancaster bomber called P for Peggy, which is how he got his nickname. But we never discover his real name in **A Man Made of Tin**. When his plane caught fire after crash-landing, Peggy received horrific facial burns and won the DFC for bravery. (**Fig. 63**) Crosbie Dahl belonged to the same squadron as Peggy, idolising him before the accident and feeling sorry for him afterward. He and his wife Freda employed Peggy as the barman at The Tyrian Traveller. While he was "as tireless as a beaver and strong as an ox,"[35] he understandably felt persecuted and the victim of injustice. Consequently, Peggy would drink too much, and as he got steadily sloshed, his banter with the customers would digress from good-natured humour to stinging sarcasm to

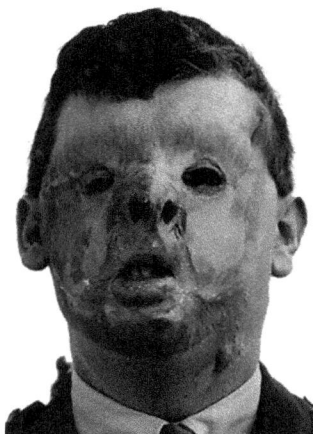

Fig. 63 The type of injuries suffered by Peggy – Lieutenant Norman E. Wallace received horrific facial burns when his RAF plane crashed in World War I.

189

Fig. 64 Boris Karloff as The Monster *(left)* and the angry villagers.

offensive and obscene comments. Peggy would also become "a great, hulking Don Juan trying to make a pass at every woman he sees — and frightening most of them out of their wits!"[36]

Professor Challis described Dahl as "a deluded but well-intentioned Frankenstein" and Peggy as "the Monster."[37] He also described a scene that echoed the hostile attitude of the angry villagers who pursued the Monster in **Frankenstein** (1931), the first of three classic horror films starring the English actor Boris Karloff (1887-1969) as the Monster. (**Fig. 64**) According to the Professor, "If [Susan Deane] were to die, who among the people of Gadsden, aware of [Peggy's] strength and latent brutality, knowing his reputation and the fact that he had tried to force his attentions on [her] — what single one of them would believe that it was not he who had violently assaulted and murdered her, but the girl's own husband, the scholarly, respectable, unobtrusive Norris Deane?"[38]

But the Monster created by the English writer Mary Shelley (1797-1851) in **Frankenstein or the Modern Prometheus** (1818) was not George Johnston's only model for Peggy. During World War I, Johnston's mother, Minnie, was a Voluntary Aid Detachment (VAD) nurse at South Caulfield Hospital in Melbourne. As part of her after-care duties, she often took maimed and wounded soldiers whose families were not nearby home with her to boost their morale.[39] As did the mother of Johnston's alter ego David Meredith in **My Brother Jack** (1964), who was also named Minnie and a VAD nurse. "The nightmarish one in this remembered gallery is Gabby Dixon," recalled Meredith, "because he kept in the background and was never seen much, and I don't suppose he wanted to be [...] because he had suffered terrible facial burns with mustard gas and his face was no longer really like a face at all. He used to frighten me with his staring silences, and he is about the only one I remember as a cheerless figure because sometimes at night, through the thin partitions of the wall, we could hear him sobbing in his room."[40] Thus, Johnston modelled Peggy also on the man he later called Gabby Dixon. It is yet another example of him trying out an idea in a Challis novel first and then using it in something else later.

Sam Jackett

The most likeable character in **The Man Made of Tin** is the Professor's Gadsden landlord, Sam Jackett. He was a very squat, square, solid man with a pear-shaped head, thick arms, and pale skin. Sam's face was pear-shaped, too, and "sagged into a complicated wattle of dewlaps and chins."[41] Jackett had bright black eyes like shiny buttons and a perpetual squint. He was getting on a bit and suffered from chronic rheumatism, using traditional folk remedies to ease the pain, strapping an arum lily leaf to each shin, and sewing strips of grey flannel around his joints. Jackett was no fashion plate, wearing a grey check cloth cap pressed down tightly and an over-large khaki greatcoat purchased for "thirty-five bob at army disposals."[42] Professor Challis suspected he was bald but could not say for sure as he never removed his "flat 'at."[43] Jackett's only vices were smoking a pipe and drinking at the Tyrian Traveller.

Jackett started as a barrow-boy around Stepney and Whitechapel before ending up at the pinnacle of the costermonger trade, Covent

Garden. He was very proud that he could simultaneously carry nine baskets of fruit and vegetables on his head, which Challis believed accounted for "the extraordinary flatness of the man's skull."[44] During World War II, Jackett served in the Home Guard in London, describing it as "playing with fire-crackers."[45] Then, late in life, he won a modest prize in a football pool, which enabled him to retire and purchase Laurel Cottage in Gadsden. "By the sale of his cauliflowers, the letting of rooms and the provision of afternoon teas to summer visitors, and part-time employment as the village sexton and caretaker of the little church," Jackett and his wife were able to live with "an enviable measure of security and contentment."[46]

> Mrs. Jackett looked and probably was very much older than her husband. Her skin had the almost waxen transparency [...] one associates with great age, her eyes that pale, watery, fading look as if one were seeing them in an actual process of dissolving. Her nose was bone-thin, with wide damp nostrils; there were three moles on her chin; the joints of her thin, brown-flecked fingers were painfully arthritic; her smile of welcome, exposing two rows of ill-fitting but youthfully glittering teeth, gave the eroded face a fleeting air of caricature.[47]

Mrs. Jacket had been a missionary in China in her younger days but was now bedridden. She had spent much of her time recently watching the comings and goings at Susan Deane's cottage next door from the window of her "heavily chintzed" and "herbaceously wall-papered" bedroom, happily communicating what she saw to Professor Challis. Since Mrs. Jackett could no longer do domestic chores, they were all left to Sam. He was a wholesome, if plain, cook. For example, breakfast consisted of "porridge and cream, toast, homemade preserves, eggs and bacon, and a fried collage of yesterday's scraps called bubble and squeak."[48] And lunch typically consisted of "tripe and onions with plain boiled potatoes, preceded by a thick mulligatawny soup, and with a steamed cabinet pudding to follow."[49] Sam also made good Cornish pasties. "This 'ere is the common or garden variety — just the meat an' onions and plenty of spuds," he told Challis, "but you can pretty well stuff 'em with whatever you fancy. Egg-and-bacon, rabbit-and-leeks, dates, egg-and-currants, apple-and-bacon, jam … bit of mackerel or 'erring is real tasty for a change,"[50] While the Professor's bedroom in Laurel Cottage was a testament to Sam's housekeeping skills and tastes in furnishings — as well as George Johnston's descriptive mastery and sense of place:

> The room itself was small, spotlessly clean, and frigidly cold. The only floor covering was a shiny linoleum which smelt overwhelmingly of wax polish and which was patterned all over with an intricate design of what seemed to be dark-brown sea slugs writhing through a twisted jungle of some green fungus which, while unidentifiable, was unquestionably poisonous. The furnishings comprised a large iron bedstead enamelled white; the 'linen chest,' a wardrobe, wash-stand and two chairs, all in an atrocious figured veneer; an ornate toilet set in heavy china bearing an overall decoration of flowers, robins, and cupids and consisting of four articles — water-jug, wash-basin, soap-bowl, and chamber-pot — all of which were meticulously arranged in a well-spaced row along the top of the wash-stand; and a thick glass ash-tray bearing the improbably exotic invitation: 'Take Next Year's Vacation in the Dead Heart of Australia!' Hanging from a tasselled silk cord above the door was a framed oblong of embroidery which said, rather enigmatically, "He Is Always With Us."[51]

With no deception whatsoever, George Johnston named Sam Jackett after his fellow journalist Sam Jackett (1909-1979), who was "a Cornishman through and through."[52] In 1935, Jackett left Cornwall to join the **Evening News** (1881-1980) in London as a reporter. He became a war correspondent in the Far East for Reuters in 1943, re-joining the **Evening News** after World War II and becoming a crime reporter, news editor, and eventually managing editor. (**Fig. 65**) Jacket and Johnston may have met when they were both war correspondents in the Far East. Afterward, Jackett was a leading member of the London Press Club, where he and Johnston no doubt drank occasionally. Jackett retired from Fleet Street and returned to his native Cornwall, dying there aged seventy in 1979.[53] Perhaps he opened a bed and breakfast like his namesake in **The Man Made of Tin**.

Sam Jackett

continues his weekly series, revealing the triumphs of Britain's counter-espionage system.

Fig. 65 One of Sam Jackett's by-lines (1954).

Charlie Fallenden

Around midnight on 26 July 1954, the *Traute Sarnow*, a three-hundred-ton freighter trading out of Flensburg, Germany, ran aground in heavy fog off Gurnard's Head, four miles south-west of Zennor while carrying coal from Cardiff to Ostend. The captain fired a distress signal, the St. Ives lifeboat stood by, and rescue teams had to make their way along cliff paths for about a mile to reach the spot. Visibility was almost nil. The five members of the crew were hauled to safety up an eighty-foot-high cliff by a breeches buoy. But within hours of hitting the rocks, gale-force winds turned the ship broadside against the cliffs, and heavy seas smashed it to smithereens. (**Fig. 66**) A fortnight later, George Johnston visited Gurnard's Head and reported on the shipwreck:

> Immediately the wreck was notified, a Customs officer was sent down hot foot, and the usual notices were posted on the coastguard station warning allcomers against the "seizure of the wreck." In the fortnight since then, hurricane lanterns have been bobbing about mysteriously by night amid the gorse and the ling along the rugged Cornish headlands. I was down there at the weekend, while the *Traute Sarnow* has broken into three sections, I am happy to report that nothing of any value has been lost to the voracious sea. But quite a number of dairy farms appear to have their cowsheds stacked with valuable coils of rope, pumps, timber, dynamos, electrical equipment, teak doors, mattresses, bed linen, furnishings, ships' stores, navigating instruments, and so on. I gather that the Customs man made only one attempt to check the plague of Cornishmen. At the bottom of the cliff, he was confronted by a huge, weather-beaten farmer who had just lugged ashore about a

Fig. 66 The wreck of the *Traute Sarnow* in 1954.

ton of timber, coils of rope, the ship's wheel, and a tangle of wire hawser. The Cornishman scowled at the representative of officialdom, spat into the water, and growled, 'You want the stuff, eh? OK. Then you carry it up the cliff!' The Customs officer retired and has not been seen since.[54]

I believe the smashing of the Danish freighter *Thekla* in **The Man Made of Tin** was inspired by the breaking up of German cargo ship the *Traute Sarnow* in a storm off Gurnard's Head. Furthermore, the likeable Gadsden spiv, Charlie Fallenden, was based on the enterprising Cornishmen who completely stripped the *Traute Sarnow* — although, "he was built to a scale quite different from that of his diminutive, quick-eyed, Cornish companions."[55] Fallenden was over six feet tall and built like a Mallee bull. He had a rough-cut head, a wild mop of wiry hair, a rich baritone voice, and "huge hands that only displayed their delicacy when the slender feathered darts spun from his fingers."[56] He wore a dandyishly cut and abominably pattered jacket with a full-blown rose in the lapel.

196

A bunch of seals hung from a gold fob chain at his waist. And his "long thin pointed tan shoes [were] polished to a lacquered gloss."[57] In the opinion of Sam Jackett, "Women, singing, dancing, boats, darts, drinking — Charlie's the boy."[58] Fallenden and Challis started being wary of each other but became trusting friends. So much so that Fallenden showed the Professor the shed where he stored his loot:

> Awed and admiring, the Professor allowed his eyes to drift over the stacked shelves and piled-up racks, the corners packed with coils of rope and lengths of cable, with oars and boathooks and wire tackle; the ships' binnacles and chronometers, the brass lamps in gimbals, the sextants and aneroid barometers, the transformers and light-switches and generators and electric pumps, the Thermos flasks and toilet seats. In racks below the ceiling were thousands of superficial feet of Baltic planking. Part of a ship's radar equipment made an improbable futuristic clutter in one corner of the shed. The Professor himself sat comfortably in a fine mahogany chair which doubtless had once graced a captain's cabin. The wall facing him was shelved floor to ceiling and every shelf was packed with proofs of Fallenden's audacity and ingenuity — Dutch cheeses, cans of Californian fruit, French wines, Danish butter and bacon, tins of Australian meat, bolts of cloth, lengths of sponge-rubber, sheets of canvas, hanks of cordage, spools of copper wire, boxes of tools, cans of lubricating oil, rolls of navigation charts. From one corner, painted eyes stared across at the Professor from a battered ship's figurehead — the solitary evidence in all the cluttered shed that Charlie Fallenden possessed a sentimental as well as a practical turn of mind.[59]

Fig 67 George Cole as Arthur Daley in *The Minder*.

Fallenden's shed reminded Challis "of the stores along the coast of Maine — half ship-chandlers, half grocery shops — where he had spent childhood holidays."[60] It reminded me of the lock-up where dodgy Arthur Daley, played by the English actor George Cole (1925-2015), stored his ill-gotten gains in the TV series *Minder* (1979-1991). In fact, to some extent, Daley was an older Cockney version of Fallenden. (**Fig. 67**)

The Man Made of Tin did not make as much money as George Johnston hoped. But he pushed on regardless because he had faith in Professor Challis. As soon as Johnston finished writing **The Man Made of Tin**, Johnston started the fourth — and arguably the best — book in the series, **The Myth is Murder** (1959).

Endnotes

[1] 'Crime Corner,' **Manchester Evening News** (Manchester, UK), 29 May 1958, p. 3

[2] Collins advertisement, **Daily Telegraph** (London, UK), 16 May 1958, p. 14.

[3] Frances Iles, 'Criminal Records,' **The Guardian** (London, UK), 6 June 1958, p. 4.

[4] Shane Martin (George Johnston), **The Man Made of Tin**, London: Collins, 1958, p. 220.

[5] George Johnston, Letter to David Higham, 25 April 1954, at the Harry Ransom Center, University of Texas.

[6] George H. Johnston, 'London Diary: Frolicsome Air in Britain: Great Weather — And Peace,' **Newcastle Sun** (Newcastle, Australia), 6 August 1953, p. 12.

[7] Shane Martin, 1958, pp. 9-11.

[8] Shane Martin, **Twelve Girls in the Garden**, New York: William Morrow & Company, 1957, p. 7.

[9] Shane Martin, 1958, p. 233.

[10] Ibid., p. 18.

[11] Ibid., p. 233.

[12] Ibid., p. 10.

[13] Ibid., pp. 12-13.

[14] Ibid. p. 35.

[15] Ibid., unpaged.

16 Ibid., p. 36.

17 Gilly Wyatt Smith (Warden of St. Senara's Church), Email to Derham Groves, 30 May 2023.

18 George H. Johnston, 'London Diary: Frolicsome Air in Britain: Great Weather — And Peace.

19 Shane Martin, 1958, p. 37.

20 Ibid., p. 38.

21 Ibid., p. 42.

22 Ibid., p. 43.

23 Ibid., pp. 56-57.

24 Ibid., p. 42.

25 Ibid., p. 23.

26 Ibid., p. 24.

27 Ibid., pp. 14-15.

28 Ibid., p. 25.

29 Ibid., p. 234.

30 Ibid.

31 Sir Arthur Conan Doyle (1905), 'Black Peter,' in William S. Baring-Gould (ed.), (1968), **The Annotated Sherlock Holmes**, London: John Murray, 1973, vol. II, p. 398.

32 Ibid., (1891), 'The Man with the Twisted Lip,' vol. I, pp. 370-371.

33 George Johnston, **The Darkness Outside**, London: Collins, 1959.

34 Garry Kinnane, **George Johnston: A Biography**, Melbourne: Nelson, 1986, p. 174.

35 Shane Martin, 1958, p. 73.

36 Ibid., p. 74.

37 Ibid., p. 148.

38 Ibid., p. 208.

39 Garry Kinnane, pp. 6-7.

40 George Johnston, **My Brother Jack**, London: Collins, 1964, p. 13.

41 Shane Martin, 1958, p. 40.

42 Ibid., p. 92.

43 Ibid., p. 53.

44 Ibid., p. 54.

45 Ibid., p. 95.

46 Ibid., pp. 53-54.

47 Ibid., p. 79.

[48] Ibid., pp. 56-57.

[49] Ibid., p. 84.

[50] Ibid., p. 151.

[51] Ibid., p. 49.

[52] 'Eldon,' 'Press Man's Punchline,' **Evening Chronicle**, 14 March 1979, p. 14.

[53] 'Eldon,' 'Sam Jackett, Newsman,' **Evening Chronicle**, 27 February 1979, p. 12.

[54] George Johnston, 'London Diary: "Silly" Season Rumors,' **Sun** (Sydney, Australia), 11 August 1954, p. 28.

[55] Shane Martin, 1958, p. 44.

[56] Ibid.

[57] Ibid.

[58] Ibid., p. 43.

[59] Ibid., p. 132.

[60] Ibid.

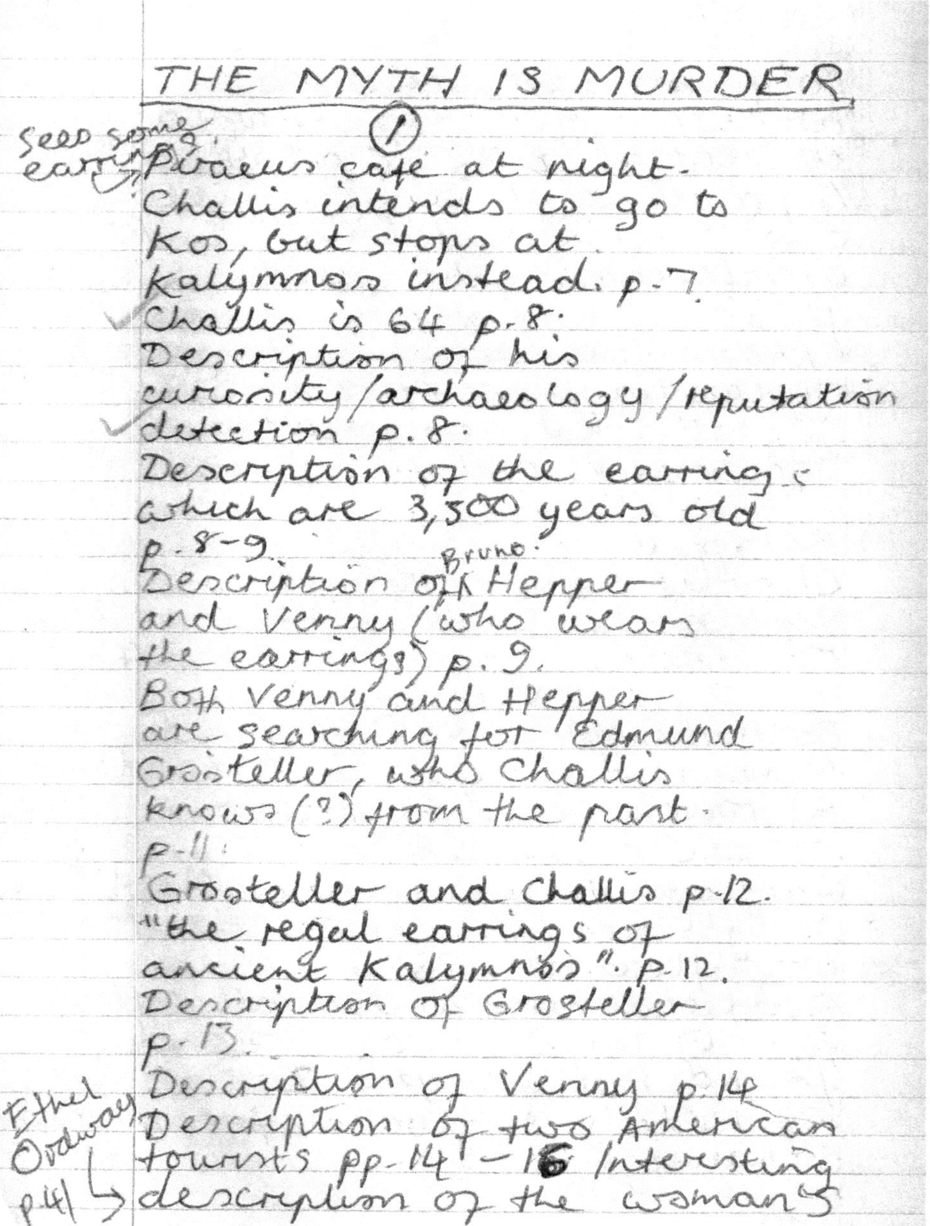

THE MYTH IS MURDER

(1)

seed some earns → Piraeus café at night.
Challis intends to go to
Kos, but stops at
Kalymnos instead. p. 7.
✓ Challis is 64 p. 8.
Description of his
curiosity/archaeology/reputation
✓ detection p. 8.
Description of the earring
which are 3,500 years old
p. 8-9.
Bruno.
Description of Hepper
and Venny (who wears
the earrings) p. 9.
Both Venny and Hepper
are searching for Edmund
Grosteller, who Challis
knows (?) from the past.
p. 11.
Grosteller and Challis p. 12.
"the regal earrings of
ancient Kalymnos". p. 12.
Description of Grosteller
p. 13.
Ethel Ordway → Description of Venny p. 14
Description of two American
tourists pp. 14 - 16 / Interesting
p. 41 → description of the woman's

Plate 5 Page from Derham Groves' notebook.

4. The Myth is Murder

The Myth is Murder (1959) by Shane Martin/George Johnston is the fourth and arguably the best of the five Professor Challis novels. It takes place over a week in 1955 on the Greek island of Kalymnos — where the Johnstons lived for not quite a year before moving to Hydra in 1956. Collins published it in the UK and William Morrow in the USA as The Third Statue (1959), but no Australian edition was published. While it is out of print, it is still possible to pick up a second-hand copy, but the prices sometimes asked would have astonished its cash-strapped author. Following is a summary of The Myth is Murder, with comments, opinions, and reviews later.

Dramatis Personae

Professor Ronald Challis	An archaeologist and amateur detective.
Edmund Quincy Grosteller	A German archaeologist who was once the Professor's colleague.
Nino Vivaldo	An Italian art dealer and Grosteller's former publisher.
Ethel Ordway	Grosteller's former American assistant.
Veronica 'Venny' Ordway	Ordway's American daughter.
Mark Kermit Glassop	Ordway's American boyfriend.
Bruno Hepper	A small-time American crook and Venny's boyfriend.
Johnny Franz	A shady American art dealer and Hepper's boss.
Constantine Krafos	A Greek amateur archaeologist and friend of Challis and Grosteller.
Anthony Krafos	Krafos's son.
Sophia	Krafos's housekeeper.
Miquelon	A French archaeologist.
Corporal Vassilis	A Greek policeman.
Pavlov	A Greek fisherman.

Chapter I

Professor Ronald Challis waits in a coffee house in Piraeus, Athens, for the steamer to the Greek island of Kos, where he is to do some work for the Flenzberger Foundation. At a nearby table is a twenty-two-year-old woman wearing a pair of wafer-thin gold pendant earrings in the shape of myrtle leaves, which are from Kalymnos and about three thousand five hundred years old. Surprised to see such treasure in such a grungy place, the Professor eavesdrops on her, an American called Venny, and her American companion, a redheaded man whom she calls Hepper, who tells her his boss, Johnny Franz, is coming from Istanbul to meet Edmund Grosteller, "a screwy old crackpot who's got a bug about Phidias." (**Fig. 68**)

Fig. 68 Phidias, the ancient Greek architect and sculptor.

"Edmund Grosteller?" asks Venny. "But that's who we were looking for. I want to know about this man, Grosteller."

"I'm sorry, Venny, there's nothing I can tell you," says Hepper. "I don't even know the guy. Let's skip it."

Challis worked with Grosteller almost thirty years ago. He had been an excellent scholar, but things had not gone his way. There had been a string of disasters — a big scandal in Dusseldorf, that sordid business in Bologna, and an annihilating failure in Milan — followed by total obscurity. Challis thought Grosteller was dead, but apparently, he isn't.

The Professor believes Venny is with two American tourists at a nearby table who also attract his attention. One is a woman named Ethel, who he deduces is a college lecturer, while the other is an older man in his early fifties, whom Challis finds harder to place. He is carrying two cameras and a light metre in a leather case and wearing a striped Mykonos shirt that does not suit him. They are talking about how Pericles (495-429 BC), an ancient Greek general and politician, built the Long Walls from Athens to Piraeus.

Hepper introduces Venny to a short man about five feet tall who joins them. "You've heard me talk about my friend Johnny," says Hepper. "This is Johnny Franz." Venny then leaves them to join Ethel and the man in the Mykonos shirt, who are now checking the schedule for Greek island steamers. Challis overhears Ethel saying, "Kalymnos."

A large dark man sees Hepper and Franz through the coffee house door and abruptly runs off, his legs comically going up and down like pistons. "Vivaldo!" cries Franz before he and Hepper hastily depart to try and catch him, but he avoids them.

The Professor waits another twenty minutes in case Grosteller shows up, then leaves the coffee house. The affairs of the Flenzberger Foundation can wait, he decides. Instead of going to Kos, he will go to Kalymnos.

Chapter II

Johnny Franz and Bruno Hepper visit Edmund Grosteller's run-down house in Athens. But he is not at home, so they break in and look around. The place has been closed for a long time and smells of damp. Books and newspapers are piled on the table, the floor, and the few battered pieces of cheap furniture. A heap of dirty blankets and bed linen patched and frayed at the edges is in one corner, and a pile of dirty plates is in the cement sink. "I had the oddest feeling that we were not the only ones anxious to find your Mr. Grosteller," says Franz.

> I recognised him from photographs in archaeologist publications. He has a face that would be difficult to forget. Ronald Challis is a distinguished archaeologist who sometimes works for governments. I find it a remarkable coincidence, Bruno, that on the same night we are to persuade Mr. Grosteller to go with us to Kalymnos, this man Challis is also there.

Chapter III

Boarding the steamer to Kalymnos, Professor Challis sees Ethel and the man in the Mykonos shirt among the passengers and Venny waiting for someone on the dock. Challis asks the steward whether anyone named Krafos still lives on Kalymnos. "The young Mr. Krafos travels often to Piraeus and back with us," replies the steward. But the Professor means his father, Constantine Krafos. "He is blind and unwell," says the steward. "The old Mr. Krafos has not left the house for many years, I understand."

"Does a gentleman named Grosteller travel often with you?" Challis also asks.

"This person I do not remember," says the steward.

By chance, later that night, Professor Challis meets Ethel alone on the deck. "This is the way to see Greece," he says to break the ice. "I should introduce myself. I am Challis. Ronald Challis."

"I am Ethel Ordway," she nervously replies. Suddenly, the boat lurches and Ordway drops her imitation alligator handbag, its contents scattering over the deck — a chequebook, a handkerchief, keys, makeup, a passport, a purse, a roll of film, snapshots, and a small, heavy, snub-nosed automatic. (**Fig. 69**)

Fig. 69 Ethel Ordway's handbag and gun.

Chapter IV

The next day, Bruno Hepper calls Venny at her hotel in Athens to say he will be tied up for a few days working for Johnny Franz. "But I have to see you, Hepper," says Venny. "I must talk to you. I want to talk to you about that man, Grosteller."

But Hepper's hands are tied. "You see, Johnny and I, we've got some business to do, and it concerns something this mad crackpot Grosteller was on to a long while back, and … well, candidly, Venny, I wouldn't like Johnny to get the idea I'd been blabbing to a girl about the company's business." As she will not take no for an answer, he warns her of the dangers of getting mixed up with Franz and Grosteller. "This is a queer situation we're dealing with," Hepper says. "It isn't for you, Venny. Keep out of it. I think somebody's going to get hurt. I don't want it to be you."

Chapter V

Professor Challis arrives on the island of Kalymnos, which has not changed much since he visited twenty-five years ago. There are more caiques in the harbour now. And they have painted the once bone-white houses pink, yellow, and ultramarine. (**Fig. 70**)

Fig. 70 Kalymnos (2018).

After eating a disappointing lunch of lukewarm squid and oil-soaked spinach, Challis makes his way to the house of Constantine Krafos, who probably knows Edmund Grosteller better than any man alive and might know where to find him. "I have called to see Mr. Krafos," Challis tells the elderly housekeeper, Sophia.

"He is in Athens," says Sophia. "He will return the day after tomorrow."

"I am speaking of Mr. Constantine Krafos," he says.

"The old Mr. Krafos sees nobody," she says. "He is unwell. The doctor forbids visits." And with that, Sophia closes the door in the Professor's face. So he spends the next day searching Kalymnos for Grosteller but does not see him or any of the people from the Piraeus coffee house.

At two o'clock on his third day on Kalymnos, Professor Challis returns to Constantine Krafos's house, but again Sophia closes the door in his face. So Challis retreats to a waterfront café and considers going to Kos for the Flenzberger Foundation after all when he sees Ethel Ordway, Venny, the man in the Mykonos shirt, and the man who ran off at the coffee house, Nino Vivaldo, strolling along the promenade.

But before Challis can follow them, Anthony Krafos approaches his table and introduces himself. "I understand you have been inquiring about me," says the thirty-year-old son of Constantine Krafos. While Challis wants to meet him, he wishes it could have been at a better time because he loses sight of his quarry.

"Of course, my father has frequently spoken of you," says Anthony. However, "Visitors are out of the question." But when Challis mentions Edmund Grosteller, he suddenly changes his mind and invites him to his father's house at eleven-thirty tomorrow morning. "I cannot promise anything, you understand," says Anthony. "If he seems improved, perhaps you could see him briefly."

Chapter VI

Johnny Franz and Bruno Hepper make their way to Kalymnos separately by private boat. Even though Hepper is in Franz's debt and Franz needs Hepper's help, they dislike and distrust each other. "You are the laboratory assistant to the scientist, the artist's apprentice, the scholar's secretary, and sometimes perhaps only the janitor," Franz tells Hepper before comparing him to the Greek shadow puppet Karagiósis. "He has a great gift for understanding life, and he also has an arm which is three times the length of a normal arm, which has the dual virtue of being both an instrument of protection and a great aid to the pilfering. I am not making too much of a riddle of this, am I, Bruno?" (**Fig. 71**) Whatever the caper is, Franz knows all about it. "We need to get to Edmund Grosteller before Nino Vivaldo does," Franz suggests. And since Vivaldo trusts Hepper, Franz wants him to kill him.

Fig. 71 Karagiósis with his oversized arm.

Chapter VII

Once Anthony Krafos departs, Professor Challis tries to find the man in the Mykonos shirt and Nino Vivaldo. While randomly asking people in the street if they have seen them is slow and tedious, he ends up at the shipyard at Lefassi at about ten o'clock at night. When he hears footsteps, he quickly hides behind a clump of tamarisk. Walking away like a somnambulist in the moonlight is Ethel Ordway. When the coast is clear, the Professor proceeds to a long workshop building and peers through the window. While he sees no one, he hears the man in the Mykonos shirt and Vivaldo arguing. Then someone fires two shots at Challis from behind.

Chapter VIII

Although shaken by the previous night, Professor Challis returns to Lefassi the next day. On the way, a crowd outside the police station attracts his attention. The man in the Mykonos shirt is lying under a wet blanket in the courtyard. Someone shot him in the back and dumped him in the water. Corporal Vassilis tells Challis he was Mark Kermit Glassop, born in St. Louis, Missouri, on 21 July 1903.[1] "If this man is known to you, I will take you to see the captain," Vassilis tells the Professor.

"I do not know him," says Challis before continuing to Lefassi, now accompanied by Pavlov, the fisherman who found Glassop's body.

"About here," says Pavlov, showing Challis the place. "It was not floating, just washing around on the shallow beds." The Professor follows the trail of blood to where Glassop fell and died. Nearby, a boy is making gulls from the torn pages of a battered book. Challis picks it up and reads the title page, "The Lost Truth, A Study of Phidias, By Edmund Quincey Grosteller, Forum Editions — Nino Vivaldo, Milano, MCMXXXIII." Written on the flyleaf is the name of the book's owner — Ethel Ordway.

Challis does not wish to get involved with the Greek authorities but feels obliged to say something, so he returns to the police station and tells Vassilis, "An American woman on this island named Ethel Ordway knew the person killed."

"Wait here, please," Vassilis tells Challis before going upstairs to speak to his boss. "You have made a mistake," he says when he returns. "The captain has already talked to her. She was unable to give any information. She had never seen him before."

Chapter IX

Constantine Krafos has been bedridden for eleven years and blind for the last seven. Anthony Krafos tells him Professor Challis wishes to see him about Edmund Grosteller. "But why does everyone want to talk about poor Grosteller?" asks Constantine. "There was that Englishman whose name I can never remember, and the other day, that French fellow, Miquelon."

"It was not the other day but before the War, and it has been twenty years since Miquelon was here," says Anthony. "It might be best if you do not see the Professor, Father. I can explain how ill you have been and send him off."

But Constantine will have nothing of it. "Nonsense, Anthony!" he protests. "I feel better than I have felt in many a long day. Of course, I shall see Challis. Have him come early this evening after I have my camomile tea."

Chapter X

Professor Challis talked with Constantine Krafos for nearly an hour before he fell asleep. "Did you learn anything?" asks Anthony Krafos.

"Not really," says the Professor. "I already knew Miquelon was looking for a cave."

"Are you also looking for a cave?" asks Anthony.

"No, I'm looking for Edmund Grosteller," says Challis. "I would not like to see any harm come to him. I suppose you remember Grosteller, Mr. Krafos?" As a boy, he remembers seeing a great bull of a man with a wild beard in a monk-grey robe of rough grey cloth, gazing down at gold, jewels, and scraps of pottery lying on the desk in the study. "Would I bore you if I spoke to you about Edmund Grosteller?" asks Challis.

"Certainly not," says Anthony. "I would like to hear what you have to say."

Chapter XI

Professor Challis has known Edmund Grosteller since 1929. He was anti-social, hostile, offensive, and ungracious. Grosteller's only friend was Constantine Krafos, and his one obsession was Phidias. Then, in 1932, he announced he had found two small sculptures by Phidias in the ruined precincts of a temple to Poseidon in Kalymnos. But if that were not enough, Grosteller asserted the bronze one was Phidias's original model for the lost great statue of Zeus, one of the Seven Wonders of the Ancient World. (**Fig. 72**) Consequently, academia came down on Grosteller like a ton of bricks. A committee of eminent archaeologists in Dusseldorf examined his claims, ultimately discrediting them. As a result, he lost his lectureship at the University of Bologna, although the pretext was an earlier scandal involving some girl.

Next, Grosteller moved to Milan and wrote **The Lost Truth: A Study of Phidias**. According to Challis, it was

Fig. 72 Statue of Zeus at Olympia (c. 435 BC) by Phidias.

the perfect distillation of Grosteller's extraordinary scholarship and his equally remarkable prejudice, written from too much pent-up passion and emotion and too much self-pity and downright vindictiveness to be taken seriously. Finally, he settled in Athens and fell into obscurity.

The Professor ends by asking Anthony if he saw Grosteller in Athens and whether he is responsible for him not keeping his appointments. "I have no information on Doctor Grosteller," says Anthony. So after getting nowhere, Challis changes tack.

"I'd give a great deal to be able to spend a night or two in this house once more, for old times' sake," the Professor tells Anthony. "You don't, I suppose, accept guests … paying guests, if necessary. I would love to rummage through this place, looking for things."

"We are not very comfortable for guests," says Anthony. But then he suddenly changes his mind again. "I will have the woman make up a room for you," he says. "If you really wish to stay, that is?"

"I do. Oh yes, I do," answers Challis, rubbing his hands together.

Chapter XII

Since Edmund Grosteller is obsessed with Phidias, Professor Challis reminds Anthony Krafos that Phidias designed but did not make the Parthenon sculptures, better known as the Elgin Marbles, now in the British Museum. (**Fig. 73**) He made the thirty-foot bronze of the *Athena Promachos* and the great *Athena Parthenos,* although neither has survived. Likewise, the Zeus of Olympia, Phidias's masterpiece, is only a memory, described in **Hellados Periegesis** by the ancient Greek geographer Pausanius (110-180). Thus, people believed that nothing survived from the hand of Phidias until Grosteller came along, claiming to have found two statues he had made.

Fig. 73 The Elgin Marbles in the British Museum.

"According to Grosteller, Phidias was imprisoned for impiety in Athens until his friends smuggled him to Kalymnos, where he lived and worked in a cave for fifteen years," explains Challis. "When he died, they buried him in this cave with all his works of art, which Grosteller has been looking for all these years and may have found."

"And you believe it?" asks Anthony.

"People have," says Challis, citing Miquelon for one.

"Where are the two little statues that Grosteller found?" asks Anthony.

"I was hoping you might be able to inform me," says Challis, suspecting Anthony knows more than he admits before warning him that shady people like Johnny Franz are now involved. "You know him?" asks the Professor.

"Yes, I know him," answers Anthony. "He is an art dealer. Antiques, old manuscripts, rugs, that sort of stuff. He was from Izmir when I knew him." Then Anthony drops a bombshell. "The lost cave of Phidias was found and then lost again," says Anthony, explaining that his father told Grosteller he had found the cave but not everything about it. "Then he had a stroke, became paralysed, went blind, and could not remember anything about the cave. That is all I want to say," says Anthony, complaining of a migraine and going to bed.

Even though it is nighttime, Challis has arranged to pick up his things from his hotel. But first, he hides in the garden and waits. Soon, Anthony emerges, a carafe of wine in his hand and a bag of food over his shoulder, and leaves through the big iron gate.

Chapter XIII

Nino Vivaldo lost a lot of money publishing books by the likes of Edmund Grosteller, Baretti, Giacomo the poet, and a Mexican futurist introduced to him by the Italian writer Gabriele d'Annuzio (1863-1938) himself. (**Fig. 74**) "I must choose to do something else before all my father's money is gone on these people with expensive visions!" says Vivaldo. "So I become an art dealer, specialising in antiquities." However, Vivaldo has been smuggling antique works of art with the help of Grosteller, Bruno Hepper, and Johnny Franz to sell at his *Galleria Nino Vivaldo* on Via Scaffeti in Milan.

Vivaldo met Mark Glassop, Ethel Ordway, and Venny when they visited his gallery by chance, purchasing the ancient Kalymnos earrings as a graduation present for Venny. He sent them to their hotel with Hepper, who took a fancy to Venny. Now, somehow, they are all in Kalymnos looking for Grosteller.

Fig. 74 The Italian writer Gabriele d'Annuzio.

Vivaldo wanted Glassop to be his intermediary because Franz scared him. But since the murder of Glassop, Vivaldo has been terrified to leave his hotel room. So he asks the hotel boy to bring Ethel Ordway to his room because he now wants her to be his intermediary. But she refuses, saying she even denied knowing Glassop at the police station. "Had I involved myself with identifying his body, the delays and complications would have been endless," says Ordway. "I do not expect you to appreciate this, Signor Vivaldo, but he would have understood what I did."

Suddenly, someone knocks on the door. Vivaldo imagines the police and panics. But it is Professor Challis. He found out where Vivaldo was living from Corporal Vassilis. "I came merely to extend an invitation," says the Professor. "At eleven o'clock tomorrow morning, I shall have Edmund Grosteller at the house of Mr. Constantine Krafos. I was hoping you, as his former publisher, could be there. The invitation, of course, goes for you also, Miss Ordway."

Chapter XIV

Bruno Hepper finds the house where Venny is staying. He wants to tell her he loves her and warn her to leave. "This place is going to get hot from now on, Venny," he says. "It's not going to be a good place to be. So you've got to get out of it. That's what I came to tell you. You've got to get away from here — you and your mother."

"We have to find Doctor Grosteller," says Venny. "He's in danger, isn't he?"

"Listen, Venny," says Hepper, "Johnny Franz has got his eye on Grosteller like a fox on chickens because Grosteller seems like the biggest, cheapest, and dirtiest bargain in his life, and he's scared someone will try to peel it away from him."

"Bruno, what does Doctor Grosteller look like?" asks Venny. Hepper silently stares at his hands and recalls the night it all started at Grosteller's house some time ago.

Flashback to that meeting in Athens: "I have not been unappreciative of Vivaldo's great patience and support," Grosteller tells Hepper. "So tell him he will have his reward very soon. I have been returning to Kalymnos and working secretly, and the results have been rewarding." Hidden under Grosteller's mattress is a tin box containing forty-seven pieces of ancient Kalymnos gold jewellery, including the earrings later bought for Venny, and a crudely fashioned statuette in some black metal of a nude male figure standing on a small square pedestal. "Throughout the Classical period in Kalymnos, it was customary to present an honoured visitor with three effigies — one in iron, one in marble, and one in gold — which he would leave at any shrine he favoured," says Grosteller.

> I found this one in the ruins of a Poseidon temple on the north coast of Kalymnos. It is from the late Fourth Century BC. The great interest lies in the lettered inscription on the pedestal, which is always just the name of the honoured recipient. On this one, it is Phidias, establishing quite incontrovertibly that he did visit the island of Kalymnos, whatever the opinion of conservative scholarship. (**Fig. 75**)

Fig. 75 "Phidias" inscribed on the statuette.

Grosteller asks Hepper to give the box and the contents to Vivaldo, saying it is only a token of things to come and triggering the whole caper.

"What have you been thinking about, Bruno?" asks Venny. "You've been sitting there so long looking down at your hands. I asked you what Doctor Grosteller looked like, and you didn't answer."

"You can see for yourself what he looks like," says Hepper. "I'll take you to see him." Since Grosteller talked to Hepper over the years about his search for the cave of Phidias and showed him charts, drawings, maps, and photographs, Hepper believes he knows where Grosteller might be. Suddenly, Johnny Franz walks into the room. He was getting suspicious of Hepper and tracked him down. "Come, Bruno," says Franz. "Say good night. Let us be on our way."

Chapter XV

After leaving Venny, Johnny Franz and Bruno Hepper walk through the dreamy streets of Kalymnos. Franz tells him they should do something about Vivaldo, visit Constantine Krafos, and do something about Venny. "I am confirmed in my belief that she is not good for you, Bruno," says, Franz, causing Hepper to snap. He takes Franz by the shoulder, spins him around, and repeatedly punches his face, leaving him crumpled and limp like a cast-off ventriloquist's doll.

Chapter XVI

It is after midnight when Professor Challis returns to the house. As Anthony has not returned, Challis searches the house for anything related to Edmund Grosteller. Out of respect for his host, he searches Constantine's bedroom last. While the frail old patriarch sleeps fitfully in his massive four-poster-bed, Challis rummages through the illogical, jumbled paraphernalia of somebody else's life. He finds three small, weighty bundles, two in canvas and one in newspaper, in a corner cupboard behind an old amphora, heavy as stone. Constantine wakes up and asks whether it is his late daughter Ketty. "No, it isn't Ketty, Constantine," says the Professor. "It's Ronald Challis. I came to see how you were."

"She will have gone for her English lesson," says Constantine, his mind wandering. "It is very kind of that girl to give Ketty the English lessons. Poor Edmund! He doesn't like it, you know. I have no idea whether he begrudges the time she spends with Ketty as time lost which otherwise might be devoted to attending to his whims, or it is just this bitter prejudice he harbours against anything connected with England and the English."

Challis asks Constantine for the name of Ketty's English teacher, but before he can answer, Anthony returns. "Why are you here," he angrily asks Challis. "And what's that?" he adds, looking at the looted cupboard. They move to the drawing room, taking the three bundles. They contain three small statues — an ivory figure of a naked athlete, a bronze figure of a seated god, and a marble figure of a naked man standing on a square pedestal inscribed with the name Phidias, which is one of the three statuettes presented to the great architect and sculptor when he visited Kalymnos.

"Now, the example in marble we have here before us," says Challis. "The facsimile in iron, I learned this evening, is now the property of Signor Vivaldo. He received it last year as a gift from Edmund Grosteller. I wonder where the figure in gold can be?" he asks Anthony.

Fig. 76 The American expert on etiquette, Emily Post (1872-1960).

"I haven't the least idea," says Anthony, who reprimands Challis for rifling through his father's bedroom and ransacking the house of his host while he was absent.

"I am aware of the breach of manners. Mr. Krafos," says Challis, "which I both regret and deplore, but we are not dealing with a case in which Emily Post is the arbiter." (**Fig. 76**)

Suddenly, there is a knock on the door. It is ten to three in the morning. "This lady has called on you," says Anthony. Ethel Ordway is seeking help from Challis because Venny is missing.

"I am sorry to have come at this hour," says Ordway. "You're the only one who can help me, I think." Venny left Ordway a note saying, 'Hepper knows where Grosteller is. He's taking me to him. Don't worry, darling.' You don't know Hepper," Ordway tells Challis. "You don't know what he is, what he represents!"

While Challis and Ordway talk, Anthony quietly slips out of the house and away through the big iron gate. "Now, where the devil are you going," thinks the Professor.

Chapter XVII

Since there is nothing that Professor Challis can do about Venny until daybreak, he and Ethel Ordway talk about the past. Twenty-six years ago, as a recent graduate of Columbia University, aged twenty-two, she was Edmund Grosteller's assistant in Kalymnos and taught English to Ketty. Ordway was also at the centre of the scandal at the University of Bologna — they had been lovers. Furthermore, Grosteller is Venny's father. "Is the girl aware of this?" asks Challis.

"Yes," says Ordway, who returned to America before Venny was born and never saw Grosteller again until she spotted him on the boat from Piraeus to Kalymnos. "At first, I didn't recognise him at all, and then gradually I realised who it was and watched him for a long time, although it was terrible, horrible because he was in a shabby old coat and looked feeble, timid, and helpless."

After Venny was born, Ordway left her parents' farm in New Hampshire, USA, to teach college in the Midwest, where she met Mark Glassop. "He was very kind to Veronica and became a sort of guardian to her," she says. "We were more than friends, I suppose."

When Glassop bought the earrings for Venny, Nino Vivaldo said Grosteller found them in 1931, but Ordway knew he did not. That and other things Bruno Hepper told Venny made her suspect something fishy. Ordway followed Grosteller to Lefassi after they landed, but given their history, she was reluctant to speak to him. So she took Glassop to see him later, but only Vivaldo was there. Ordway does not know who shot Glassop, although according to Challis, the possible suspects are Vivaldo, Johnny Franz, Hepper,

Grosteller, Ordway, and himself. It is now four a.m. Ordway falls asleep on the sofa, while Anthony Krafos has still not shown up.

Chapter XVIII

Bruno Hepper and Venny trudge through the rugged landscape to where they hope to find Edmund Grosteller. "It isn't easy, Venny," says Hepper. "And the further we go, the worse it gets. Up there below that cave, I think there's an old sheepfold. If it's there, we can get out of the wind, and maybe you can get some rest." But as Venny does not feel much like sleeping, she asks Hepper to tell her about this place. "Down there to the right is the important place," says Hepper. "That's the old city of Damos. It's all carved out of solid rock — houses, streets, graveyards, everything. That's where old Grosteller digs up his golden jewels. That's where your earrings came from. And the other side of that, there's a ridge with the old watch tower on it, and after that, the sea."

Venny tells Hepper that Grosteller is her father. But she has never seen him. According to Venny, her mother loved her father so much that she could not burden him with a baby, especially as he had already suffered more than he could bear. But Ordway had been haunted by old ghosts ever since. "You see, she always thought she'd failed him, that she had done the wrong thing in running away — that it was her desertion of him at the time of his trouble, when he most needed her, that had permanently embittered him and driven him into obscurity," says Venny. When Hepper says they are like the Babes in the Wood, Venny kisses him passionately.

Chapter XIX

Despite having a sleepless night, Professor Challis sets out at seven o'clock in the morning after questioning Sophia and learning that time is now his prime enemy. Firstly, he visits the Hotel Apollon, where Johnny Franz and Bruno Hepper are staying.

Fig. 77 The Apollon Hotel on Kalymnos? (recent photograph).

(**Fig. 77**) "I have seen your picture in various publications," says Franz, still bearing the bruises from Hepper's beating. "I have for many years been an admirer. There was some particular matter on which you desired to see me?"

Challis wanted to invite Franz to meet Edmund Grosteller at eleven o'clock at Constantine Krafos's house, but "we simply cannot find Doctor Grosteller," he says. "A friend of mine, a young lady, has gone to round him up, and your friend Hepper was gracious enough to offer his assistance."

"Would you prefer to talk up in my room, or shall we go elsewhere?" asks Franz, tense and alert.

"Outside, I think," says Challis. "I always feel happier with lots of people around." So, they find a coffee house to continue their discussion. "It would save time if I came straight to the point," says the Professor amicably. "A steamer is leaving for Piraeus at ten this morning, the *Kyklades*, a nice ship. I am suggesting, Mr.

Franz, that you should take it. Otherwise, I will inform the police that you murdered Mark Glassop and took two potshots at me. I would prefer not to do this since the police inquiries would involve my colleague Grosteller, whom it would be best not to interrogate too closely."

Challis and Franz then play cat and mouse with each other until the Professor calls time and cuts to the chase. "About four years ago, you visited Kalymnos and met Anthony Krafos, who was living a lonely life with no companionship but a half-mad old servant and a bedridden old man," says Challis. "So he sold you his father's collection of antiquities since he could not work under the circumstances and needed some money. Perhaps one might shop around Istanbul and find bits of it here and there," remarks Challis.

> Then, about two years ago, Grosteller made it known he had located the lost cave of Phidias. He gave the iron statue he found in the Poseidon temple to Nino Vivaldo, his long-time business associate, as proof that Phidias had visited Kalymnos and the gold and marble statues to Anthony Krafos for safekeeping. Rumours of Grosteller's discovery reached you, although not via Vivaldo, who was your business associate, too. He wanted to keep you in the dark because he hoped to finally receive a big pay-off for all the years of supporting Grosteller, which he did not wish to share. When Anthony learned you were also interested in the lost cave of Phidias, he sold you the gold statue that Grosteller had given him for safekeeping. Anthony also wanted to impress you with the promise of further riches despite having nothing more to sell. So he invented a story about his father finding the cave before becoming ill and then forgetting where it was,

and now Grosteller was hot on the scent of the cave based on what Constantine had told him.

Anthony does not want Franz to meet Grosteller and discover his lie. Furthermore, since he is guilty of aiding and abetting the smuggling of archaic works of art, a crime in Greece, he can ill afford to have a lot of strangers rummaging around his island on business with Grosteller. Enter Ethel Ordway and Venny and Mark Glassop, who became involved to find closure more than treasure, and Challis, who got involved initially out of curiosity and now out of loyalty to old friends and colleagues. But it is made more complicated because everyone knows everyone else. Consequently, it has become a desperate race to find Grosteller first. However, the Professor's account of events does not persuade Franz to leave Kalymnos. "I have no intention of taking that ship," he tells Challis. "I take it that the purpose of your absurd and rambling story is merely to tell me that there is no lost cave of Phidias."

"Oh, but there is!" says Challis cheerfully. "The trouble is that I am the only one who knows where to find it!"

Chapter XX

At daybreak, Bruno Hepper goes to get food and water. An hour later, Venny sees Anthony Krafos coming slowly and cautiously up the slope towards the sheepfold, moving from one clump of scrub to another in a devious way. "Who are you?" Anthony asks Venny. "What are you doing here?"

"Are people not supposed to be here?" says Venny.

"You must go down there," says Anthony before he sees Grosteller approaching in the distance and changes his mind. "Don't move from here!" he says and hastily departs.

Now that it is daylight, Venny sees a cave above the sheepfold and a crude ramp leading up to it thirty yards away. "I must find Bruno and tell him!" Venny thinks.

But after walking about a quarter of a mile, Anthony stops her and says, "I told you to stay where you were. Go back up there!" He means business and points a pistol at Venny. Then she sees a weird-looking man with a bulbous caricature of a face, bright inquiring eyes, and wildly matted coarse grey hair peering at them from behind a tangled thorn bush — the illusive Edmund Grosteller. Venny is not out of danger yet, however. After returning to the safety of the sheepfold and sitting down, she notices Anthony watching her from the cave above.

Chapter XXI

Nino Vivaldo is the only person Edmund Grosteller trusts. "What you must realise is that you are now the only contact with reality he has," Professor Challis tells Vivaldo, hoping to set up a meeting between them at a pottery factory outside the ancient city of Damos. "I cannot be your intermediary, but I shall try to scare Johnny Franz into leaving Kalymnos on the ten o'clock steamer tomorrow morning," the Professor tells Vivaldo, who greatly fears Franz. "Either I or Franz or Grosteller will come," explains Challis. "If it is Franz who comes, you will have to face him." Vivaldo waits over three hours at the pottery factory before a car pulls up, and Johnny Franz steps out.

Chapter XXII

From behind a wall at the upper edge of the ancient burial ground of Damos, Bruno Hepper watches Johnny Franz and Nino Vivaldo below, picking their way carefully between the open graves. Then, suddenly, someone softly calls his name from the aloe plants on his left. It is Professor Challis. "What the hell!" gasps Hepper, his heart in his mouth.

"Shhh! We must be quiet!" whispers the Professor. "I have been watching here for an hour. I saw you coming. I want you to take me to Venny, you see. Not at the moment, of course. Later. We must see what happens here." Vivaldo and Franz enter a tomb and disappear from view. A few minutes later, only Vivaldo emerges. He rolls a boulder over the entrance and collapses on the ground.

Challis and Hepper race down the slope. Vivaldo tells them he killed Franz in self-defence by hitting him many times with a rock. "He would have killed me," says Vivaldo. "I saw him kill that other man on the beach. He would have killed me like that."

"You saw him kill Mark Glassop?" asks Challis. Vivaldo anticipated trouble after talking with Glassop and hid. He saw Franz and Glassop arguing. Then, as Glassop walked away, Franz cold-bloodedly shot him in the back.

Chapter XXIII

Venny is the bait in a trap set by Anthony Krafos. In the distance, she sees Bruno Hepper approaching the sheepfold with someone she thinks is Johnny Franz but is Professor Challis. What Venny first thought was Franz's white hat was the Professor's mop of white hair. "You will make no sound and do nothing that might attract their attention," Anthony, armed and ready, tells Venny.

But Venny feels she must warn Hepper somehow. So, when she thinks it is the right time, she races out of the sheepfold and down the slope in a shower of dust and flying pebbles. Hepper rushes past Venny and yells at Anthony, "Don't do it, man! For Christ's sake, don't! There isn't any need!" But Anthony fires his gun and hits Hepper, who still reaches the cave and grapples with him. Anthony appears to have the upper hand until he trips, falls off the ledge at the mouth of the cave, and breaks his neck.

Spooked by the commotion, Edmund Grosteller flees. "I guess it scared him away," says Challis. "He's vanished again into the mountains somewhere."

Chapter XXIV

The police retrieve the bodies of Johnny Franz and Anthony Krafos and conclude that Nino Vivaldo killed Franz in self-defence and Anthony's death was accidental. It is nighttime when Professor Challis returns to Constantine Krafos's house. Ethel Ordway is sitting on the Chintz chair in the drawing room, staring into space. Challis assures her that Venny is fine and with Hepper at the hospital. "He'll be all right, but it will take a few weeks," says the Professor. Ordway tells Challis she might stay and nurse Constantine since he was always very kind to her.

The marble, ivory, and bronze figures are on the table, so Challis returns them to Constantine's bedroom. He replaces the marble and ivory ones in the corner cupboard. But something about the bronze statuette catches his attention, something that Edmund Grosteller and the committee of eminent archaeologists in Dusseldorf missed — two tiny limpet shells embedded in the bronze and very difficult to see because of the bronze patina.

Fig. 78 The island of Telendos off the coast of Kalymnos.

"We used to talk a lot, Constantine," Challis tells his sleeping or perhaps unconscious friend lying in bed. "Well, maybe this will be the last time, so here is something interesting. Something you'll enjoy. You see, Constantine, I believe Phidias did come here, and Grosteller's research was perfectly valid, and his reconstruction of the case brilliantly accurate — up to a point." The Professor explains that the island of Telendos was severed from Kalymnos by an earthquake in 211 BC. **(Fig. 78)** "Even now, you can see on the sandy bottom the ruins of old houses and part of the long walls of the ancient city where Phidias lived," says Challis. "And the two minuscule sea shells indicate that someone long ago, but after Phidias, retrieved the three statuettes from the sea and cleaned them of almost all of their sea growth before taking them to the temple of Poseidon, in the ruins of which Grosteller later found them. Thus, not only did Phidias's adopted city sink below the sea but probably also his cave that would have been nearby."

But Challis decides to say nothing about this. "I think we'll let Grosteller go on looking, Constantine," says the Professor. "He's lived for nearly seventy years, and they haven't been all that happy, and there isn't much longer to go. After all, this is the only dream he has ever had. We must not take that away from him, too."

THE END.

Comments, Opinions, Reviews

Anything But The Long Walls

In 1959, Collins published **The Myth is Murder**, the fourth Professor Challis novel by George Johnston/Shane Martin, in Great Britain. Johnston had wanted to call the book **The Long Walls** — a reference to the six-kilometre-long defensive walls between Athens and Piraeus built by the ancient Greek general Pericles (d. 429 BC) — which Ethel Ordway and Mark Glassop talked about in the coffee house at the start of the book.[2] (**Fig. 79**) Perhaps he had initially envisioned more of the action happening in Athens. But as he mentioned the Long Walls only this one time, Collins asked him to change the book's title to something more general.[3]

Fig. 79 Piraeus with the Long Walls beyond.

Once again, Collins hired William Randell to design the dust jacket. In his previous designs for **Twelve Girls in the Garden**, **The Saracen Shadow**, and **The Man Made of Tin,** he depicted dramatic scenes from the novels — the fistfight between Brandon Flett and Bimbo Grasset for the first, Jaquiline Lemaignan holding a smoking gun for the second, and Norris Dean strangling his wife Susan for the third. But for **The Myth is Murder**, Randell did a conceptual design based on the ancient Greek amphora in the bedroom of Constantine Krafos, showing the vessel casting a shadow on the floor of a man with his hands in the air. In keeping with the book's Greek setting, he chose a Greek-style font for the title and name of the author. I believe Randell's dust jacket for **A Myth is Murder** is the best of the four he did, and I am fortunate to own his original artwork, dated 29 September 1958, rescued from a rubbish tip. (**Fig. 80**)

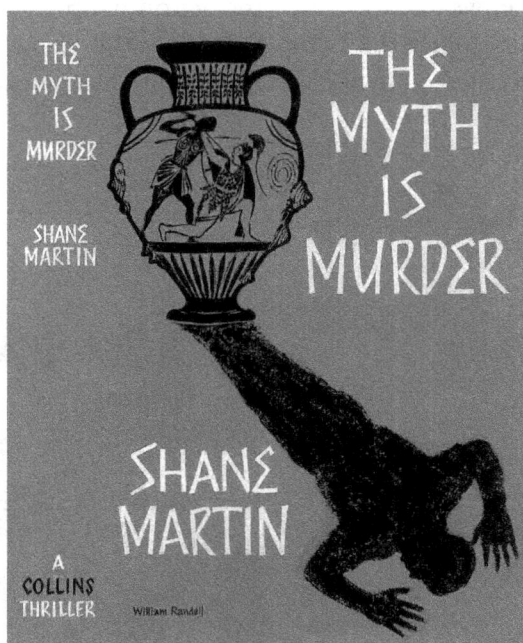

Fig. 80 Dust jacket by William Randell.

After a two-year absence of Professor Challis in the USA, William Morrow published an American edition of **The Myth is Murder** in 1959, but with a different title, **The Third Statue**. James Hill (1930-2004), the first Canadian illustrator to receive membership in the American Illustrators' Association, designed the dust jacket. It featured the cobwebby heads of the three statues found by Edmund Grosteller, framed inside a stylised ionic column. (**Fig. 81**) Since Morrow did not publish American editions of **The Saracen Sword** and **The Man Made of Tin**, Shane Martin was described on the dust jacket of **The Third Statue** as the "Author of **Twelve Girls in the Garden**," suggesting there were only two Challis novels instead of four.

We know more about Hill than Randell. He was notoriously unreliable due to his alcoholism. So, whenever his agent got Hill a commission, he had to keep checking on the artist to be sure he was focused and on schedule, which was even more difficult

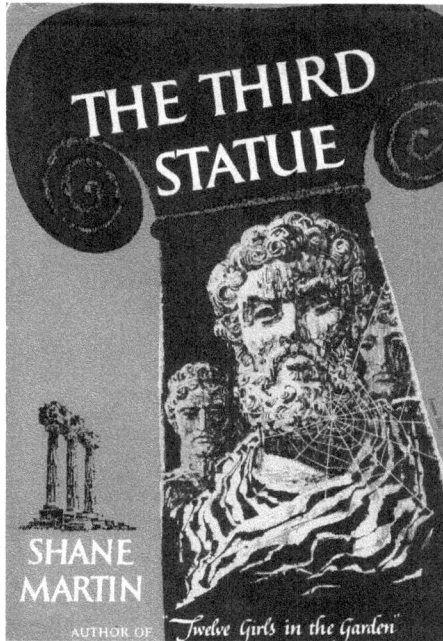

Fig. 81 Dust jacket by James Hill.

because Hill did not have a telephone. On one occasion, his agent visited him the night before a painting was due. Hill only had to fine-tune one or two things to complete it. But when his agent arrived to collect the artwork the next day, Hill had painted over it because he thought it "looked like shit."[4]

George Johnston dedicated **The Myth is Murder** to Niko and Despina Famakides,[5] a cosmopolitan couple who were the Johnstons' part-time neighbours on Hydra, spending their weekends and summer holidays there while living and working the rest of the time in Athens. Niko and Despina spoke excellent English and got on like a house on fire with George and his wife, the writer Charmian Clift.[6]

Niko Famakides (b. 1911) was a director of the Bank of Athens. He later became the General Secretary and Minister of Industry

Fig. 82 Niko and Despina Famakides.

in the Transitional Government (October-November 1974) and the President of Olympic Airways (1978).[7] In **Clean Straw for Nothing**, Johnston's alter ego, David Meredith, has a "banker friend in Athens"[8] named Stephanos, who I suspect George based on Niko. On one occasion, Stephanos asked Meredith, "Don't you ever feel you want to [return] to your own country [...] your own people? [...] I have travelled [...] a good deal, and there are places, other than Greece, that I like very much. If I [like] them too much, I pack at once, and hurry home."[9] I can hear Niko also saying this to George. Indeed, it would not surprise me if the sympathetic and wealthy Famakideses helped the Johnstons when their coffers were low — sadly a frequent occurrence — which might explain why George went as far as dedicating **The Myth is Murder** to them.

Kalymnos

In September 1954, the British broadcaster Wilfred Thomas (1904-1991) told George Johnston of an Australian government plan to bring sponge divers from Kalymnos to work in the pearl-diving industry in Darwin because cheap synthetic sponges were quickly replacing more expensive natural ones harvested from the sea. (**Fig. 83**) "I've been looking for a book to write that would get me out of Fleet Street, and this is the one!"[10] Johnston told Thomas enthusiastically. The Johnstons made plans to move to Kalymnos, and George quit his job.

Arriving late to the Johnstons' farewell party in London, Thomas dampened the celebrations by announcing he had just heard the government had cancelled the plan because the sponge divers had decided "the prospect of deep waters, sharks, and leaving their familiar way of life too daunting, and they felt it would be better to look for work on the Greek mainland."[11] But George was cheerfully philosophical about this bad news. "What the hell!" he declared. "We'll go anyway! It's too late to change. We'll have to see just what happens."[12] So, on 2 December 1954, the Johnstons sailed

Fig. 83 Natural sponges for sale on Kalymnos (2018).

Fig. 84 The Johnstons' house on Kalymnos (recent photograph).

for Kalymnos. By all accounts, their living conditions were pretty grim. The yellow terrace house they had rented sight unseen from Athens was unfurnished and unheated, with a leaky roof and no water or sewerage to connect to the toilet cistern, for which they paid an exorbitant rent of six hundred drachmas per month.[13] (**Fig. 84**)

The Johnstons lived on Kalymnos for less than a year before moving to Hydra for a better life. But while there, George heard the legend of the lost cave of Phidias. As the story goes, a shepherd followed some sheep into a cave on the island of Telendos and discovered lots of treasure inside, believed to belong to Phidias. The shepherd left to seek help from his relatives to carry the loot away but could not find the cave again, and his relatives disbelieved his story. But, from time to time, after heavy rains, people have found gold coins on the slopes of the tiny mountainous island.[14] This intriguing folk tale provided Johnston with the bones of a plot for **The Myth is Murder**. Like the Kalymnos shepherd, Constantine Krafos found the cave of Phidias and then forgot where it was. But the same folk tale also may have influenced the previous Challis novel, **The Man Made of Tin**, because Mad Jolly likewise found the tomb of the Tyrian Traveller and then forgot where it was. Interestingly, in **Clean Straw for Nothing**, Johnston's surrogate, David Meredith, also considered writing a book about Phidias.[15]

George Johnston and Charmian Clift co-wrote the novel **The Sponge Divers** (1955), which they set on the island of Kalymnos and wrote while living there. It featured yet another Johnston proxy, the Australian journalist Morgan Leigh, who thought Kalymnos looked "like a kid's painting of a town, the sort of painting they would put up in an exhibition of child art to illustrate the perceptiveness of the young mind before some damn-fool teacher came along to strangle it with convention."

> Cubes of different colours, crazy colours, wonderful colours, not laid on flat and clear but all washed out into streaks and blotches, like an amateur's watercolour — bright blues and pinks and very pale blues like the faded eyes of old fishermen, and yellow and orange and grey and white and green — all piled on top of one another, with the rugs hanging vivid and gay from the balconies. A town in abstract: toy blocks with little square windows ruled in white, spread between the rock wall of the mountains and the harbour, green as a jewel and shining in the sun.[16]

I have shown how Johnston often tried something out in a Challis novel first and then reused it in another book later. But this time, he tried out describing Kalymnos in **The Sponge Divers** first and then reused it in **The Myth is Murder** later. Mimicking Leigh's sentiments exactly, Professor Challis said that Kalymnos "looked less like a real town than a child's painting of a town, with the colours laid on in streaks and blotches, and all the windows and doors square and ruled out in white, and the outlines not quite well-drawn enough, and the perspectives tilted this way and that ... he remembered it in the evening light and at sunrise as a town in abstract, built up out of a set of children's building blocks — it was the direct sun of noon that washed everything out, like an amateur's watercolour."[17]

Since Johnston wrote **The Myth is Murder** while living on Hydra, I suspect he based many specific buildings in the book on ones there rather than on Kalymnos. Take the house of Constantine Krafos on Kalymnos, for example. It was located "at the extreme eastern end of the town, the very uppermost of all the houses and larger, too, than any: it sat high above the harbour on a steep, walled

Fig. 85 The Lazaros Kountouriotus mansion on Hydra (2018).

parapet with nothing above it but the gaunt rock cliffs and it had the grim, forbidding look of some feudal keep of an earlier overlord."[18] This house reminded me of the grand, eighteenth-century stone mansion on Hydra that belonged to the shipowner and politician, Lazaros Kountouriotus (1769-1852), far more than any houses I saw on Kalymnos. (**Fig. 85**) Nowadays, the mansion is open to the public and well maintained, but in Johnston's day, the Kountouriotus family still lived there, and it was much shabbier like Krafos's house.[19]

Edmund Grossteller

George Johnston created some of his most colourful characters for **The Myth is Murder**, and at the top of the list is the archaeologist Edmund Grosteller. Born in Zurich in 1889, he was the only child of a German professor of anatomy and an English governess. Soon after Grosteller was born, however, his father deserted his mother. Grosteller spent his childhood in England, where his mother taught him before he won a scholarship to Oxford, graduating with first-class honours in Greats (i.e., Greek and Latin languages and the history, literature, and philosophy of Greece and Rome) in 1912, the same year his mother died of tuberculosis — the same disease that eventually also killed Johnston.

When World War I started in 1914, "not having taken the precaution to change his name, and having a German father,"[20] Grosteller was interred in Dublin for eight months. After the war, he returned to Switzerland to teach at various schools until an unexpected legacy from his repentant father allowed him to go to Greece to study classical life. He became an expert on — although Professor Challis said he was obsessed with — the great ancient Greek architect and sculptor Phidias. On the strength of that, Grosteller gained a lectureship at the University of Bologna. Then, in 1932, he announced he had found two sculptures by Phidias, which brought the wrath of academia down upon him. After losing his position at the university, Grosteller retreated to Athens and wrote **The Lost Truth, A Study of Phidias**, which only made things worse for him. He was 'cancelled' and fell into obscurity for almost thirty years.

All these misfortunes finally took a heavy physical toll on Grosteller. When his former assistant and lover, Ethel Ordway, saw him for the first time after many years on the steamer to Kalymnos, she could hardly recognise him. "I watched him for a long time, although it was terrible ... horrible, too horrible even to be tragic ... degrading somehow," she told Challis. "He was in a shabby old coat, so feeble and timid and ... helpless — there on that crowded forward deck, groping around in the darkness, trying to find a place to sit. They kept pushing him away and laughing at him. I couldn't look at it. I had to run away."[21]

But according to the Professor, in his heyday, Grosteller was "a huge man, six-feet-six, I should say, with a wild beard, broad, thick shoulders, and arms that seemed too long even for his huge body, swinging from thrust-forward bone sockets, which gave his spine an almost hunchback look. With his tormented blue eyes, and thick lips, and crushed ears, and unkept hair and beard, and a complexion that looked like thick cream which has been left too long in the bowl, he was monstrously ugly — I'd almost say, the ugliest man I have ever set eyes on."[22]

I believe George Johnston modelled Edmund Grosteller on the aggressive, hot-tempered, domineering zoologist Professor George Edward Challenger, who appeared in three science fiction novels by Sir Arthur Conan Doyle — **The Lost World** (1912), **The Poison Belt** (1913), and **The Land of Mist** (1926). It seems that **The Lost World** was a boyhood favourite of Johnston's since he referred to it at least twice in newspaper articles he wrote later in life. There is undoubtedly a strong physical resemblance between Grosteller and Challenger. Compare the description of Grosteller by Challis above to the following description of Challenger by the narrator of **The Lost World**, the journalist Edward Malone:

> His appearance made me gasp. I was prepared for something strange, but not for so overpowering a personality as this. It was his size, which took one's breath away — his size and his imposing presence. His head was enormous, the largest I have ever seen upon a human being. I am sure that his top hat, had I ventured to don it, would have slipped over me entirely and rested on my shoulders. He had the face and beard, which I associate with an Assyrian bull; the former florid, the latter so black as almost to have a suspicion of blue, spade-shaped and rippling down over his chest. The hair was peculiar, plastered down in front in a long, curving wisp over his massive forehead. The eyes were blue-grey under great black tufts, very clear, very critical, and very masterful. A huge spread of shoulders and a chest like a barrel were the other parts of him which appeared above the table, save for two enormous hands covered with long black hair. This and a bellowing, roaring, rumbling voice made up my first impression of the notorious Professor Challenger.[23]

Fig. 86 Sir Arthur Conan Doyle made up as Professor Challenger (1912).

At the front of the first edition of **The Lost World** is a photograph of the novel's four protagonists — Professor Summerlee, Malone, and Lord John Roxton, all played by actors, and Challenger, played by Doyle, heavily made up as the Professor, demonstrating his great affection for the character. But if I said it was a photo of Grosteller, I don't think anyone would disagree. (**Fig. 86**)

Johnny Franz

Johnny Franz had a difficult start in life, growing up in the Greek port city of Smyrna, "a bad city in which to be poor," but surviving thanks to his cunning and ruthlessness. According to Nino Vivaldo, he was like a snake or a worm that burrows and burrows and lives on death.[24] Bruno Hepper agreed but put it more kindly. "Johnny's a queer sort of character," he said. "He burrows around. He likes to find out what's going on."[25]

Franz described himself as "a Levantine merchant," telling Professor Challis it was "the only thing in the world I care about … the only thing worth doing." However, his passion for wheeling and dealing did not hide the fact he was a psychopath, unhesitatingly shooting Mark Glassop in the back in cold blood, for example. Indeed, there was something very creepy about Franz.

> He was a tiny man, smaller even than Challis himself, no more than an inch or so over five feet — a geometrical little man who seemed to be composed of nothing but lines and points and angles … a clean exposition of some problem by Pythagoras. A man scrupulously clean and scrupulously pressed, the features and the clothes equally pale and equally pointed … as if the colour had been almost scrubbed out of the faintly off-white suit and the faintly off-white complexion, and both had been ironed under a damp cloth to an almost polished smoothness.[26]

But despite Franz's brutality and cruelty, it did not stop Hepper from punching him unconscious or Vivaldo from bashing him to death with a rock. Perhaps it was his diminutive size and effeminate ways — suggested by subtle things like his catlike cleanliness, crisp white suits, and "soft and dreamy"[27] voice — that prevented him from being a classic tough guy. And for these reasons, Franz reminds me of Joel Cairo as played by the Hungarian-American actor Peter Lorre (1904-1964) in the 1941 film version of the Dashiell Hammett (1894-1961) thriller, **The Maltese Falcon** (1930). (**Fig. 87**) Even when Cairo threatened Private Eye Sam Spade (Humphrey Bogart) with a gun, it did not stop Spade from slapping Cairo and telling him, "You'll take it and like it."[28]

Fig. 87 Peter Lorre as Joel Cairo in **The Maltese Falcon**.

There were other things reminiscent of **The Maltese Falcon**, too. For example, big and fat Nino Vivaldo was the ally-turned-enemy of Franz, and Kasper Gutman (Sidney Greenstreet), known as The Fat Man, was the enemy-turned-ally of Cairo. Secondly, Hepper hated Franz and was happy to be rid of him after Vivaldo bashed him to death. While Spade detested his partner, Miles Archer (Jerome Cowan), and was glad to be rid of him after Brigid O'Shaughnessy (Mary Astor) shot him to death. The search for the lost cave of Phidias does not end when the book ends, and the quest for the gold and jewel-encrusted Maltese falcon does not finish when the film finishes. However, in both cases, the cause seems hopeless. Finally, **The Myth is Murder** contains some classic film noir moments, like when Hepper watches "the flat ellipse of moonlight moving on the cabin wall"[29] of the boat he and Franz sailed aboard to Kalymnos. In the hands of someone like John Huston (1906-1987), the director of **The Maltese Falcon**, **The Myth is Murder** could have made a great movie.

All this makes me wonder whether George Johnston had Joel Cairo and **The Maltese Falcon** in mind when he wrote **The Myth is**

Murder. It would certainly not surprise me if he did. But I am not the only person who noticed a similarity between them because the person who reviewed crime novels for the **Philadelphia Enquirer** said **The Myth is Murder** had "a set of suspects as disparate as those in **The Maltese Falcon**."[30]

Bruno Hepper

Bruno Hepper was the emotional heart of **The Myth is Murder**. He grew up in Wisconsin before joining the Air Transport Command (ATC) during World War II, flying C-46s — big, fat-bellied, US Air Force cargo planes — carrying strategic war supplies from Assam in north-east India over 'The Hump' — the name given to the eastern end of the Himalayas by Allied WWII pilots — into China. (**Fig. 88**) It was exceedingly dangerous work, although not primarily due to Japanese fighters and flak, but "the mountain peaks, mist-filled ravines, sudden storms, wild air-currents, and the implacable jungle."[31]

Like many of his buddies in the ATC, Hepper got involved in black marketeering and smuggling. "At first, it had been fountain

Fig. 88 A C-46 US Air Force World War II cargo plane.

pens — Parker 51s, and wristwatches, and Ronson lighters, and the sort of harmless drugs they liked to peddle around the black market in Kunming, in the side alleys off Chin Pi Lu,"[32] recalled Hepper. As a newspaper correspondent during the War, George Johnston reported on these rackets since 'The Hump' was his patch. For example, in 'Giant Smuggling Ring Smashed: Contraband Flown Over "The Hump" to China' (1944), he reported, "In one American troop carrier squadron, some officers from the commanding officer down, were involved in cigarette smuggling which cleared an estimated \$50,000 profit."[33] A large amount of illicit money was there to be made.

But Hepper was lucky because, despite "a whole army of FBI out to clean up the Hump rackets,"[34] they never caught him, and he was honourably discharged from the US Air Force after two tours of duty, "with one-thousand-one-hundred-and thirty-two days of service on the ticket — and not one of these days when people some place or other weren't killing each other like crazy … millions and millions of people [were] killed while he'd been spending them going up and over across 'The Hump' — and he'd never once been in the position of having to kill anybody at all."[35]

After the War, Hepper was involved in a lot of shady stuff and was in "very serious trouble"[36] when Franz found him in Isfahan, Iran, and took him in. But he felt he had just about repaid that debt when he met Venny and fell hopelessly in love. While he was not the most unusual male love interest in the Challis novels — that was Peggy in **The Man Made of Tin** — he was not a typical leading man either. Hepper was "a young-old, red-haired, rather good-looking man," according to Professor Challis.

> He had eyes that swaggered anxiously, and he wore a rumpled seersucker suit. He gave the impression of being deeply interested in the girl — whom he called Venny — but a little uncertain of his standing. There were certain nervous tensions

which kept his thick, freckled fingers drumming on the table-top, which in less than an hour had practically filled the ashtray with the twisted stubs of cigarettes rejected before they were half smoked, which moved his grey eyes in a ceaseless, restless questing about the room [...].[37]

Johnston probably based Hepper on the ATC pilots he met as a war correspondent covering 'The Hump.' He also appears to have been his dry run, so to speak, at writing about these unsung heroes. In 1960, the same year he began his fifth Professor Challis novel, **A Wake for Mourning** (1962), Johnston also started another book, **The Far Face of the Moon** (1965),[38] which drew heavily on his wartime experiences and was "dedicated, with respect, to those many young men of the Air Transport Command, who once upon a time risked, and in many cases gave, their lives flying 'The Hump' out of North Assam."[39] Unfortunately, its male protagonist, the English reporter Jacob Strickland, was not a rough diamond like Hepper. However, its female protagonist, the Hollywood entertainer Jane Carson, was like Frenzy Talmadge in **A Wake for Mourning**. Finally, it is worth noting that, while they were completely different in many respects, Hepper and Jack Meredith, the brother of David Meredith in **My Brother Jack** (1964), were similar in that they both served in World War II and struggled to find their feet in civilian life.

Speculating where a character's name came from is an amusing game. So I wonder whether George Johnston borrowed the name Hepper from the English artist William Sanchez de Pina

Hepper (1892-1954), who was found guilty of the rape and murder of eleven-year-old Margaret Spevick and hanged in 1954? Suggestively, perhaps, the combination of Latin given names and this German surname was rather unusual. Since Hepper's trial dominated English newspaper headlines for much of that year, Johnston would have been well aware of him. (**Fig. 89**) The case might have even brought back memories of the murder of Molly Dean involving his friend, the Australian artist Colin Colahan (see the chapter on **Twelve Girls in the Garden**).

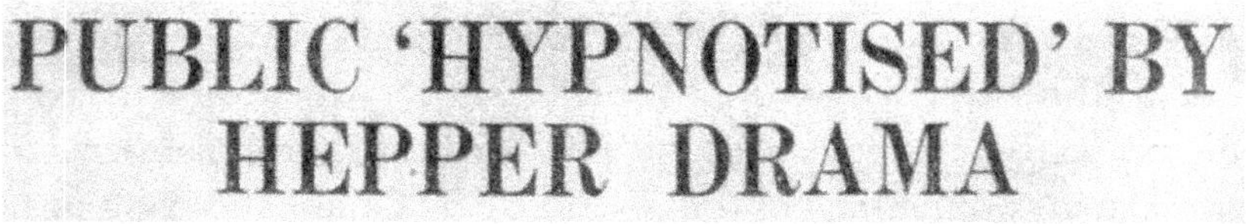

PUBLIC 'HYPNOTISED' BY HEPPER DRAMA

Fig. 89 Headline from **The Daily Mail**, 4 May 1954.

Reviews

Like **Twelve Girls in the Garden**, **The Myth is Murder** or **The Third Statue** was reviewed widely in the USA, less in the UK, and not in Australia. As they did not publish the two previous Challis novels in the USA, American book reviewers thought **The Myth is Murder** was the second instead of the fourth in the series. Thus, the **Tulsa World** in Oklahoma said, "Shane Martin's last novel was **Twelve Girls in the Garden**."[40] The **Daily Press** in Virginia wrote, "Greece is setting for archaeologist Ronald Challis's second adventure."[41] And the **News Tribune** in Tacoma, Washington, described the Professor as "a newcomer,"[42] despite having four cases under his belt.

As was customary then, many reviews of **The Myth is Murder** consisted of only three or four lines. Nevertheless, some were amusingly colourful. For example, the **Daily Press** described Edith Ordway as "Yank lady professor who packs gat."[43]

248

The Myth is Murder received generally good reviews. "An absorbing novel in which suspense-filled incident and polished story-telling lead hand-in-hand to a provocative climax,"[44] said Ruth Smith of the **Orlando-Sentinel** in Florida. Likewise, the **Wichita Falls Times** in Texas said, "A meatier than average mystery involving an archaeologist and a search for the lost cave of Phidias."[45] But some were critical. For example, the **Times Literary Supplement** thought, "Mr. Shane Martin uses words excellently, but he uses too many of them for too little story."[46]

Many reviewers praised the Greek setting of **The Myth is Murder**. For example, John T. Osborne of the **Rutland Daily Herald** in Vermont wrote, "A good plot and the Grecian setting make a refreshingly different mystery story."[47] While Maurice Richardson of the **Observer** in London, England, said, "Mr. Martin is holding up nicely as the poor man's Hellenic Cruise."[48] However, it was not all smooth sailing. Richardson also criticised **The Myth is Murder** for being "drily written."[49] Avis DeVoto of the **Boston Globe** in Massachusetts believed it was excessively wordy.[50] And the **Daily Press** said the "stage is overloaded."[51] While the **Oakland Tribune** in California damned **The Myth is Murder** with faint praise: "This is a mystery, of sorts, that will probably be of more interest to the classical scholar or the student of archaeology than to the avid reader of who-done-its."[52]

After writing four Professor Challis novels in three years, George Johnston had a break from his archaeologist-detective for a few months before starting the fifth and final Challis novel, **A Wake for Mourning**, in late 1960.

Endnotes

[1] Before we discover his name in **The Myth is Murder** (1959), Mark Glassop is known as "the man in the Mykonos shirt." Similarly, before we learn his name in **Closer to the Sun** (1960), Clem Kettering is identified as "a lesser man, wearing a Mykonos shirt." It is yet another example of Johnston trying something in a Challis novel first and then using it in another book later. See George Johnston, **Closer to the Sun**, London: Collins, 1960, p. 74.

[2] Shane Martin (George Johnston), **The Myth is Murder**, London: Collins, 1959, p. 15.

[3] Garry Kinnane, **George Johnston: A Biography**, Melbourne: Nelson Publishers, 1986, p. 174.

[4] Dan Milligan (Pupil of James Hill), Email to Derham Groves, 4 August 2023.

[5] Shane Martin, Dedication, unpaged.

[6] Ioanna Ralli (Nino and Despina Famikades's daughter-in-law), Interview with Derham Groves, 3 September 2020.

[7] The Australian Embassy of Greece, Email to Derham Groves, 7 September 2020.

[8] George Johnston, **Clean Straw for Nothing**, London: Collins, 1969, p. 175.

[9] Ibid., pp. 120-121.

[10] Garry Kinnane, p. 137.

[11] Ibid., p. 139.

[12] Ibid.

[13] Garry Kinnane, p. 142.

[14] George Hatzismalis (Officer, Kalymnos Tourist Office), Email to Derham Groves, 6 September 2023.

[15] George Johnston, **Clean Straw for Nothing**, p. 37.

[16] Charmian Clift and George Johnston, **The Sponge Divers**, London: Collins, 1955, pp. 19-20.

[17] Shane Martin, pp. 46-47.

[18] Ibid., p. 47.

[19] Venia Vogiatzi (Curator, National Historical Museum), Email to Derham Groves, 16 September 2023.

20 Shane Martin, p. 100.

21 Ibid., pp. 180-181.

22 Ibid., pp. 101-102.

23 Arthur Conan Doyle, **The Lost World**, London: Hodder and Stoughton, n.d. (1912), pp. 32-33.

24 Shane Martin, p. 136.

25 Ibid., p. 45.

26 Ibid., p. 17.

27 Ibid., p. 34.

28 John Huston (Director), **The Maltese Falcon**, Warner Bros., 1941.

29 Shane Martin, p. 55.

30 'Mysteries Solved By Slick Sleuths,' **Philadelphia Enquirer**, 17 May 1959, p. 89.

31 Maurice Vinter, 'Novel Set in Assam,' **Sydney Morning Herald** (Sydney, Australia), 13 March 1965, p. 15.

32 Shane Martin, p. 64.

33 George H. Johnston, 'Giant Smuggling Ring Smashed: Contraband Flown Over "The Hump" to China,' **Argus** (Melbourne, Australia). 18 December 1944, p. 16.

34 Shane Martin, p. 65.

35 Ibid. pp. 56-57.

36 Ibid., p. 61.

37 Ibid., p. 9.

38 Garry Kinnane, p. 189.

39 George Johnston, 'Author's Note,' **The Far Side of the Moon**, London: Collins, 1965, unpaged.

40 'Island Intrigue,' **Tulsa World** (Tulsa, Oklahoma), 12 July 1959, p. 87.

41 'Crime Corner: **The Third Statue**. By Shane Martin. Morrow. $3.50,' **Daily Press** (Newport News, Virginia) 19 July 1959, p. 46.

42 '**The Third Statue**. By Shane Martin. Morrow,' **News Tribune**, (Tacoma, Washington), 26 April 1959, p. 66.

43 **Daily Press**.

44 Ruth Smith, 'Books New and Good: The Third Statue — by Shane Martin [Morrow — $3.50]. **Orlando-Sentinel** (Orlando, Florida), 24 April 1959, p. 34.

45 **Wichita Falls Times** (Wichita Falls, Texas), 2 August 1959, p. 65.

46 'Cosmopolitan Crime,' **Times Literary Supplement**, 29 May 1959, p. 326.

47 John T. Osborne, 'Books for Vermonters,' **Rutland Daily Herald** (Rutland, Vermont), 12 May 1959, p. 4.

48 Maurice Richardson, 'Crime Ration: **The Myth is Murder**. By Shane Martin (Collins. 10s 6d),' **Observer** (London, UK), 31 May 1959, p. 24.

49 Ibid.

50 Avis DeVoto, 'The Third Statue,' by Shane Martin: Morrow,' **Boston Globe** (Boston, Massachusetts), 10 May 1959, p. 93.

51 **Daily Press**.

52 'The Third Statue,' by Shane Martin, William Morrow and Co., N.Y., $3.50,' **Oakland Tribune** (Oakland, California), 21 June 1959, p. 107.

(5) MOURNER'S JOURNEY
(I)
✓ Challis pp. 1-2
Naples architecture pp. 1-2.
Challis was bored so captain
Sam Brewster came to his rescue p. 2.
✓ Challis p. 3.
Galleria p. 3.
                Josephine
Miss Portland p. 3.
Scott Fitzgerald & Irwin Shaw p. 4.
Josephine Portland has been
hired as private secretary and
Professor Challis as "custodian
✓ of culture ... Advisor on classical
antiquities. p. 4.
Tony Saben pp. 4-5.
Challis drinking with Portland
at the Corelle's cafe. p. 6.
Description of man next to challis
who is shot pp. 4, 6-7.
Description of the Galleria pp. 6-7.
Sam Brewster p. 8.
(II)
→ Description of the Meltemi pp. 9.-10
Josephine Portland p. 10.
Tony Saben p. 10.
Sam Brewster p. 11
Giuseppe Simione and his
wife pp. 11-12.

"Meltemi" a type
of wind in Greek.

Plate 6 Page from Derham Groves' notebook.

5. A Wake for Mourning

A Wake for Mourning *(1962) by George Johnston/Shane Martin is the fifth, the final, and arguably the edgiest Professor Challis novel. It takes place on a schooner cruising the Mediterranean over a week in July 1960. Collins published it in the UK and Doubleday in the USA as* **Mourners' Voyage** *(1963). However, yet again, no Australian edition was published. Second-hand copies are difficult to find. Indeed, I have never seen a copy of the English edition. A summary follows, with comments, opinions, and reviews later.*

Dramatis Personae

Professor Ronald Challis	An archaeologist and amateur detective.
Sam Brewster	The captain of the *Meltemi*.
Petros	Brewster's deckhand.
Tony Saben	A shady playboy who charters the *Meltemi*.
Josephine Portland	Saben's temporary private secretary.
Major Vancouter	Saben's business adviser and lawyer.
Willard Xavier Crestfall	Saben's personal adviser and style consultant.
'Drips' Faversham	Saben's yes-man and jester.
Bullbeat	Saben's strong arm and gopher.
T. Curtis 'Dizzy' Brandenburg	A journalist writing an article about Saben.
Rudy Callahan	Brandenburg's mentor, murdered by Saben.
Giuseppe Simione	A New York gangster, also murdered by Saben.
Veronica 'Frenzy' Talmadge	An exotic dancer and mistress of Simione and Saben.
Thorold Shackleton	Simione's stock broker.
Angelo Tintolli	Kastókos's mayor, magistrate, school teacher, Socialist Party secretary, and vet.

Chapter I

The American gangster and playboy, Tony Saben, is chartering Captain Sam Brewster's schooner, *Meltemi*, for a Mediterranean cruise with six associates. Saben needs a private secretary and a tour guide on the cruise, so Brewster hires two friends, momentarily both bored and at loose ends — the young and beautiful Josephine Portland and the old and queer-looking Professor Ronald Challis.

The four shipmates agree to meet at Corelli's Café in the Galleria Umberto in Naples to discuss arrangements for the cruise. (**Fig. 90**) Portland and Challis arrive first. While they have never met, she recognises him from Brewster's succinct description of the Professor, "Sixtyish, about as big as your thumb, white hair all over the place, mischievous eyes — rather like a delinquent pixie."

Fig. 90 Galleria Umberto (1891), Naples (recent photograph)

At the adjoining table, a large man in a beige suit with a briefcase and a TWA airline bag takes up more than his fair share of room, forcing Challis to move his chair twice. Suddenly, a shot fired from a first-floor window hits him in the back, causing the man to slump against the Professor before collapsing on the floor and causing a commotion in the cafe. Two policemen arrive and take the man to hospital. However, Challis suspects he is already dead.

"I should be very grateful that whoever shot him was a good marksman," says the Professor wryly. "There couldn't be more than a few inches between his shoulder and mine."

"Well, hello, you two," says Brewster, arriving late and unaware of what occurred. "I must say, you look subdued. What's the matter? Not hitting it off?" When they tell him about the shooting, he puts it down to "Good old Napoli! These beggars are always at that sort of thing." Suspiciously, Saben never shows up for the meeting.

Chapter II

The next day aboard the *Meltemi,* Sam Brewster wants to brief Josephine Portland and Professor Challis before Tony Saben and his party arrive, but the Professor is running late. Brewster is still annoyed with Tony Saben for not turning up at Corelli's Café yesterday because he had to arrange Saben's friends' passports and papers at the port authority without his help. "You can imagine the trouble I could have had at Customs with this damned thing!" says Brewster, taking a white porcelain urn shaped like a cider jar from a cupboard and showing it to Portland. "It contains the ashes of Saben's friend Giuseppe Simione (1924-1960). My booking agent looked up some old newspaper articles about him. Simione was murdered in Riverside Drive, New York, six months ago. I'm sure you're pleased to know we have a Customs clearance for his remains. I described them on the manifest as a jar of best quality antifouling boottopping." (**Fig. 91**)

Fig. 91 Giuseppe Simione's ashes (left) and
a tin of antifouling boottopping.

Challis is half an hour late after having a busy morning. He visited Corelli's Café once again, showed the police where the shot had come from, helped them locate the spent shell on the floor of the office of the Calabrian Group for Peasant Reform, and found nearby a book of matches from the Golden Flute Cabaret Bar, wherever that is, he wonders. Since the police had no interest in the matchbook, Challis discreetly pocketed it. He also confirmed the victim, an American named Giuseppe Simione, was dead.

"I think there has been some mistake," says Portland, somewhat puzzled. "Because Giuseppe Simione is in a white jar in that cupboard."

"There's something very queer about all this," says Brewster. Challis advises him to say nothing at all to Saben about this.

Chapter III

Later that morning, Tony Saben and his party board the *Meltemi*. Major Vancouter is Saben's legal adviser. Willard Crestfall is his personal adviser and style consultant. T. Curtis 'Dizzy' Brandenburg is a journalist writing an article on Saben. 'Drips' Faversham is Saben's yes-man and court jester. Bullbeat is his strong arm and gopher. And Veronica 'Frenzy' Talmage is his sometime girlfriend.

"The main thing to be clear about is that you'll be under my orders," Saben tells Brewster. "I tell you what to do and where to go, and you take us there. Check?" Brewster agrees so long as it will not jeopardise the safety of the *Meltemi*.

Josephine Portland turns heads when she appears on deck with coffee for everyone, while Vancouter insults Professor Challis by warning him not to expect any tips on the cruise. "I'm quite confident you'll have no cause for complaint, Mr. Vancouter," says the Professor servilely, not wishing to rock the boat just yet. "I know I'll give you entirely satisfactory service."

Chapter IV

After the *Meltemi* sets sail, Professor Challis sums up Tony Saben's associates with fishy analogies. "Vancouter — something hairy and horrible. Faversham — jellyfish. Frenzy — a clinging creature, extremely beautiful and possibly dangerous, like a sea anemone. Bullbeat — barracuda. Crestfall — whale. And Brandenburg — fish out of water." Challis is looking for a possible source of information among them and decides that Curtis Brandenburg is his best bet.

In the meantime, Sam Brewster's dislike for his passengers steadily mounts. He thinks Josephine Portland is far too interested in Saben, and he does not like what Major Vancouter said to the Professor. But as Challis suspects there is some connection between Saben, the shooting last night of the man — whoever he was — and the urn of ashes on board — whoever they belong to — the Professor tells Brewster he prefers they see him as "some stupid little third-rate hack of a professional guide."

Since Brewster still does not know where Saben wants to go, he asks, "Would you like to go over the chart with me?"

"Where we go, for the moment, is quite immaterial to me," says Sabin before rolling over on his stomach and sunbaking on the deck.

Chapter V

Professor Challis finds Curtis Brandenburg alone on deck and subtly pumps him for information. He tells the Professor he is writing a feature article about Tony Saben for the New York magazine **Viewpoint**, which explains why he is not as close to him as the others.

In the old days, Saben would have been brutal, original, rough, and vulgar like Al Capone (1899-1947) or John Dillinger (1903-1934). "But nowadays, he has to be all smoothed out and polished up," says Brandenburg. "Last year, they judged him one of America's best-dressed men. **Life** wrote about his collection of paintings by Pierre Bonnard (1867-1947). And **Esquire** interviewed him about fine food and wine. How do you like that?" (**Fig. 92**)

Fig. 92 (L-R) Al Capone, John Dillinger, and Pierre Bonnard.

When Challis has Brandenburg in the mood to talk, he takes a risk and asks, "On the subject of violence, what is Saben's connection with Giuseppe Simione?"

"What do you know about Simione?" says Brandenburg warily.

"Well, I know we have his ashes on board," says the Professor. "I know we are taking them on a sort of pilgrimage somewhere. That is why I asked."

"If I were you, I'd wait for the wake," advises Brandenburg, who is onto the Professor.

> Suppose we stop trying to kid each other. I went to Harvard, too. So I know about your work and have even read one or two of your books. I also know about your hobbies — the Grosteller case and the Rocamadour Reliefs business. Let's leave it at that for the moment. Maybe tonight sometime we could get together. Right now, we'd better discuss something else because here comes Vancouter, Mr. Trouble.

Chapter VI

Without a destination, Sam Brewster and his deckhand Petros aimlessly sails the *Meltemi* to-and-fro while Tony Saben and his cronies drunkenly party, and Professor Challis hatches a plan. The Professor finds Josephine Portland alone in the ship's tiny galley, struggling to grill ten steaks for everyone's dinner. He wants her to question Saben about Giuseppe Simone when she sees him later, but without mentioning the shooting at Corelli's Café. Then Challis finds Brewster lying in his bunk and reading a copy of **The Rudder**. (**Fig. 93**) "Sam, I have a hunch," says the Professor.

"Ah, I was waiting for this," says Brewster sceptically. Challis asks him to play along with Saben and the others for the time being, but before he can say anymore, they hear a strange noise on deck and go to investigate. It is Drips Faversham playing his clarinet.

Fig. 93 Cover of the July 1960 edition of **The Rudder** (1891-1977).

Playfully, Frenzy takes the Professor in her arms and hugs him tightly to her breast. "For Pete's sake, Frenzy, you'll kill the poor guy," says Saben.

Frenzy suggests someone should take a photo of her and Challis, who she calls 'Poppet.' "Can't you see it in a swell gilt frame there, back of the bar in the Golden Flute," jokes Bullbeat, which upsets Faversham and causes a fight, resulting in his clarinet going overboard. When things finally calm down, Challis and Curtis Brandenburg sneak off to the bow for a quiet chat.

Chapter VII

Curtis Brandenburg takes Professor Challis into his confidence because they might be able to help each other. Brandenburg is a sort of double agent, pretending to be on the side of Tony Saben but wanting to nail him for murder. "Saben and Giuseppe Simione were partners in all kinds of nefarious activities — blackmail, drugs, gambling, oil, politics, vice, you name it," explains Brandenburg. "But the year before last, Simione had a change of heart, travelling to the island of Kastókos, where he was born, to give the poor villagers money and build them a new church for the Virgin Mary. When he returned to New York, he wanted to end their partnership, so Saben killed him."

Furthermore, Brandenburg's mentor, the crusading New York journalist Rudy Callahan, was beaten up and stabbed in a back street in Greenwich Village. "They said Puerto Ricans murdered Callahan, but I know Saben was behind it," says Brandenburg.

"Wait!" whispers Challis, suddenly sensing they are not alone. Sleeping in a hammock below the bowsprit is Major Vancouter.

"Suppose he heard," says Brandenburg before walking off without saying another word.

"There are always some guys who talk too much," says Vancouter ominously, still lying in the hammock.

Chapter VIII

Josephine Portland feels uncomfortable sharing sleeping quarters with three men — Sam Brewster, Petros, and Professor Challis. "I assure you I don't like undressing in Grand Central Station," she tells Brewster.

"One thing I must say — you look awfully decorative down there," says Brewster unhelpfully. "I've had females on cruises before — for the cooking. None of them looked in the least like you." But then later, he hits the roof when she tells him Tony Saben is happy for her to share a cabin with Frenzy. "Of all the confounded impertinence!" says Brewster jealous of Saben. "I've never heard of such brazen cheek in all my life!"

Chapter IX

The next day is perfect for sailing. Still unsure of their destination, Sam Brewster heads south for Sicily. Then, at eleven a.m., Tony Saben announces, "I want to buy a newspaper, Captain. A Rome newspaper. In English. The latest."

"I don't see a kiosk about," says Brewster sarcastically.

"Drop the wise-guy business, Brewster," says Saben angrily. "I don't pay out two hundred bucks a day plus extras just for the fun of listening to your cracks." Suitably chastened, Brewster sails for Palermo.

Chapter X

Professor Challis wants to contact Curtis Brandenburg to warn him that Major Vancouter heard at least some of their conversations last night, but he gets no response when he knocks on his cabin door. Perhaps Brandenburg is seasick, thinks the Professor. Or he is afraid to come out. Or Vancouter and company are holding him prisoner. Seeing Challis snooping around their sleeping quarters, Willard Crestfall tells him to mind his business and go away.

In the meantime, Tony Saben gives Sam Brewster new instructions about Palermo. Brewster will drop anchor outside the breakwater, and Petros will take the dinghy and drop Saben ashore to buy a newspaper. "If I refuse, all Saben has to do is sue me for breach of contract," Brewster tells the Professor.

"It is obvious Saben wants this newspaper because of the shooting in the Galleria Umberto," says Challis.

"I thought of that, too," says Brewster. "He tried to feed me a line about stock market reports."

Challis has already begun to solve the mystery. "Kastókos, that's where we're going," he tells Brewster. "But you will be told in due course, don't worry. I also discovered they all know about the Golden Flute. I believe it is where Frenzy performs her tassel dances."

"For God's sake, what is it all about?" begs Brewster.

"All I'm prepared to say is that it isn't peanuts," says Challis.

Chapter XI

At seven p.m., the *Meltemi* anchors off the coast of Palermo, the loveliest headland in the world according to the German poet Goethe (1749-1832), says Professor Challis. (**Fig. 94**) "Suppose we skip the scholastic notes and get this guy Petros organised," says Tony Saben.

Since Saben does not speak Greek, he asks Challis to give Petros his instructions. But the Professor also tells him to pick up another newspaper without Saben knowing. About an hour later, they return to the *Meltemi* in the dinghy. "Where to now?" asks Brewster.

"Just head out," says Saben. "But I'd like to look at the charts with you in your cabin later." Just as Challis predicted, Saben tells Brewster to sail for Kastókos. Although it will take about three days, Saben wants to travel there non-stop.

"The normal practice is for us to put in at ports here and there to pick up fresh provisions and water," says Brewster.

Fig. 94 The bluff of Monte Pellegrino, Palermo.

"Hell, we can do all that at Kastókos," protests Saben.

"It's a very out-of-the-way place," says Brewster. And very primitive. We won't be able to get much there. But it's your charter, Mr. Saben. I guess we'll get by."

Chapter XII

Sam Brewster, Josephine Portland, and Professor Challis read of the shooting at Corelli's Café in the newspaper smuggled aboard by Petros before the Professor gives his latest thoughts on the mystery. "Mr. X, the man shot at Corelli's, was hostile to Saben and his cronies, so they lured him to the café to kill him," he says.

> What could be easier than to leak our meeting about visiting Giuseppe Simione's birthplace to him? Mr. X comes to the café and identifies me and Miss Portland by the descriptions of us someone gave him, but while eavesdropping on our conversation, he is shot dead. But then something happens that

makes getting to Kastókos a matter of urgency. I suspect it was when Saben read the newspaper in Palermo and learned that Mr. X was masquerading as Simione. Curtis Brandenburg might be able to tell me the identity of Mr. X, but nobody has seen him for thirteen hours. He is very seasick, so they say, and Faversham and Bullbeat have moved in with Frenzy to leave him alone in the cabin. But they may have roughed him up to make him talk.

Chapter XIII

The *Meltemi* meets with gale-force winds and rough seas upon rounding the Cape San Vito, so Captain Brewster does the rounds of the ship to check everything is fast and secure when he sees a dark figure on the weather side of the deck, clutching the forward shrouds. (**Fig. 95**)

Fig. 95 The *Stormie Seas* – the model for the *Meltemi*.

"What the hell are you doing here?" demands Brewster. "You'll go overboard, you fool!" It is Major Vancouter, looking for Curtis Brandenburg, who cannot be found anywhere and might have gone overboard in the rough weather. Brewster orders a thorough search of the *Meltemi* but to no avail. Afterward, he has a private tete-a-tete with Professor Challis. "Look, the last thing I want is to appear dramatic, but I have to ask you this. Is it possible they did this to him? After all, nothing could be easier." However, they are interrupted by Vancouter, Willard Crestfall, and Tony Saben, who object to returning to Palermo to report Brandenburg's disappearance.

"You'll report it in the ship's log, and we'll send details by telegram from Kastókos," orders Saben. "I still want to get there as quickly as possible." Since they can do nothing for the missing man, and Challis wants Brewster to play along with Saben, Brewster reluctantly agrees before he and the Professor collect Brandenburg's things and go through them. But the others may have already done that.

According to his airline ticket, Brandenburg flew from New York to Italy on TWA flight six-eight-two on Friday, 11 July — probably the same flight as Mr. X, surmises the Professor — while on the back of the ticket, Brandenburg wrote, "Shackleton — Hotel Vulcan, via Sistina, 32." Also among his belongings, they find some match-books from the Golden Flute Cabaret Bar, but not his passport or cash and traveller's cheques. "Now, can you imagine an American travelling in Italy without a passport or any money?" asks the Professor sceptically.

Chapter XIV

The next day, the sea is rough, but the wind has eased. Despite the futility of it, Sam Brewster and Professor Challis search the *Meltemi* again for Curtis Brandenburg, but still to no avail. Then Brewster writes a straightforward report and takes it to Tony Saben.

"I'd like you to sign it as the charterer and Major Vancouter as a witness," says Brewster. "I'll post copies of the report to the United States Consul in Rome and the Italian Maritime Police from the first port we call at."

"The first port after Kastókos, you mean Captain," says Saben. "I hope you understand that very clearly."

Brewster agrees. "You wouldn't have any clues about Brandenburg's next of kin?" he asks.

"He was a stranger to us," says Saben. "His editor suggested he should come. I do not wish to be hard-hearted, but the guy is gone, and I cannot get too worked up about it. On other matters, I would like to see Challis later. I want to make use of him. And about Miss Portland. I have decided she had better share the cabin with Frenzy. She feels a bit low and would appreciate the company."

"I formed the impression she had company already," says Brewster sarcastically, referring to Faversham and Bullbeat.

"Those two bums shifted back to where they were," says Saben. "I hadn't realised, Captain, that you were also responsible for morality on board the ship. But you have my guarantee they won't bother Miss Portland."

Chapter XV

Professor Challis meets with Tony Saben, Major Vancouter, and Willard Crestfall. "I asked Captain Brewster to hire someone who could speak Italian and Greek and knew the local geography and customs, and you got the job," says Saben.

> I want to discuss our visit to Kastókos. I understand you already know something of this from Brandenburg. But it might help if we were a little more frank about things than he was. Giuseppe Simione was our colleague, and we are taking his ashes back to Kastókos, his birthplace. But you

don't know he was a no-good, dirty, two-timing rat who cheated everyone, including the three of us. About two years ago, Simione visited Kastókos. You know the drill — rich man returns to the scene of humble origins. But he hid a million and a quarter dollars somewhere on the island because he saw that things might eventually go against him in New York. Since he died before he could return to collect it, the hoard is still there — a lot in cash and jewellery, but the bulk in bonds and securities.

"Why are you telling me this?" asks the Professor.

"We need this ship to get to Kastókos, and we need you to act as our go-between," answers Saben. "Very simple, I'd say."

Afterward, Brewster asks Challis how it went. "Splendidly!" he says. "They told me almost everything! Now, all we have to do is work out how much of it is true. They seem to think the money isn't Simione's but theirs. But in a sense, nobody has a legal claim to it. Indeed, I'll lay you even money now that I'm the one who gets it!"

"Well, if you aren't the most incredible, immoral, interfering, and unscrupulous old bastard!" says Brewster. "What now?" Challis thinks Josephine Portland should move in with Frenzy and try to discover a few things from her.

"Such as?" asks Brewster.

"I'd like to find out who Shackleton is," says the Professor. "He might be Mr. X. I'd also like to know more about a New York newspaperman named Rudy Callahan. He's dead, and I think Saben was responsible, but I would like to know for certain."

Even though Brewster disapproves of the move, Josephine Portland is determined to share the cabin with Frenzy. "This may be a man's world, Captain Brewster, but I think it's time for a salient female," says Portland. "You're too domineering, that's the trouble!"

Chapter XVI

In the afternoon, Josephine Portland moves into the cabin with Frenzy. Tony Saben, Major Vancouter, Willard Crestfall, Drips Faversham, and Bullbeat play poker on deck. Sam Brewster cleans the guns he keeps on board while Professor Challis watches him. There are two revolvers — a Luger and a Colt — a double-barrelled twelve-bore shotgun, and a Remington automatic .303 rifle. "A useful little arsenal," remarks the Professor. (**Fig. 96**)

Fig. 96 Sam Brewster's "useful little arsenal."

Frenzy and Josephine Portland have a girl-to-girl chat in their cabin. "I've slept around with the whole bunch of them, from Tony down to Drips," she tells Portland. "No, not with Mister Crestfall … believe me, I can draw the line somewhere, too!" Frenzy took the disappearance of Curtis Brandenburg badly because, contrary to what Tony Saben told Sam Brewster, she has known him "since God knows. We went around a bit together once."

Saben arrives and orders Frenzy up on deck. He makes a move on Portland that "startles her by being not entirely unpleasant." Saben asks her to act as his confidential secretary, someone he can trust. "You see, you can be useful to me," he tells Portland. "Maybe you might even be necessary to me. Let me tell you something, Miss Portland. That guy Brandenburg — he didn't go over the side by accident. Someone on this ship pushed him over. And we're going to find out who that someone was. So you're going to tell me, in confidence, anything you hear from these others, aren't you?"

Then Frenzy bursts in, senses something is perhaps afoot, and orders Saben out. "You keep out of this," Frenzy warns Portland afterward. "Don't get yourself mixed up in this."

Chapter XVII

With the *Meltemi* sailing steadily for Kastókos, everyone settles into sunbaking, reading, fishing, drinking, and dozing, almost like any other cruising party, but for the anxiety of all on board. Yet there are some details Professor Challis still might clear up. So he locates Captain Brewster in the after-cabin. "Open that locker, and let's look at Mr. Simione's urn," Challis tells Brewster. "If we break the wax seal, do you have anything on board that might simulate it?"

"We have a plastic caulking compound that might do the trick," says Brewster. "But you can't be serious! For heaven's sake, it would be like grave-robbing!"

"Don't be tiresome," says Challis before breaking the seal with a knife and turning the urn upside-down. "Voila!"

"Empty!" declares Brewster. "What's the point if there's nothing in it?"

"Neither the urn nor Mr. X is Giuseppe Simione," says the Professor. "One is an empty ... pickle jar, and I think the other is a New York stockbroker named Shackleton. But we mustn't let Tony Saben and the others know we're aware this is just a blind. Now you'd better get that caulking compound."

Chapter XVIII

Professor Challis makes sure the charterers are occupied on deck before he enters Tony Saben's cabin on the pretext of making up the bunks but really to look around. He opens a drawer and removes a pigskin briefcase containing letters, papers, and a cutting from the **Rome-American** headed, 'MYSTERY SURROUNDING NAPLES KILLING.' As the Professor sits and reads them, Saben bursts in, rushing him from behind and flinging him against a bunk. "What the hell are you up to?" snarls Saben.

"I was making up the bunks," says the Professor. "Or that was what I was supposed to be doing. But I'm an incorrigible stickybeak, I'm afraid."

"What are you looking for, Challis?" asks Saben.

"I thought I might find poor Brandenburg's passport and traveller's cheques," says the Professor. "I also wanted to check on Shackleton. Was he Simione's stockbroker? And the one murdered in the Galleria?"

"Thorold Shackleton was a two-timing bastard," says Saben.

I planned this deal a year ago to look after all of Simione's victims. Not just the big losers like me, Crestfall, and that goddam Shackleton. But also the little people like Frenzy and Faversham. It didn't occur to me then that where money is concerned, guys like Shackleton don't like sharing. He wanted to play it his way. The rest of us went ahead with the deal as planned. The problem was to find out where Simione had hidden the loot on Kastókos. So, I came up with idea of returning his ashes to the island to get in the locals' good books. Shackleton arrived in Italy. Somehow, he had gotten hold of Simione's passport. Shackleton was nosing in, doing it his way. However, something happened, and someone murdered him in Naples. But I knew nothing about it — and I like to know what is happening. Then Vancouter overheard you talking to Brandenburg, so I spoke to him. OK, maybe I roughed him up a little. Anyway, I first learned about Shackleton's murder from him. Then he disappeared over the side. The way I see it, that was no goddam accident. That guy didn't fall. Somebody who didn't care for what Brandenburg knew pushed him. Somebody aboard this ship, Challis.

However, the Professor is sceptical about Saben's innocence. "How could Brandenburg have known about the shooting since there was nothing in the Naples newspapers before they left," asks Challis, besides pointing out that Saben has as good a motive to kill Shackleton and Brandenburg as anyone else — over a million dollars.

Finally, Saben proposes he, Challis, and Josephine Portland scout Kastókos first before the others follow. "Why should you take Miss Portland," asks the Professor.

"It could be I just like the dame," says Saben.

Chapter XIX

The Meltemi drops anchor in a little cove about a mile west of Kastókos. Petros rows Tony Saben, Professor Challis, and Josephine Portland to the shore in the dinghy, then returns to the ship. It is hot and dry. As they pass through thorny undergrowth and an ill-tended olive grove, Challis feels someone is watching them, stealthily moving from tree to tree. After walking almost three miles, they see Kastókos ahead:

> The houses were mostly block-shaped, cubes and prisms, sun-glaring, eye-aching planes of whitewashed plaster under the fierce sun, scattered around sandy streets, parched gardens, and scraggy orchards, spreading back into more dispersed farm properties at the one extremity and huddling into a tight, almost urban compactness at the end abutting the harbour.

"Do you want to go into the town?" asks Challis.

Since everyone is taking a siesta and nothing appears open, Saben elects to return to the ship. "This is what I primarily came for," says Saben, his bravado gone. "I just wanted an idea of the layout of the place. It is quite a bit bigger than I thought it would be." As they head back, someone starts shooting at them, hitting Saben in the left arm. As he appears to be the gunman's target, Challis tells him and Portland to take cover and stay put while he tries to make it to the beach, but the gunman shoots at him, too, and has them pinned down. The Professor believes he knows who it is.

Chapter XX

When Petros returns to the *Meltemi*, the others demand he take them ashore, too. Major Vancourter and Willard Crestfall take their guns, hoping to shoot a quail or two, while Drips Faversham, Bullbeat, and Frenzy want to sunbathe on the beach. So Petros obligingly drops them on Kastókos and rows back to the ship. But after not seeing or hearing from anyone on the island for more than four hours, Sam Brewster starts to worry. "Where the devil are they," he wonders. "Keep an eye on things," he tells Petros. "I'm taking the dingy ashore."

It does not take long before Brewster discovers the body of Vancourter, stretched out flat on his back with his arms flung wide, one knee bent, his eyes open, and his gun nowhere to be seen. (**Fig. 97**) Brewster can do nothing for him, so he returns to the *Meltemi* to get his rifle and Petros and comes back. They push Vancourter's body down to the beach, wrap it in canvas, and Petros takes it back to the ship.

Brewster wanders into the olive grove and shouts Portland's name. She hears him, but Saben stops her from answering. "You just keep quiet!" he says. "Let him get closer. A diversion is what we need. He'll draw this other bastard's fire, and we can make a break for it." But Portland refuses to play along, screaming, "Take cover, Sam!" The gunman shoots, grazing Saben on the left temple this time and knocking him out. In the meantime, Brewster and

Fig. 97 The body of Major Vancouter.

Professor Challis dash to where Portland and Saben are hiding. "Look after him," Brewster tells them. "I'll try to break this up." He fires twice at the gunman, forcing him to break cover. "He's running out," cries Brewster. "You two stay here."

Brewster searches the olive grove but only finds two spent rifle shells. "Best we get out of here," he says on his return. "This is no place to loiter, and Saben needs some attention." They find Faversham, Bullbeat, and Frenzy waiting impatiently on the beach, totally unaware of the drama that has just taken place. Brewster whistles for Petros to bring the dinghy.

Chapter XXI

After bandaging Tony Saben's wounds, Sam Brewster tells him, "The Professor and I propose to go ashore and look around. Then we're going into the port, regardless of whether Mr. Crestfall has returned, and hand the whole matter to the police."

As they clamber ashore, each armed with a rifle, Challis tells Brewster they are "dealing with a madman. Someone whose reason is impaired."

"Crestfall, you mean?" says Brewster.

"No, Brandenburg," replies the Professor. "He murdered Shackleton in Naples and had to come here to finish the job and kill the others, especially Saben."

"But Brandenburg went over the side," says Brewster.

"That's true," says Challis. "But of his own volition, right after Saben attacked him on the ship. Remember, it was standing off the breakwater at Palermo for nearly an hour. What could have been simpler for Brandenburg than to wrap his passport and traveller's cheques in plastic, put on his swimming trunks, go up on deck when nobody was looking, and swim ashore? He would have looked like any other foreign tourist strolling back from his evening dip. All he had to do then was buy some clothes, head to Kastókos, and wait for your big, beautiful, white schooner to show up."

Chapter XXII

Curtis Brandenburg watches Professor Challis and Sam Brewster from a thorny patch in the olive grove. He has the second-hand, long-barrelled Schneider rifle he bought in Brindisi on his way to Kastókos trained on them, but he doesn't shoot. (**Fig. 98**) Instead, he recalls his hatred of Tony Saben and affection for Frenzy.

> Poor, screwed-up Frenzy! The dame Saben had always treated like a used toothbrush. Frenzy, who'd always come running when he snapped his fingers. The dame he'd sleep with when it suited him and hand around among his bullies when it didn't, who he treated like dirt, and who kept on loving him. Still, Frenzy knew on which side her bread was buttered. She'd played her part damned well in Palermo — keeping those other jerks in the cabin, making sure the decks were clear so he could get up and away without anyone being the wiser. She was smart if you treated her right.

Brandenburg watches Challis and Brewster row back to the *Meltemi*, which then circles the cove at half-speed and heads to sea. Brandenburg tells himself to look for Crestfall and Vancourter.

Fig. 98 Curtis Brandenburg's second-hand, long-barrelled Schneider rifle.

Chapter XXIII

The *Meltemi* is in the harbour, Curtis Brandenburg is at large, and Willard Crestfall is missing. Professor Challis goes ashore to arrange a memorial ceremony for Giuseppe Simione with the Mayor of Kastókos, Angelo Tintolli. When he returns to the ship at around ten p.m., he tells Sam Brewster and Tony Saben that Simione's ashes will be buried at sea in the morning, leaving them tomorrow afternoon to find his money before the police from Otranto arrive in the evening. "No doubt you've located that too," says Brewster sarcastically.

"Oh, I've known for days," says Challis, explaining that for the person who discovered the Gournian Treasury, finding Simione's stash was child's play! According to the Professor, Simione imported his own hiding place.

> He presented the town of Kastókos with a new church. Simione was not a religious man, but he was a very cunning one, so he took the precaution of ensuring that the building of the new church was not a local enterprise, bringing the workers and materials across from the mainland. I had a look at it tonight. As a practising archaeologist, I think that is where I should dig.

Sam Brewster feels obliged to look for his missing passenger, Willard Crestfall, so he puts the outboard motor on the dinghy and, accompanied by Professor Challis, heads back to the cove where they found Major Vancourter's body earlier. Curtis Brandenburg watches them disembark from the high cliff on the town side of the bay. They search by moonlight, thinking it is safer to keep the torch off. "We've been taking it for granted that Brandenburg killed Vancourter," says Challis.

> But supposing he didn't. Don't you see, if Vancourter was ambushed and shot down here by Brandenburg, then Crestfall would have been shot down too. There's no cover here close enough for him to have reached. Perhaps Crestfall saw Brandenburg leave the ship and kept mum about it. Then he could do his own killing and conveniently, at the right moment, see that Brandenburg got blamed for it. I'm afraid we will need the flashlight.

The Professor sees the copper shell of a rifle bullet in the grass out of the corner of his eye. "Same calibre and make as the ones I found in the olive grove," says Brewster. They soon find Crestfall's body nearby, shot in the back below the left shoulder blade. "We can't get him up from there and drag him back," says Brewster. "We'd better tell Tintolli, and he can send a party out in the morning." As they walk towards the dinghy, they suddenly hear the sound of the outboard motor. "Brandenburg!" cries Challis.

Chapter XXIV

On the *Meltemi,* Frenzy is remorseful for helping Curtis 'Dizzy' Brandenburg. "Dizzy was kind, kinder than that damned Tony Saben ever was," she tells Josephine Portland. However, Frenzy now realises that Brandenburg deceived her. "They flew out together — Dizzy and Shackleton — did you know that?" she asks.

> And when Dizzy got me to get Tony to take us all around the nightspots so he would miss that meeting he had at the cafe in Naples, how was I to

know he wanted to get Shackleton there? I didn't know about it until later, here on the boat. I knew there was something crazy about the bastard then. He'd say things I didn't even know about, things I couldn't understand, about retribution, his pay-off, and a crusade that Rudy Callahan had begun, which he was going to finish. It was all crazy talk you couldn't make head or tail of.

"Don't worry about it, Frenzy," says Portland reassuringly. "You don't have to tear yourself to pieces about it now. You're not to blame. Brandenburg is out of his mind." Then she hears the outboard motor approaching the ship. "Listen, they're coming back!" she says happily. "Wait here. I'll meet them, and then I'll get you a sleeping pill."

Josephine Portland suspects something is wrong when the dinghy heads to the jetty instead of the *Meltemi*. "Why should Sam want to put in there?" she wonders, thinking perhaps he or the Professor has been hurt, or they found Crestfall dead and are taking his body to the shed behind the jetty. "Are you alright, Sam?" calls Portland.

In the meantime, Tony Saben, armed with his stubby Remington automatic, pushes past Portland and heads for the jetty. Curtis Brandenburg fires his rifle at him but misses in the dark. "Hold it there, Saben, where you are, clear against the sky," he orders. "I won't miss you this time, you son-of-a-bitch."

As Portland cautiously proceeds towards the jetty, both men fire their guns at each other. In the eerie silence that follows, she sees Saben lying dead on the planking, still holding his pistol, and Brandenburg lying face-up in the shallows, the barrel of his rifle leaning against the side of the dinghy.

Chapter XXV

Very early the next day, Professor Challis and Angelo Tintolli visit Giuseppe Simione's church and find the million and a quarter dollars he stashed there a year earlier under the foundation stone. The Professor asks the Mayor to take charge of the money to build "a good new school, a little hospital, a dam for the summer water, a medical clinic for the kids," etc. Later, Sam Brewster tells Challis what he thinks of his plan.

> A year from now, they'll all be fighting over the money. The Church, the municipality, and the Government will all want it. There will be aunts, uncles, cousins, and great-grandmothers, all named Simione, all lining up to claim it. There'll be Tintolli trying to grab it for the Socialist Party. While up there, on his marble plinth, Giuseppe Simione will be laughing his Carrara pants off!

"Yes, but some of it will get around, Sam," says the Professor optimistically. "Some of it will do some good."

Giuseppe Simione's memorial service is held onboard the *Meltemi* and watched by the residents of Kastókos packed on the quay. While they are somewhat bewildered by it all, "Everybody puts on his best for a wake," observes Professor Challis. Following stirring speeches by him and Tintolli, the Mayor ceremoniously throws the urn — supposedly containing Simione's ashes but filled with best-quality, anti-fouling boottopping to make it sink — into the sea.

THE END.

Comments, Opinions, Reviews

The Lucky Last

A Wake for Mourning was the fifth and final Professor Challis novel by George Johnston writing as Shane Martin, which he finished in early February 1961.[1] It was an Agatha Christie-style mystery with a twist — rather than a group of people isolated in an English country house, they were on a yacht cruising the Mediterranean. Furthermore, as they were packed on the ship like sardines with nowhere to go but overboard, it was the edgiest of the five Challis mysteries. The body count was also high for a Challis novel — (1) Thorold Shackleton, (2) Major Vancourter, (3) Willard Crestfall, (4) Tony Saben, and (5) Curtis Brandenburg.

Collins published **A Wake for Mourning** in the United Kingdom, but only after their crime fiction editor, Lord Hardinge of Penshurst (1921-1997) — renowned for spotting flaws in storylines no matter how small[2] — asked for changes to the novel, delaying the cash-strapped author receiving his advance from the publisher. (**Fig. 99**) In desperate need of money, Johnston "sent out an S.O.S." to Collins for three hundred pounds, which he received as a loan to avoid tax.[3]

When Collins was unhappy with the title **Press the Rue for Wine**, Johnston changed it to **The Saracen Shadow** (1958). Likewise, when Collins was displeased with the title **The Long Walls**, he changed it to **The Myth is Murder** (1959). So, whatever

Fig. 99 The formidable Lord Hardinge of Penshurst.

Collins disliked about **A Wake for Mourning**, it was presumably not the title, for a change. But, yet again, Johnston could not take a trick with the Challis novels as far as his biographer, Garry Kinnane, was concerned, who described **A Wake for Mourning** as "dreadfully titled."[4] Did he read the novel? What did Kinnane expect? The title is perfectly adequate for the story. It is also phonetically ironic — 'Awake for Morning.'

According to Kinnane, **A Wake for Mourning** "was, he [Johnston] knew, one of his worst 'Shane Martin' efforts, for which he could not find enough interest to make the changes Collins were demanding; in the end, they gave up and published it anyway."[5] Johnston may well have dragged his feet but allowing a novel that the very demanding Lord Hardinge thought "was awful,"[6] according to Kinnane, slip through does not sound like something he would have done to me. Frankly, Kinnane is so biased against the Challis novels that I find many of his comments about them open to doubt.

Instead of hiring William Randell to design the dust jacket again as he had done for the previous four Challis books, Collins hired another highly accomplished British illustrator, Barbara Walton, of whom not a lot is known either.[7] Besides Collins, she also worked for the British publishers Robert Hale and John Long, which both specialised in crime fiction. Walton's sister, Eileen, was also a talented and prolific dust jacket artist.

Barbara Walton's dust jacket for **A Wake for Mourning** depicted Sam Brewster looking for Josephine Portland and the Professor on Kastókos after he found Major Vancourter's body. (**Fig. 100**) It is a terrific image, showing Brewster holding a rifle and squinting to avoid the blazing sun. I am pleased to own Walton's original artwork (dated 1962), one of hundreds inexplicably tossed out by Collins and found in a dumpster.

Fig. 100 Dust jacket by Barbara Walton.

American editions of three Challis novels were published —
Twelve Girls in the Garden (1957), **The Myth is Murder** (1959)
with the title **The Third Statue**, and **A Wake for Murder** with the
title **Mourners' Voyage** (1963). Since William Morrow published
the first two, it was surprising they did not do the third. Doubleday
published that as part of its Crime Club series.

Doubleday hired the Irish-Canadian illustrator James
McMullan (b. 1934) to design the dust jacket for **Mourners'
Voyage**, which featured Sam Brewster's schooner, the *Meltemi*.
(**Fig. 101**) Recalling the artwork in 2022, McMullan said, "It's

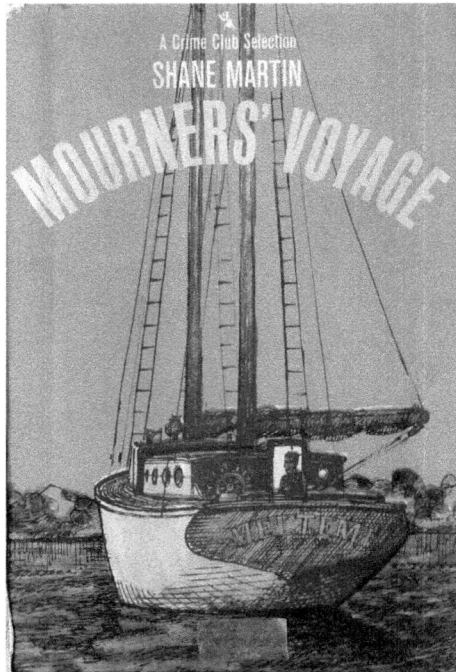

Fig. 101 Dust jacket by James McMullan.

interesting to see the cover – not a typical style for me in that there doesn't seem to be much watercolour."[8] McMullan is perhaps best known for the many posters he designed for the Lincoln Center Theater in New York.[9]

When Curtis Brandenburg and Professor Challis have a long, heart-to-heart chat onboard the *Meltemi,* the ex-Harvard journalist tells the much older ex-Harvard archaeologist, "I know about your work, of course. I've even read one or two of your books. And I've read other things about you, too — your hobbies, shall we say? The Grosteller Case. The Business About the Rocamadour Reliefs."[10]

It is worth noting that Johnston referenced only the two Challis novels published in the USA — **The Myth is Murder** ("The Grosteller Case") and **Twelve Girls in the Garden** ("The Business About the Rocamadour Reliefs") — and not the two that hadn't — **The Saracen Shadow** and **The Man Made of Tin** (1958). It appears he did not wish to confuse or upset his American readers, knowing full well which side his bread was buttered. While **A Wake for Mourning/Mourners' Voyage** proved to be the final Challis mystery Johnston wrote, perhaps at the time, he felt he still had more in him.

Other People's Houses

George Johnston wrote **Twelve Girls in the Garden**, **The Saracen Shadow**, **The Man Made of Tin**, and **The Myth is Murder** while living in the Johnston's house on the island of Hydra in Greece — hence the title of this book **Homicide on Hydra**. But he wrote **A Wake for Mourning** while living in the Tudor farmhouse, Charity Farm, owned by his comfortably well-off friends Peter and Didi Cameron in Stanton, England. (**Fig. 102**)

The Johnstons and the Camerons first met on Hydra during the summer of 1960. While they got on extremely well, the Camerons were shocked by how the Johnstons were living, always short of money and rarely able to afford 'luxuries' like a tin of corned

Fig. 102 Charity Farm,

beef.[11] So they decided to swap houses for six months, between November 1960 and April 1961, to give each other, but mainly the Johnstons, a break. The Camerons and their four children lived in the Johnstons' house on Hydra, and the Johnstons and their three children lived in the Camerons' house in Stanton. They thought George might even return to Fleet Street if everything worked out.

Unfortunately, the house swap was a disaster. George felt humiliated when he looked up old journalist friends in London who virtually told him, "Don't call us. We'll call you."[12] While Charmian Clift felt uneasy living in the Camerons' house because "what actually happened was […] we began living their lives," she explained in her marvellous essay, 'Other People's Houses' (1966).

> We began playing at landed gentry and hobnobbing around with other landed gentry, and our conversation became knowledgeable about sheep and lambing and crops and point-to-point meetings and field labour, and their friends became our friends and their retainers became our retainers

286

and their problems became our problems. While on the island they became islanders to the manner born and took on our role as completely as we were taking on theirs.[13]

In addition, George and Charmian's marriage was on the slide, and George was seriously ill with tuberculosis but continued to drink and smoke heavily regardless. But despite all his troubles, he still knuckled down and wrote — contrary to Garry Kinnane's assessment of **A Wake for Mourning** — a fast-paced and suspenseful Professor Challis thriller.

Take That! Charmian

Like many heroines and female love interests in his novels, George Johnston modelled Josephine Portland in **A Wake for Mourning** on his wife, Charmian Clift. Even the following brief description of Portland — "she moved the big straw hat over her eyes and turned away from the sea"[14] — speaks loudly of Clift. Furthermore, Portland's friends, whom she described as "a crazy bunch of my brilliant, exiled compatriots who don't know whether they belong to the lost generation of Scott Fitzgerald or [...] Irwin Shaw,"[15] sounded very much like the friends of Clift and Johnston on Hydra.[16] (**Fig. 103**)

Even though Johnston idolised Clift in this way, their marriage was a classic case of can't live with you and can't live without you. Many people thought of Clift as promiscuous, including Johnston, who said cruel and hurtful things to her about this when drunk. However, he was not faithful to her either. In 1954, when Clift and their two children (Jason was not born until 1956) were on holiday in Cornwall, Johnston had an affair with an attractive young typist named Patricia Simione in his newspaper's office. (**Fig. 104**) "Since everyone in the office knew about the affair, it is possible that Clift did too,"[17] said Garry Kinnane.

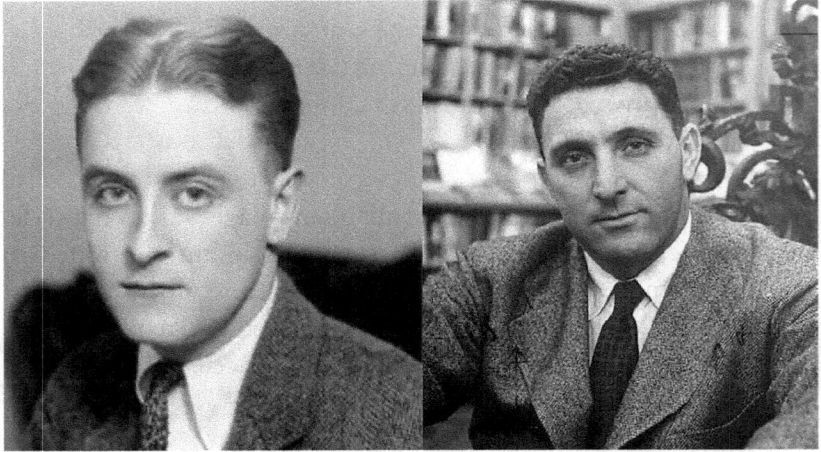

Fig. 103 F. Scott Fitzgerald (1896-1940) (left) and Irwin Shaw (1913-1984).

Fig. 104 Patricia Simione.

Not long before moving to Charity Farm, Clift resumed an affair with an American named Chip Chadwick on Hydra, which caused a lot of angst between her and Johnston. "Jealousy, public rows, drunken scenes, friends dragged in to take sides, except that this time it was so much worse, the confrontations were that much more bitter, and at times violent,"[18] said Kinnane. To make matters worse for Johnston, "Sexually, his illness had broken [him]. He and Clift were rarely lovers, and this was exacerbated by the fact that Clift, at [thirty-seven], was desperate to prove that she had not lost her sex appeal."[19]

How did Johnston try to get back at Clift over her affairs with Chadwick and the others? Writing **A Wake for Mourning** at a low point in their marriage, he named the absent but omnipotent villain of the novel, Giuseppe Simione, after Patricia Simione with whom he had had an affair. Since we are not talking about a name like Smith or Jones, Johnston precisely knew what he was doing — sending Clift the pointed message, "Remember, Darling, I've had affairs too!" hidden in plain sight of the pages of his latest Professor Challis novel. It must have been like a red rag to a bull and would not have helped the atmosphere, one bit, inside Charity Farm.

Tony Saben, Celebrity Gangster

The 'mourners' who travelled on the *Meltemi* were very colourful characters. There was T. Curtis Brandenburg — a crazy, young, well-educated, New York newspaperman-cum-vigilante on a homicidal mission. Major (his name, not his title) Vancourter — an arboreal-looking, thick-set, literally hairy-chested lawyer who handled his New York celebrity gangster boss, Tony Saben, like a corporation. Willard Xavier Crestfall — a double-crossing, murderous, overweight 'guru' from Westport, Connecticut, who looked and sometimes dressed like a Sumo wrestler and collected erotic paintings. Drips Faversham — a clarinet-playing,

Hawaiian shirt-wearing, marihuana-smoking lush with freckles. Frenzy Talmage — a beautiful, toffee-colour-haired, tassel dancer who was drunk for much of the time. And Bullbeat, an athletic, jazz-loving, multiracial thug who could run a hundred metres in ten-point-two seconds. "An unlikelier group of mourners has never been accumulated,"[20] remarked the **Gustine Standard** in California.

But since Saben had brought all these oddballs together, I shall focus on him. He was forty-three years old, of average height but solidly built, with broad shoulders and "the lithe, quick-looking good body of the good athlete."[21] Saben was uncommonly charming and personable. Although he had an insincere smile, "the sort you might pick up in a business college or by watching Hollywood films."[22]

Saben was the darling of the gossip writers, providing them enough material on who was sharing his bed to keep their "hot little prattling fingers rattling on their typewriters for a month of Sundays!"[23] The fact that Saben was something of a Lothario concerned Sam Brewster when he thought Josephine Portland was paying him far too much attention. However, Brewster "was somewhat mollified to observe that, in spite of the man's striking physique, he had skin of that grey-pink, inclined-to-freckle type that often went with reddish hair."[24]

Saben was wealthy and happy to throw his money around. However, it came from highly illegal and dubious enterprises, such as the Golden Flute Cabaret Bar, where Frenzy performed her tassel dances. Therefore, Saben employed Vancouter and Crestfall to help him launder his money by purchasing art and making him appear legitimate in public.

If social media had existed in Saben's day, he would have undoubtedly taken to it like a duck to water. He liked sitting around swimming pools with Hollywood starlets. Attending first nights on Broadway, concerts and prize fights at Madison Square Garden, horse races at Belmont Park, and "those Italian film premiers where it's all décolletage and defamation."[25] Being interviewed by fashionable magazines like **Esquire**, **Life**, and **Viewpoints**, which employed Brandenburg. Partying with the Irish theatrical group, the Abbey Players, then very popular with US high society. Travelling on the luxury liner, *Queen Elizabeth*. Being one of America's ten-best dressed men. Eating at the finest restaurants. Reading classical literature like **The Aeneid** (19 BC) by Virgil (70-19 BC) — and so on. But as Professor Challis poignantly noted, "You don't necessarily have to be interested in culture if you can afford to buy it."[26]

Perhaps all gangsters are alike, but Tony Saben reminds me of Abe Saffron (1919-2006), the long-time Mister Big of Australian crime who owned numerous businesses in Sydney's redlight district, Kings Cross. (**Fig. 105**) Saffron was involved in various criminal

Fig. 105 Abe Saffron at the Roosevelt Club, King's Cross, Sydney (1951).

activities, including trading stolen goods, drug dealing, extortion, illicit gambling, prostitution, illegally selling alcohol, and tax evasion. He avoided prosecution for so long because he bribed politicians and police with money and sexual favours. George Johnston would have undoubtedly known of him, especially as Saffron owned the Roosevelt Club, a notorious hang-out for high society and underworld identities alike — possibly the inspiration for the Golden Flute — and since Johnston wrote five articles about crime and vice in Sydney for a controversial series called 'The Naked City' published by the **Sun** in 1949.[27]

Sam Brewster and the Meltemi

Sam Brewster was the English captain of the schooner, *Meltemi,* in Greek, meaning the strong, dry, seasonal winds found over the Aegean Sea. He was blond, blue-eyed, very tall, and excessively thin with a lean, sea-creased, sunburned face and a good-natured grin and, according to Professor Challis, would have looked incongruous everywhere except on the deck of his ship. Brewster was brave, gallant, and honest. He hated anything happening onboard that he did not know about or which in some way did not stem directly from his orders, clashing numerous times over this with its charterer, Tony Saben. By the end of **A Wake for Mourning**, Brewster was head-over-heels in love with Josephine Portland.

Challis described Brewster's upbringing as "limited and austere." He attended school in Norfolk before joining the Royal Navy. Despite being "little more than a schoolboy" when World War II started in 1939, Brewster had "some hair-raising experiences in the Mediterranean with small boat commandos."[28] He was somewhat old-fashioned in that he firmly believed "right always triumphed over wrong, that villains invariably got their deserts, that crime never paid in the long run, that virtue was its own reward, and that of all the world's people, Britishers were the most deserving of respect."[29]

Brewster virtually built the *Meltemi* himself in the old shipyard at Paramé, on the north coast of Brittany in France,[30] but I think Johnston meant to write Perama, near the Athens port of Piraeus. It had a backup Mercedes diesel engine capable of a maximum speed of eight knots, but when under sail and propelled by the winds that gave the ship its name, the *Meltemi* could do twelve knots and looked magnificent:

> By dawn the wind had freshened considerably, and the *Meltemi*, under one jib, one staysail, and the mainsail, which Brewster and Petros had reefed down at first light, was boiling along on a southward course at a fine clip. She sailed with wet decks and an exhilarating rhythm, lunging and plunging into the crisp, dark roll of the seas. From taut, soaked sails the wind boomed. Rigging drummed and whined. Spars and timbers creaked. It was, to Sam Brewster, a perfect day for sailing. Standing wide-legged to take the kick of the wheel, he sang to himself an exultant, tuneless song.[31]

Since space was a premium onboard the *Meltemi*, there was a place for everything and everything in its place. Indeed, Challis was particularly impressed with "the complex compression of racks, shelves, cupboards, stoves, water tanks, gas bottles, crockery, equipment, and foodstuffs"[32] in the ship's tiny galley or kitchen, telling Portland that if the world put its city planning problems in the hands of marine architects, there would not be any of these issues with urbanism or overcrowding. "They would pack it all in like this."[33] But not everything onboard was practical. For example, decorating the walls of the ship's little saloon or living room was a lithograph of the Blackwall frigate *Arundel Castle* by Clarkson Stanfield (1793-1867), a clock and barometer in a mahogany frame carved like knotted ropes, and a calendar featuring a reproduction

Fig. 106 *Aerial and Taeping* by Jack Spurling.

of a painting by Jack Spurling (1870-1933) of the *Ariel* and the *Taeping* racing each other in 1866. (**Fig. 106**)

George Johnston modelled Sam Brewster on one of his expatriate friends on Hydra, the English yachtsman Sam Barclay (1920-2000), and Brewster's schooner *Meltemi* on Barclay's schooner *Stormie Seas*. Furthermore, he dedicated **A Wake for Mourning** to them, writing "For the other Sam … and the *Stormie Seas*."[34] (**Fig. 107**)

Like Sam Brewster, Sam Barclay came from Norfolk, enlisted in the Royal Navy, and became a small boat commando during World War II. In 1943, he was a very bored Sub-Lieutenant on a destroyer in the North Atlantic when he saw a notice calling for volunteers with sailing experience to join the Levant Schooner Fleet, set up in 1942, the year after Germany invaded Greece, to harass and eventually re-occupy the Greek islands. After the War, Barclay returned to England, bought a small black ketch named *Bessie,* and sailed to Greece.

Barclay found the last great sailing shipbuilder in Greece, Evangelos Koutalis, and in partnership with his ex-Royal Navy chum John Leatham, they built the *Stormie Seas,* making the frame from well-seasoned Cypress and hard pine, the deck from teak salvaged from the wreck of the *Giovanni Batista* (1668), and the deckhouse from teak recovered from a German tug.[35] Despite Barclay's family ties to the eponymous famous bank founded in London in 1690, he and Leatham ran out of money halfway through building *Stormie Seas.* Consequently, they agreed to run anti-communist groups into Albania on the ship for MI6 in return for the British Secret Intelligence Service taking over the cost of its construction.[36]

Fig. 107 Sam Barclay and his schooner, *Stormie Seas.*

For George Johnston, **A Wake for Mourning** was a nostalgic return to the very beginnings of his journalistic career. While learning lithography as a teenager, he developed a passion for sailing ships and spent much of his leisure time drawing, painting, and reading about them. At sixteen, while still an apprentice lithographer, Johnston started writing historical articles about sailing ships on the side for the **Argus** in Melbourne. In 1930, he became the founding secretary of the Ship-Lovers' Society of Victoria,[37] which occasionally held its meeting in the newspaper's office lounge.[38] In 1933, the **Argus** hired Johnston as a cadet reporter responsible for covering the shipping round. This job led him to write articles about the Australian Navy at the start of the War and become the newspaper's official war correspondent in 1941. These links between sailing ships and journalism may have prompted Johnston to name the newspaper editor his surrogate, David Meredith, worked for in his autobiographical trilogy, Bernard Brewster, after Sam Brewster. While living on Hydra, Johnston owned two fishing boats — the *Agios Bunyip,* which sunk, and the *Slithey Tove.* He was also friends with Sam Barclay and no doubt sailed on his yacht *Stormie Seas.* With all this nautical experience, Johnston wrote about Sam Brewster's yacht *Meltemi* with great authority. I would not be surprised if **A Wake for Mourning** was his favourite Professor Challis novel due to its sailing ship connections.

Reviews

The pattern with **A Wake for Mourning** or **Mourners' Voyage** was similar to George Johnston's other Challis novels. It got more publicity in the USA than in Great Britain or Australia, and most reviews were only one or two-line summaries. For example, Mary

Castle of the **Boston Globe** in Massachusetts said, "Captain of schooner, chartered by intimates of late gangster accompanying ashes on Mediterranean pilgrimage, is startled by false information of murder on previous day in Naples."[39] Likewise, Lois Wilson of the **Miami News** in Florida wrote, "Another Crime Club selection is Shane Martin's **Mourners' Voyage**. A Mediterranean voyage to carry the ashes of murdered gangster Giuseppe Simione to his home city involves a lot of people in murder and a search for a million dollars."[40]

A few reviewers were complimentary. J.R.C. of the **Chattanooga Daily Times** in Tennessee thought it had "a fast-moving plot" and was "good."[41] Ken Carnahan of the **San Bernadino County Sun** said, "I don't think you'll get this one."[42] And Peter Phillips of the **Daily Herald** in London, UK wrote, "Small yacht atmosphere and storm at sea episodes are excellently done. By no means a strain to read."[43]

But most reviewers found something to criticise. R.D.B. of the **Sydney Morning Herald** in Australia concluded, "Not a first-class effort, but an acceptable run-of-the-mill thriller."[44] Shirley Combs of the **Evansville Press** in Indiana said, "Involved and a mite beyond credulity, this is not a good'ern."[45] Vivian Mort of the **Chicago Tribune** in Illinois wrote, "Unfortunately, it seems at times as if poster paints were used in the colouring."[46] While the reviewer at the **Star Tribune** in Minneapolis, Minnesota, said, "When girl with 'raven hair' 'crinkled her nose when she laughed' on page two, this reader gave up!"[47]

In those days, American lending libraries published lists of their newly acquired books in newspapers, and it is evident from these that many purchased **Mourners' Voyage**, probably because it was part of Doubleday's Crime Club series and seen as a safe bet. Indeed, my second-hand copy of **Mourners' Voyage** originally belonged to the Greeley Public Library in Colorado.

George Johnston wrote no more Professor Challis novels after **A Wake for Mourning** because he didn't have to – the publication of **My Brother Jack** in 1964 and **Clean Straw for Nothing** in 1969, which both won Miles Franklin Awards, finally provided him with the financial security and literary accolades he longed for. But his five Challis novels were much better thrillers and revealed much more about the man and the writer than most people have assumed. Anyone interested in Australian crime fiction or the life and work of George Johnston should read them. If the Challis novels are "pot-boilers," they are bloody good ones!

Endnotes

[1] Garry Kinnane, **George Johnston: A Biography**, Melbourne, Australia: Nelson Publishers, 1986, p. 202.

[2] Robin Deniston, 'Lord Hardinge of Penshurst, **Independent** (London, UK), 17 July 1997, p. 18.

[3] Garry Kinnane, p. 202.

[4] Ibid.

[5] Ibid., p. 208.

[6] Ibid., p. 202.

[7] Rachel Brett (British Library), Email to Derham Groves, 7 September 2023.

[8] James McMullan, Email to Derham Groves, 14 February 2022.

[9] See James McMullan, 'McMullan,' https://www.jamesmcmullan.com, accessed 5 September 2023.

[10] Shane Martin (George Johnston) (1962), **Mourners' Voyage**, Garden City, New York: Doubleday & Company, Inc., 1963, p. 38.

[11] Garry Kinnane, p. 191.

[12] Ibid., p. 199.

[13] Charmian Clift (1966), 'Other People's Houses,' in Nadia Wheatley (ed.), **Sneaky Little Revolutions: Selected Essays of Charmian Clift**, Sydney, Australia: NewSouth Publishing, 2022, pp. 202-203.

[14] Shane Martin, p. 133.

[15] Ibid., pp. 3-4.

[16] See Paul Genoni and Tanya Dalziell, **Half the Perfect World: Writers, Dreamers and Drifters on Hydra, 1955-1964**, Clayton, Australia: Monash University Publishing, 2018.

[17] Garry Kinnane, p. 130.

[18] Ibid., pp. 210-211.

[19] Ibid., p. 210.

[20] 'New Books at Gustine Library,' **Gustine Standard** (Gustine, California), 6 June 1963, p. 10.

[21] Shane Martin, p. 21.

[22] Ibid., pp. 31-32.

[23] Ibid., p. 54.

[24] Ibid., p. 31.

[25] Ibid., p. 4.

[26] Ibid., p. 5.

[27] George H. Johnston, **The Naked City** (series): 'Predatory Men Worst Blot in City's Growing Vice,' **Sun** (Sydney), 15 June 1949, p. 3; 'Vice Drives Girls into Depravity, Poverty, **Sun**, 16 June 1949, p. 3; 'City's "Dark Perimeter" of Vice is Easy Step to Depravity's Depths, **Sun**, 17 June 1949, p. 3; 'Night in a Pick-Up Joint,' **Sun**, 19 June 1949, p. 5; 'Easy Money the Lure: Sordid Court Scene the End,' **Sun**, 20 June 1949, p. 3.

[28] Shane Martin, pp. 108-109.

[29] Ibid., pp. 108-109.

[30] Ibid., p. 31.

[31] Ibid., p. 62.

[32] Ibid., pp. 39-40.

[33] Ibid., pp. 39-40.

[34] Ibid., dedication, unpaged.

[35] See Peter Throckmorton, '*Stormie Seas:* An Unfinished Saga,' **Sea History**, No. 18, Fall 1980, pp. 24-25.

[36] William Bland and Ian Price, **A Tangled Web: A History of Anglo-American Relations with Albania**, London: The Albanian Society, 1986, p. 277.

[37] 'Meetings, Lectures, etc. Ship-Lovers' Society of Victoria,' **Argus** (Melbourne, Australia), 16 June 1930, p. 1.

[38] Ibid., 11 March 1931, p. 1.

[39] Mary Castle, 'Thrills and Chills, **Mourners' Voyage** by Shane Martin, Crime Club,' **Boston Globe** (Boston, Massachusetts) 24 February 1963, p. 125.

[40] Lois Wilson, 'Diplomacy is Murder,' **Miami News** (Miami, Florida), 10 March 1963, p. 24.

[41] J.R.C., 'Skiing Compared to Life Journey, **Mourners' Voyage** by Shane Martin, 181 pp. Garden City: Doubleday and Co. (Crime Club) $3.50,' **Chattanooga Daily Times** (Chattanooga, Tennessee), 7 April 1963, p. 18.

[42] Ken Carnahan, 'Turning the Pages,' **San Bernadino County Sun** (San Bernadino, California), 31 March 1963, p. 49.

[43] Peter Phillips, 'Crime Shelf, **A Wake for Mourning** by Shane Martin, Collins, 12s. 6d.," **Daily Herald** (London, UK), 19 May 1962, p. 6.

[44] R.D.B., 'Mainly Murder,' **Sydney Morning Herald** (Sydney), 20 October 1962, p. 14.

[45] Shirley Combs, 'Who-Dunnit? **Mourners' Voyage** by Shane Martin (Doubleday, $3.50),' **Evansville Press** (Evansville, Indiana), 7 March 1963, p. 38.

[46] Vivian Mort, 'Crime on My Hands,' **Chicago Tribune** (Chicago, Illinois), 10 March 1963, p. 189.

[47] 'Crime Corner,' **Star Tribune** (Minneapolis, Minnesota), 10 May 1964, p. 90.

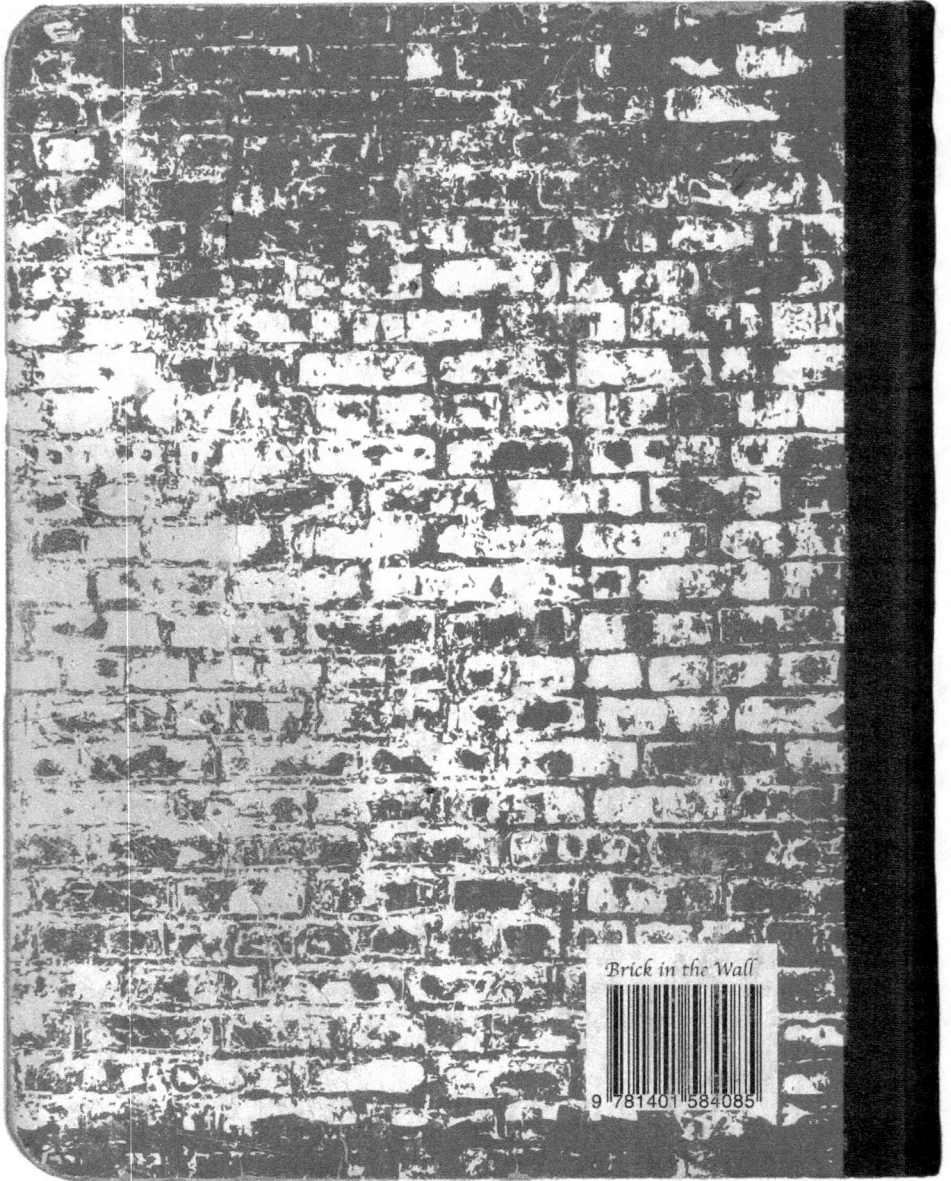

Plate 7 Back cover of Derham Groves' notebook.

The Author

Dr. Derham Groves (b. 1956) studied architecture at Deakin University and the Royal Melbourne Institute of Technology (RMIT) and art history at the University of Minnesota. He taught architecture at RMIT from 1985 until 1997 and at the University of Melbourne from 1999 until 2019. Groves is currently a Senior Fellow in the Faculty of Architecture, Building, and Planning at the University of Melbourne. He is the author of many articles and books about popular culture, architecture, and design, including, **Feng-Shui and Western Building Ceremonies** (1991), **You Bastard Moriarty** (1996), **Mail Art: The D-I-Y Letterbox from Workshop to Gatepost** (1998), **TV Houses: Television's Influence On the Australian Home** (2004), **There's No Place Like Holmes: Exploring Sense of Place Through Crime Fiction** (2008), **Victims and Villains: Barbie and Ken Meet Sherlock Holmes** (2009), **Anna May Wong's Lucky Shoes: 1939 Australia Through the Eyes of an Art Deco Diva** (2011), **Out of the Ordinary: Popular Art, Architecture and Design** (2012), **Hopalong Cassidy: A Horse Opera** (2017), **Monkeemania in Australia: Celebrating the 50th Anniversary of The Monkees' Australian Tour in 1968** (2019), **Arthur Purnell's 'Forgotten' Architecture: Canton and Cars** (2020), **Sherlock in the Seventies: A Wild Decade of Sherlock Holmes Films** (2021), **Australian Westerns in the Fifties: Kangaroo, Hopalong Cassidy on Tour, and Whiplash** (2022), and there's more to come!

www.ingramcontent.com/pod-product-compliance
Lightning Source LLC
Chambersburg PA
CBHW070247290326
41930CB00042B/2719